Playing Away

PLAYING AWAY

Australians in British Rugby League

DAVE HADFIELD

THE KINGSWOOD PRESS

First published in Great Britain in 1992
by The Kingswood Press
Michelin House, 81 Fulham Road, London SW3 6RB

A CIP catalogue record for this book
is available from the British Library
ISBN 0 413 64670 X

Photoset by Deltatype Ltd,
Ellesmere Port, Cheshire
Printed in England by Clays Ltd, St Ives plc

Contents

Foreword

From the earliest time I became aware of Rugby League football, I was fascinated by the idea of men crossing the world, from somewhere unimaginably different, to play in towns like Leigh, Workington and Huddersfield. In my privileged role of writing about the game, the influence of Australians on the 13-a-side code in Britain has seemed to me to be the most significant running story of all.

A mixture of xenophobia and pride in the native virtues of British Rugby League has led some to underestimate the positive effects of inviting players from Sydney, Brisbane and points north and south to add their abilities to our domestic game. This strikes me as a mistake. The gap which had grown between the two countries during a period of relative international isolation was there for all to see in the Ashes series of 1982, when the Australians were seen to be playing a brand of rugby not merely from the other side of the world, but from a different planet. That we now have competitive Test football again owes a great deal to the decision once more to allow movement between the two countries, and you need to take a very constricted view of the game to believe that that is a bad thing.

This is, of course, just the latest chapter in a story which runs from Albert Rosenfeld to Gene Miles and on again, I hope, to some kid throwing a ball around on a back lot in Wollongong or Wagga Wagga, of whom we have never heard but who will one day delight spectators in Wakefield or Warrington. It is a story I could not have attempted to tell without the help of many people: coaches, administrators and fellow journalists but, most of all, players present and past, and the relatives and friends of those who are no longer alive. There is sometimes a suspicion that, because they are big news back home, Australian players are prone to inflated ideas of their own importance. I have never found that to be the case. To a man, the players I have spoken to both before and after the idea of this book took seed have been approachable and helpful. That is one thing they have in common with their British counterparts.

Some special thanks are due: to Tony Pocock and Neil Tunnicliffe at The Kingswood Press, for their encouragement, faith in the project and tireless nit-picking; to the two editors during my years of association with *Rugby League Week*, Ian Heads and Norman Tasker; to Harry Edgar, the publisher of *Open Rugby*; to Robert Gate, the keeper of the archives at the Rugby Football League; to Trevor Smith of Smiths of Wigan, for his enthusiasm; to Albert Fearnley, whose passion for the game infected me fifteen years ago and planted the idea that Rugby League could be something more for me than a hobby; and to Andrew Varley, for his kind permission to reproduce all the photographs in the book except for nos. 1 and 4, courtesy of the *Huddersfield Daily Examiner*, and nos. 9 and 11, courtesy of the *Yorkshire Post*.

An apology is also called for. I have not even attempted to mention every Australian who has played professional Rugby League in Britain, nor every one, I fear, who deserves mention. So, if a particular favourite of yours is omitted – or, worse still, if you are missed out yourself – I can only plead in mitigation the impossibility of squeezing a quart into a pint pot or, if I may lapse into an Australian image for a moment, a schooner into a middy.

Dave Hadfield
May 1992

1
Playing Away

There is no annual sporting migration in the world quite to match the one which brings Australian Rugby League players to the north of England in September and October every year. It has been going on, with one or two enforced breaks for wars, international transfer bans and other inconveniences, for eighty years. In a vintage season, like 1986–87, it can involve nearly 100 players. Many of the greatest performers the code has seen have been involved in it; some have never returned home and have become part of the fabric of the game in their adopted country.

Sport, and particularly professional sport, encompasses plenty of other examples of players packing their bags and plying their trades far away from their home turf. West Indian cricketers with English counties – which are now being encouraged to manage with rather less of them – and before that in the Lancashire Leagues and other competitions, are one instance. Canadian ice-hockey players are perpetually sought after over the border in the United States. American basketball players – although not usually of the highest calibre – provide height, know-how and glamour to teams all over the world. South American footballers have long been lured to Europe by the dozen. Italian Rugby

Union clubs – although they would dispute, presumably, that they constitute professional sport – make it possible and attractive for players from all over the place to join them for the Mediterranean winter.

But nowhere is the relationship as significant within the overall context of the sport as it is between the Rugby League men of New South Wales and Queensland and the clubs of the industrial towns of Lancashire, Yorkshire and Cumbria. Every club which has ever achieved anything of note in British Rugby League has had Australians playing crucial roles for it on the field at various stages of its history. The game without them would simply not have been the same.

There is no other sport in which the distances between one hotbed and another are so immense. With the single exception of the New Zealand Rugby League players who have, from time to time, rivalled the impact of Australians in Britain, boys from Sydney and Brisbane who want to play abroad must travel further than anyone else, to a land whose climate and lifestyle is radically different from anything they have known. Even New Zealanders have a shorter-range alternative; they can advance their careers by playing in Australia, and many do. And some Australians have crossed the Tasman in the opposite direction to play in New Zealand – some even headed off to Papua New Guinea in the early days of the game's development there – but neither of those routes has ever been likely to become heavily used; there is no money in it. Nor is there very much financial gain attached to playing in France, although a handful who can cope with the concept of an underdone steak give it a try every year. Fundamentally, though, an Australian who wants to live and play abroad, and make a few dollars out of it, has only one place to go: and that is the north of England.

The reasons for that restricted choice go back to the origins of the game of Rugby League. The same motives of protecting players from financial loss that led to the breakaway of the Northern Union clubs in Britain in 1895 could, in theory, have led to the development of a professional code of rugby anywhere else in the world where rugby players had to work for a living. In fact, that happened in a part of just two countries: Britain and Australia.

Although the first New Zealand touring side to Britain in 1907–8 was an explicitly professional undertaking – hence the disparaging 'All Gold' title that stuck to them – the code in that country has developed along broadly amateur lines. The same is true of France and, to a large extent, of the fifth Test-playing nation, Papua New Guinea. In Australia, however, the principle of being paid to play was established early and has remained an intrinsic part of the game. The only other place in the world which held out the same possibility has been Britain. Australians trembling in the teeth of a Pennine winter – before they realise the overwhelming tactical importance of a good overcoat – must have often wished that their game had taken root in, say, Brazil or Bali. But it was not to be; it has been a case of Britain or nothing.

*

Australia in the late 19th century, like Australia now, did not have a national winter game. While cricket had established a sporting culture that transcended the state boundaries and the fierce rivalries that they represented, football already defined part of the differences between those states. Rugby was the popular code in New South Wales and Queensland, but the stronger Irish sporting influence in Victoria and South Australia – related to different patterns of immigration to the gold diggings in those states – led to the growth of a hybrid code derived from Gaelic football which eventually evolved into Australian Rules. The dominance of rugby on the relatively populous east coast, however, gave the clue as to how strong Australian Rugby League was destined to become when, twelve years after the British schism, similar events took place on the other side of the world.

If the catalyst in Britain was the question of broken-time payments for players obliged to take time off work to play, in Australia the problems of players incurring medical expenses played the same role. In 1907, Alick 'Bluey' Burdon, one of the country's best Rugby Union forwards, broke his collar-bone and snapped a sinew in his arm playing for New South Wales against Queensland; the conspicuous absence of any sort of help from the game's authorities during his ten weeks away from work became a major talking point in Sydney. One who took up his cause was

Victor Trumper, still regarded today as one of Australia's greatest cricketers, and it was during discussions at his sports store in the city that the idea of a new code of rugby that would look after the interests of its players rather better was born.

The key to the credibility and success of the new code was the recruitment of the most charismatic and crowd-pulling rugby player in the country at the time – H. H. 'Dally' Messenger, a centre and prodigious goal-kicker for Eastern Suburbs, New South Wales and Australia. The instigators of the breakaway accordingly persuaded him – or, perhaps more accurately, his formidable mother – to throw in his lot with the new venture. He was one of the reasons for a crowd of 20,000 at the Royal Agricultural Showground, next to the Sydney Cricket Ground, for the first game under the auspices of the new organisation in Australia. The game, Australia against the New Zealand 'All Golds', was played under Rugby Union rules, because a rulebook from the Northern Union in Britain – which had, by this time, among other changes, reduced teams to thirteen men and abolished the line-out – had not yet arrived. Australia lost 8–12, with Messenger scoring 5 of their points, and went on to lose this first series 0–3; but Messenger himself made such an impact that he became the first Australian Rugby League player to tour Britain. New Zealand took the extraordinary step of asking him to join them on their first tour of Britain in 1907–8, a decision that was vindicated by his outstanding displays during that long visit.

Messenger, in fact, could have become the first Australian League star to make his fortune by signing for a British club. It would not have been for one of the Northern Union sides, however; his kicking skills were such that leading soccer clubs Manchester United and Tottenham Hotspur each offered him £1500 to join them. The transition would not have seemed as unlikely in those days as it would now; Rugby Union and, to a slightly lesser extent, the new professional code, were still games in which the kicker was king. Most matches were settled by goal-kicking rather than try-scoring, and the skills of a renowned kicker like Messenger were seen as capable of adaptation to the game of association football, which placed a heavy premium on the speed with which a heavy leather ball could be hoofed downfield.

The offers were huge by the standards of the day, and Messenger is said to have been tempted and to have consulted his mother back home in Sydney. She discouraged the idea, however, and Messenger returned to Australia to take part in the first domestic Rugby League season, although two New Zealanders stayed in Britain to play with Northern Union clubs: George Smith with Oldham and Lance Todd, whose name is immortalised in the award for the man-of-the-match in the Challenge Cup final, with Wigan. After that, it was always certain that British clubs would look with great interest at the players who made up the first Australian tour the following year, in 1908–9.

On a tour of forty-five matches, spread over five months – which makes current tours look like real hit-and-run exercises by comparison – prospective buyers had ample opportunity for a long, careful look at the first Kangaroos; they found a good number of them most amenable to suggestions. Then, as was to be the case on subsequent tours, the eye-catching backs were the main targets. Messenger was certainly approached but turned down all offers; perhaps he knew by now what the answer would be from his mother. But the British clubs raided the rest of the Australian back-line pretty effectively.

The line-up that appeared on 20 February against Huddersfield, one of the very best of contemporary British sides, is representative of the trend. Of the backs on duty then, only the full-back, Charles Hedley, was not signed up to play in England after the tour. Mick Bolewski, from Bundaberg, played on the right wing that day, but was more often seen as a full-back: he joined Leigh. Centres Jim Devereux and Andy Morton both went to Hull; the practice of signing Australian players in pairs, to help both of them settle into a different playing and living environment, was established very early in the day. Left winger Dan Frawley, a larger-than-life Irishman, wound up at Warrington along with another Eastern Suburbs tourist, Larry O'Malley, and a team-mate who did not make the tour, right winger Jim Stuntz. And, in the week of the Huddersfield game, Oldham announced a double capture: they signed centre Sid Deane who, like Messenger, missed the Huddersfield match with an injury but was regarded as one of the tourists' very best players, and half-back Ernest Anlezark. Subsequently, they also signed from the tour party Tom McCabe, an Englishman who had emigrated to Australia.

All these players achieved a degree of success and celebrity in their British careers. Deane and Anlezark were important members of the Oldham side which won back-to-back Championships in 1909–10 and 1910–11, making them the first Australians to share in a major honour in the British game. They were also the first Australians to play for Lancashire, when the county committee showed an early willingness to integrate the newcomers still further into the fabric of the game. Devereux had a fine first season for Hull, scoring twenty-one tries as the club reached the final of what was then the Northern Union Cup – later the Challenge Cup. He missed much of the 1910–11 season with a knee injury, but proved to be one of the most durable of all the early Australian imports. He played on into the 1920s, with an enforced break for the First World War, and shared in Hull's Challenge Cup victory in 1914 and their Championship wins in 1920 and 1921. When he retired he had played 181 games for Hull, scoring 101 tries and four goals. Andy Morton, who made his debut alongside Devereux in March 1909, had a shorter career on Humberside, playing forty-four matches and scoring fifteen tries.

Mick Bolewski, a controversial inclusion in that first Kangaroo party but one who proved his worth on tour, played his first season with Leigh in the unaccustomed role of scrum-half, but was a great influence there and at full-back during the two succeeding campaigns. Contemporary accounts stress the quality of his tackling, which was regarded as some of the best of his era. Bolewski also made himself popular by devoting a good deal of his free time to coaching schoolboys in the town – a forerunner of the way in which overseas players, many of whom have found themselves with time on their hands, have often been able to contribute more in this direction than local stars. He eventually went home to Queensland after three seasons in which he made exactly 100 appearances, a total still unmatched by any overseas player at Leigh. Bolewski was always well remembered in the close-knit community and made a number of return visits to the town, the last of them towards the end of his life in the early 1960s. But, although he and his fellow-Australians did indeed play leading roles with British clubs, they had the misfortune – if misfortune it was – to have been contemporaries with a man whose achievements dwarfed all others of the age.

On that same day that Huddersfield played Australia at Fartown, the *Huddersfield Daily Examiner* announced that the club had secured the services of two of the tourists. One of them, forward Patrick Walsh, from Newcastle in New South Wales, did not play in that match although he did appear in all three Tests. The other new signing was in the line-up, however, and the Fartown spectators got their first glimpse of Albert Aaron Rosenfeld.

Rosenfeld had not been one of the stars of the tour; not a Deane or a Devereux, and certainly not a celebrity like Messenger. Indeed, he had not even been chosen for the original tour party, and it was only after some heated debate about the quality of the selection that his name was added. He played in just one of the three Tests – in the centre, although he had been brought primarily as a stand-off – and his acquisition did not exactly constitute headline news in the *Examiner*. In fact, the paper was fairly sniffy about the whole business of bringing in players from far and wide, clinging to the notion – outdated even in Edwardian times – that the ideal sports team consisted of local players. Yet Huddersfield, in assembling what was to become known as the 'Team of All the Talents', had already gone a long way down the opposite road: their great teams of this time included Welshmen galore, such as Johnny Rogers and Ben Gronow; New Zealanders such as the mighty centre, Edgar Wrigley; the Cumbrian Dougie Clark, and others from elsewhere in the Northern Union.

Echoing the debate which has been going on ever since, the *Examiner* seems to have deplored the overall trend but to have approved of the individuals who came to Huddersfield to improve the side. Commenting on the Rosenfeld and Walsh signings, the paper said: 'The Fartown team, despite its general excellence, has shown the want of a good wing threequarter and another forward. Now it has both.' Rosenfeld, although at stand-off for the tourists at Fartown, was already earmarked for the wing, and the *Examiner*, although it might have preferred him to have been born in Huddersfield, liked what it saw. It described him as 'a well-built player, on the smallish side, and an excellent runner. He played at Fartown on Saturday and made a good impression at outside-half, but will be in the threequarters for Huddersfield.'

Australia lost the match 3–5, and the report the following Monday spoke of Rosenfeld making one 'dashing run' before being cut down by Wrigley. There was a sense of anticipation that he was going to be a more than useful player for the club, but not the slightest realisation, one feels, of what a revelation he was destined to become.

*

Alby Rosenfeld had been born in the Eastern Suburbs of Sydney in 1885, the son of a struggling Jewish tailor who had emigrated from Poland not long before. Family legend has it that Rosenfeld senior originally arrived in London en route to his new life and had assumed that he was in Australia, because he had not realised that there would be a staging point for the journey. Young Albert trained as a tailor under his father but also emerged as a rugby player of high quality. When the breakaway code began to be mooted, he was one of the first to pledge himself to it, and he played in Australia's very first Test against New Zealand in 1907. He also appeared for Eastern Suburbs, along with Dan Frawley, in the first round of Sydney competition matches later that same year. He was, then, in every sense a Rugby League pioneer. But he would never have become one of the all-time legends of the game had it not been for the intrusion of a romantic sub-plot into the story of the first Kangaroo tour.

At some stage on his travels that English winter, Rosenfeld had met Ethel Barrend, the daughter of a Huddersfield mill manager, and had been mightily smitten. The Barrends were highly respectable people, with no links with professional sport, and Ethel was in no way an early manifestation of the terrace 'groupie'. Their grandson, Jim Shoesmith, says: 'I can't imagine where they met. It must have been at some sort of official function, because I can't see how their paths would have crossed otherwise.'

Dally R. Messenger, the grandson of the original Dally, tells a different story of their courtship, handed down from his grandfather, in his book *The Master*. His version has Ethel following the team from match to match, which seems unlikely, but is a good story nonetheless.

'The Australian team, as is usually the case with a group of virile young men, attracted a contingent of female admirers who followed them from match to match. One such young lady caught the eye of the young Kangaroo winger, Alby Rosenfeld. He fell deeply in love at first sight, and there was no curing him. The team was worried that the infatuation would interfere with his football, but the thought that his lady love was watching stirred Alby to even greater efforts, and he played some of the best games of his career. He found out where she lived, but a strict father and a suspicious mother refused him entry and kept their daughter safely locked away. This nearly drove Alby to desperation.'

Messenger and his team-mate, Larry O'Malley, decided that they would have to intervene on his behalf. They approached the parents for him, but were also turned away. Their trip was not entirely wasted, however, as they managed to locate Ethel's window, and they subsequently took Alby on a night-time expedition to the house. 'After her parents were asleep . . . the three of them crept around the back. Larry and Dally threw pebbles at her window-pane until a puzzled young lady eventually opened the window. Then they left Alby with his dream girl . . . [Alby and Ethel] visited Australia when they were in their 70s, and the surviving pioneer Kangaroos didn't let Alby forget how their courtship began.'

The liaison made it relatively easy for Huddersfield to persuade Rosenfeld to join them. Unlike some of his team-mates, however, he went back to Australia at the end of the tour and did not pull on the famous claret and gold jumper until the first game of the 1909–10 season. Broughton Rangers were the opposition, and Huddersfield won by a comfortable 36–0. The *Huddersfield Daily Examiner* was at it again; bemoaning the fact that not all of the brilliant local team hailed from within the town's boundaries.

They were enthusiastic enough about the new wingman, though, especially the first of his two tries, for which he dashed through the Rangers' defence after picking up a loose ball.

Rosenfeld was a major success in his first two seasons in what was already an outstanding Huddersfield side. But the Fartowners could not break the grip of Oldham who, with Anlezark and Deane, beat Wigan in the Championship finals of both 1910 and 1911. Nor could Rosenfeld's try-scoring, although already prolific, set him aside from the other great wingers of the day. He crossed twenty-four times in his first campaign, only half as often as leading scorer Jim Leytham of Wigan. The following year, his forty made him joint leading try-scorer with Miller of Wigan and his own team-mate Kitchen. It was from that point onwards that 'Rozzy', as he had become known in Huddersfield, really cut loose, and the 'Team of All the Talents' came into full bloom. In 1911–12, Huddersfield won the Championship, the Yorkshire Cup and the Yorkshire League, and Rosenfeld scored an astonishing seventy-eight tries – twenty-nine more than the previous individual record for a season. The *Examiner*, which by now regarded him as an honorary Huddersfieldian, predicted that it was a record which might never be beaten. In fact, it survived just the following season.

Rozzy managed a mere fifty-six tries in 1912–13 but, even with this paltry output, Huddersfield managed to struggle to the Championship, the Challenge Cup – beating Warrington 9–5 at Headingley – and the Yorkshire League. The season for which Albert Rosenfeld will always be remembered, however, was the next one; 1913–14 saw him at the height of his powers, and the result was a record which, although the *Huddersfield Daily Examiner* provides a warning of the rashness of these statements, will never be beaten, unless the rules of Rugby League are changed to give wingers more time and space than they have enjoyed in recent years. Rosenfeld's eighty tries that season are a sporting statistic, like Dixie Dean's goals, Bradman's Test average or Babe Ruth's home runs, which is burnt into the folk memory of the game.

The Huddersfield side overall was not quite as dominant as it had been the previous two seasons, nor as irresistible as it would prove to be a year later, but Rozzy was better than ever. He set out his stall from the very first, scoring four tries on the opening day of the campaign, against York. The *Examiner*'s Northern Union columnist, who gloried in the colourful pseudonym 'Rouge', remarked on how sharp Rosenfeld looked for so early in the season; players were rather expected to take a little time to get into their stride. He wrote of one score: 'Rozzy's try, after running from one end of the field to the other, must have satisfied the most ardent believer in individualism.'

Patrick Walsh had gone, after a relatively short stay at Fartown, but by this time Rosenfeld had a fiery-haired Australian centre named Tommy Gleeson playing inside him. Rozzy's freakish try-scoring was clearly not entirely attributable to his own solo efforts, because the writers of the day refer time and time again to the effectiveness of his combination with Gleeson. Considering that Rosenfeld had spent his early English career playing outside internationals of the calibre of Edgar Wrigley – who looks from his pictures like some ancient version of the massive Meninga or Miles-type centre – and the 'Prince of Centres', Harold Wagstaff, that was a great tribute to Gleeson. Even when things were going wrong as, even for Huddersfield, they sometimes did, the two were 'triers all the time, in defence and attack.'

Perhaps the high point of their work together came in the game against Wigan on 23 February 1914, in which a stunning 46–10 victory over one of the élite teams of the Northern Union put Huddersfield firmly on top of the table, which was calculated at the time on a system of percentages. 'Rouge' was beside himself: 'The way these two worked together was glorious,' he wrote, 'and, if asked for the best try of the game, how many would reply the try scored by Gleeson after passing and repassing with Rosenfeld? Rosenfeld was at his best. His first two tries were typical of the man, and his dart over in the second half was made when most wings would have regarded the chance as practically hopeless. But, with Rosenfeld, it is not his fault if he does not get through a whole team of players when he is near the line.'

Rozzy had timed one of the outstanding performances of his outstanding season particularly well. He was about to marry Ethel – it had not been quite the whirlwind courtship that the business at the bedroom window suggested – and the club had granted him a 'marriage testimonial'. This practice, which modern players might like to see revived, consisted of a collection at a big match to help a star player with the expense of setting up the conjugal home. The Rosenfeld nuptials were helped along by a collection of £28 17s 3d, that was, £17 8s in silver and £11 9s 3d in copper. It was one of Alby's better pay-days.

The previous week, he had scored five tries against Bramley and, the following week, he ran in seven in the 119–2 win over the unfortunate Swinton Park in the Northern Union Cup – a scoreline which is still a British Rugby League record. It was becoming clear that he was on course to top even his tally of two years earlier. A brace of tries against both Wakefield and Hull KR kept up the momentum, followed by hat-tricks against Bramley and Keighley. Against Widnes in the next round of the Cup, he came back scoreless – almost a newsworthy event in itself by this stage – but 'Rouge' was quick to absolve him from criticism, writing that it was not his fault that he had been given so few chances.

At home to Hull KR on 28 March, Rosenfeld finally broke his own record with a try in a 29–5 victory, and 'Rouge' reflected the surprise of many that his previous mark had been overhauled so quickly. 'In 1911–12,' he wrote, 'the little Sydney man left all records so far behind that we then considered his record one that was likely to last. He will doubtless leave it far behind if he uses the punt over the full-back with more discretion and less frequency.'

The suggestion that Rosenfeld could have scored even more regularly with different tactics is a striking observation about a man who had just scored his seventy-ninth try of the season. But Jim Shoesmith, who spent his formative years living in his grandfather's house and listening to his rugby stories, also believes from what Albert told him that he could have been even more prolific that season. 'It could have been a hundred,' he says. 'My grandfather told me that a textile firm in Huddersfield was offering a new overcoat to every player who scored a hat-trick. He already had plenty of overcoats that year and would quite often give the ball to a team-mate who shouted, "Give it here,

Alby: I've already scored two!" ' As for the chip over the full-back, which 'Rouge' felt was overused, Rosenfeld was an addict. His grandson recalls that he talked of it as his favourite ploy and of the tries that came from it as being his best. In later life, he particularly enjoyed players, like Huddersfield's Australian full-back after the Second World War, Johnny Hunter, who were skilled at it.

In the event, the 1913–14 season ended in anti-climax for both Rosenfeld and Huddersfield. He struggled through the rest of the campaign with an injury, scored just one more try in the game at Bradford, and played in the Cup semi-final defeat by Hull and the Championship final loss at the hands of Salford while obviously short of full fitness. 'Rouge' wrote: 'I cannot believe that he was fit to play [against Salford] because he gave a display that was quite foreign to him.' Rozzy also missed a couple of other games, and it is surely no exaggeration to say that, overcoats apart, if he had remained fit right to the end of the season, his record would have been closer to ninety than eighty.

For the Huddersfield club, 1914–15 was a season which was literally unbeatable. They became the second team, after Hunslet, to win all four cups – Championship, Challenge Cup, Yorkshire Cup and Yorkshire League – and Rosenfeld was inevitably to the fore. For the fourth season, he was out on his own as the leading try-scorer in the Northern Union with fifty-six. It was not the end of Rosenfeld as a player, but it was the end of his incredible run as the most potent scoring machine the game has ever seen.

During the First World War, Rosenfeld, who never gave up his Australian passport despite living in Britain for more than sixty years, was called up to serve in the Australian army and shipped to Gallipoli, in the theatre of war he always called 'Messpot' –Mesopotamia. 'He was never the same again,' says Jim Shoesmith. 'He didn't get wounded or sick during the war, but spending three or four years in that climate was quite debilitating. He told me that, when he got back, the sparkle had gone.' The war did produce a couple of memorable sporting interludes for Rosenfeld, however. He beat all comers in a foot-race in Gallipoli and played for the Army at Rugby Union at the inner sanctum of Twickenham, something which amused him greatly.

He resumed with Huddersfield after the war and scored thirty-one times in the first season of fully-fledged competition, but moved to Wakefield Trinity in August 1921. After two and a half seasons there, he moved on to become player-coach at Bradford Northern, but that only lasted for eighteen months before he retired from the professional game at the age of 40, his deeds before the war already the stuff of myth and legend. He coached an amateur team at Raistrick for some time but, after that, his contact with the game was restricted to watching Huddersfield's home games and following the schoolboy rugby careers of his two grandsons.

His son, a speedway rider, was killed in a racing accident at Odsal Stadium in Bradford, and another daughter died young, so his daughter Barbara was his one surviving child. Both she and her son, Jim, remember him as a strict, patrician figure. 'Even when we were in our teens we had to be back in the house by 9 o'clock at weekends, or woe betide you!' recalls Jim. 'He didn't smoke and he didn't drink and he didn't approve of people who did – especially if they were connected to him.'

He remained in the same house he had occupied as a player and worked until he died at the age of 85. The jobs he did are not the sort that you can imagine appealing to the record-breaking, truly great Rugby League players of later eras: for many years, he drove a corporation dustcart and, after he retired from that, he worked as a dyer. 'There was no sign whatsoever of him ever having made any money from Rugby League,' says his grandson. And, with his spartan lifestyle, there was little question of his having frittered a fortune away; his misfortune was that his playing days ended just as the Great Depression was gathering its destructive momentum. All his medals and mementoes were sold to help make ends meet; all that remains are a couple of faded photographs and a cap he won for playing for New South Wales against New Zealand under Rugby Union rules in 1907, which is now in the Rugby League Hall of Fame, into which he became one of only nine original inductees in 1988.

He was not a bitter or an unhappy man. The reason he worked for so long in what sound like menial jobs was that he enjoyed working and, unlike some great players of the past, he continued to enjoy watching Rugby League as well. As a spectator, as well as a player, he was a great believer in individual skill and initiative. The only time Jim Shoesmith can remember him refusing to watch Huddersfield was during one of their more successful post-war spells, in the early 1960s: he found them boring and regarded that as unforgivable. Players he relished as a spectator included Tom Van Vollenhoven and Billy Boston. 'And the first time he saw Roger Millward playing on television as a youngster, he said he was going to be a star of the future,' says Jim Shoesmith. 'Of all the players playing now, the one whose style he would really like is Andrew Ettingshausen. Style was very important to him.'

He had strong views about other things as well. 'He would never go to Wembley. He didn't approve of it: he said it was a northern game and that the money that was being made from it should be ploughed into a ground up here.' He also had a general distrust of administrators who, he believed, were failing to run the game for the benefit of either players or spectators; despite the leverage that his name would have given him and the authority that his achievements would have lent to his views, however, he never wanted to become involved in the administrative side of the game himself. 'He didn't particularly like to be recognised,' says Jim Shoesmith. 'When my brother and I were playing, he never wanted anyone to know whose grandsons we were.'

One form of continuing recognition he did appreciate, however, was the way that Australian touring teams never forgot him. 'Before every tour, a letter would arrive asking him for his measurements. They would kit him out with a blazer; not an ordinary tour one, but a special one with the word "Pioneers" on the badge. He used to go into the Australian dressing-rooms before Tests to wish them luck, but I think he always felt a little uncomfortable doing that. He did still think of himself as an Australian, even though he had developed a Yorkshire accent by that stage. He only sounded Australian when he was annoyed about something!'

In 1964, with some financial help from a benefactor, Albert and Ethel celebrated their fiftieth wedding anniversary by going to Australia – the first time in fifty-five years for him, the first time ever for her. He was welcomed and fêted wherever he went. Six years later, he died – the last member of the first Kangaroo touring team to bow out.

The *Huddersfield Daily Examiner* called him 'one of the most famous of all Rugby League players', and E. E. Christensen, in the *Daily Telegraph* in Sydney, wrote of him: 'Rosenfeld achieved football immortality in Australia and England and was a remarkable man, both in youth and old age. His record has never been approached and, nowadays, English club wingers feel proud of themselves if they can manage thirty tries in a season.' It is a measure of Rosenfeld's stature that, of all the records in the annals of the game, his is the one which would cause the greatest sensation if it was ever to be broken.

And, for all the other players who came to Britain as a direct or indirect result of that first Australian tour, he was the one who really put the gloss on the idea of recruiting from Down Under. Ever since, British clubs have, consciously or unconsciously, been looking for another Albert Rosenfeld. Some have come close to succeeding; there have even been players whose impact has been more instantaneous, and others whose period of dominance – uninterrupted by a war – has lasted longer. But there has never been one who has swept all before him over four extraordinary years like Rozzy. It is a statement which is used too glibly, of players whose achievements are great but not unique, but for him it holds good: there will never be another Albert Aaron Rosenfeld.

*

There were other players, who arrived in what might be termed the second wave after Rosenfeld and his ground-breakers, who deserve to be mentioned in the same breath. Tommy Gleeson, whose importance as Rosenfeld's centre in that immortal Huddersfield side should not be underrated, never played for Australia and could be argued as the first of a long line who lost the chance to do so by making their careers in the northern hemisphere.

Oldham, no doubt encouraged by their success with Anlezark and Deane, raided the second Kangaroo touring team of 1911–12 for the remarkable Farnsworth brothers. Bill and Viv were both former Rugby Union internationals who switched to League with the Newtown club, played in the side that won the Premiership in 1910 and represented Australia on England's first tour the same year. They thus became the first pair of brothers to take the field together for Australia in a Rugby League Test, and the last for fifty-three years until Dick and Ken Thornett matched them. The Farnsworths, like many brothers, were entirely different from each other in their approach to the game. Bill was a classical stand-off, still rated many years later by those who had seen him play as one of the very finest Australia has ever produced. Viv, however, was a good, all-round centre but one who was principally famed, and feared, for the ferocity of his tackling. An apocryphal story about him reflects the way that opposing players were frequently fretful in advance about Viv's attentions. In one match of the 1911–12 tour, a home-team player was on the field for the kick-off when he discovered that V. Farnsworth was his opposite number. He promptly got changed and went home.

Viv was more than a mere bone-shaker, however. He scored nineteen tries in twenty-nine appearances on tour, including two from stand-off in the first Test at Newcastle and one from the centre in the third Test at Birmingham; Australia won that game to take the series 2–0, with the middle Test at Edinburgh drawn. Brother Bill played stand-off in the second and third Tests and, in the thirteen matches he played on tour, was never on the losing side. The Farnsworths returned to Australia and went on to tour New Zealand before joining Oldham, where they continued their successful double act. Viv later achieved the distinction, unusual in those days of 'no turning back', by going back home and resuming his Test career against the 1920 Lions.

Bert Gilbert, who played centre in all three Tests for the powerful second Kangaroos, later joined Hull for a then record Northern Union fee of £450. That figure was topped later the same season by Hull's signing of Billy Batten from Hunslet for what then seemed an outrageous £600, but Gilbert's fee still shook the sporting world. As a centre with Wests and Souths, he had been regarded as the fastest in the game in his position and also as a natural captain. Two years later, in 1914, he became the first overseas player to captain a Challenge Cup-winning side when Hull beat Wakefield Trinity 6–0 in the final at Halifax. Also in the side that day were fellow-Australians Jim Devereux and Steve Darmody, a 1911–12 Kangaroo who was to lose a foot in Flanders during the Great War. Indeed, there were no more enthusiastic recruiters of Australian talent than Hull in the seasons immediately before the outbreak of hostilities; they also brought Sid Deane back to England to play briefly for them in 1914. But Gilbert, along with the trail-blazer Devereux, was the man who really made the impact: in his three seasons in the black and white, he played 114 games, averaging a try in every other one.

The selection of Dan Frawley for the second Kangaroo party sparked off a controversy which found echoes throughout the next seven decades of player migration between the two countries. The Australian selectors decided they wanted him for the tour, even though he was still contracted to Warrington; they could equally have called upon Rosenfeld, Devereux and the rest, one supposes, but did not do so. The wrangle went on for some while and forced Frawley to miss the early games of the tour; when it was eventually resolved, he made up for lost time by scoring eighteen tries in twelve matches. But the theme of 'club versus country' was to be a recurring one in international Rugby League, leading to much recrimination and the resort, on occasion, to international transfer bans.

Nobody had seriously considered such restrictions at this stage, however, and English clubs continued to bring in Australians and New Zealanders. Some gave admirable and memorable service; others vanished quickly and without trace. Yet few had the long-term impact on players' movements between the two hemispheres of the young centre that Leeds signed from Eastern Suburbs in 1912. Leeds have become such frequent and avaricious shoppers at the Australian counter over the years that it is hard to imagine them being quite so slow off the blocks. But they were not the power then that they were subsequently to become, and they missed out on the rich pickings from the first two Kangaroo squads. Instead, they bought 'blind', investing £350 in Dinny Campbell – a considerable sum of money, considering that an established international like Gilbert cost Hull only £100 more.

Campbell came initially for three years, but finished up staying for nine. Between 1912 and 1920, he made 258 appearances for Leeds and scored 136 tries, the last of them against Wigan at Headingley when he took the ball on his own 22 and beat the entire Wigan team; his illustrious centre partner, Welshman Willie Davies, described it as the finest he had seen on the ground. More than that, however, Campbell's legacy was the establishment of a dynasty of Australian players at Headingley, and he was to play a crucial role as Leeds's informant and recruiting agent on his return to his home country following his retirement from the game. That was something which was to change the balance of power in British Rugby League dramatically in the era between the wars.

2
The Golfer and the Ghost

On 11 February 1913, British Rugby League attempted for the first time to halt the flow of colonials – as they could then be called without it sounding disparaging – into their game. The Northern Union committee, meeting in Huddersfield, decided that in future no player who had played in New Zealand or Australia should be allowed to play under Northern Union rules in Britain without first serving a two-year residential qualification; contemporary accounts refer only to 'the object of encouraging local talent'. If the Australian or New Zealand ruling bodies had applied pressure, arguing that they stood to lose their best talent, then those representations were not mentioned. Nor do the arguments of clubs like Huddersfield and Leeds that their colonials had the very desirable effect of bringing spectators through the turnstiles – if, indeed, those arguments were advanced – rate a mention.

The ban did not affect the status of overseas players already playing in Britain, or those who had already signed contracts to come; the game's authorities have always had to take great care not to institute any measures which would put their member clubs in breach of contracts. A number of players, such as Rosenfeld and Campbell, pursued their careers in England for years after the imposition of the ban, entirely unaffected by it, and Sid Deane could still guest briefly for Hull in 1914.

Even though the inactivity of the war years added to its efficacy, the ban did prove considerably durable. It was eased briefly in 1923, but reimposed almost as quickly as it was removed after objections from New South Wales. Warrington tried to take advantage of the short respite by advertising in Sydney newspapers for players; but, according to a study of the subject by Trevor Delaney in *Code 13*, only one player, Francis Reade of Balmain, was considered to have been signed in time to beat the reimposition of the ban, and he does not appear to have played for the club that recruited him, Hull KR.

One interesting aspect of the ban is that it applied equally to Rugby Union players from Australia and New Zealand, but not to Rugby Union players from South Africa. That country, inevitably, became the major overseas recruiting ground for British Rugby League during the 1920s. Wigan led an attempt to have the ban lifted in January 1927, but the initiative failed by a single vote. That, however, was sufficient encouragement for the advocates of reform to try again in June of the same year and, this time, they were successful, despite howls of protest from Australia.

Huddersfield were, in the Australian phrase, 'first cab off the rank' when it came to exploiting the change in circumstances. Within hours of the ban being repealed, they had announced the signing of Ernest Mills. Like so many signings before and since, this remarkably rapid transaction owed a good deal to existing links between the two countries. Ben Gronow, the great Huddersfield and Great Britain forward, had coached Mills at the Grenfell club in New South Wales. Gronow described him as being faster than any winger currently playing in Britain, which was an impressive boast in an era when the likes of Johnny Ring and Alf Ellaby were scoring prolifically.

Mills did not disappoint. From his first practice game at Huddersfield, it was clear that the claims made for his pace were well founded. He made his competitive debut against Castleford on 27 August 1927 and finished his first season with thirty-one tries. The following season, in which Huddersfield won the Championship, he was the League's leading try-scorer on forty-four, a tally matched only by the New Zealander whom Wigan had signed when the ban crumbled, Lou Brown. Mills also played for the Other Nationalities side, a team hitherto dominated by Welshmen and South Africans but which was, in its other bursts of activity, to become an important showcase for expatriate Australians. He scored twenty-seven times in 1929–30, another Championship-winning campaign for Huddersfield, and was the League's leading try-scorer again in 1931–32.

Apart from his pace and obvious finishing ability, one of Ernie Mills's most notable characteristics was his durability; from December 1929 to September 1932, for example, he played in 123 consecutive matches. Along with Ray Markham and Bill Shankland, he was one of the first Australians to appear in a Challenge Cup final at Wembley, in 1933, when Huddersfield met Warrington and, fifteen minutes from the end, he became the first Australian to score a try at the famous stadium. Huddersfield had been leading only 11–10, with Warrington applying heavy pressure, and Mills's alert backing-up of a break by scrum-half Les 'Juicy' Adams put them on their way to a 21–17 victory. A knee injury in 1935 cost him a place in a second Wembley final and eventually ended his career in 1938, after a brief and unsuccessful comeback. In eight seasons, he had scored 289 tries – just the sort of thing that Huddersfield had been hoping for when they had lobbied for an end to the international transfer ban.

The second club into action with the scrapping of the ban was Leeds, and again the 'old boy' network was instrumental in them getting their men. On the recommendation of Dinny Campbell, they signed Jeff Moores from Western Suburbs in Brisbane and Frank O'Rourke, a centre from the University club, then a senior outfit in Sydney. Moores had played for Queensland at the tender age of 19 and was already being touted as the best stand-off in Australia, so the arrival of the two players in Leeds was eagerly awaited. They did not make the most auspicious of starts – Bradford Northern's 15–10 win at Headingley in autumn 1927 was their first there for almost twenty years – but that was soon forgotten as both players proved to be valuable additions.

O'Rourke was a fine player in his own right and ranks among the best centres ever to play for Leeds, scoring no less than 112 tries, but it was Moores who became one of the most influential figures in the whole of the club's long history. Within a year of his arrival he was, at the age of 22, the club captain, and he led them in that 1928–29 season to victory in the Yorkshire Cup. Moores also captained Leeds in three consecutive Championship finals, all of which they lost and, in 1932, along with O'Rourke and Eric Harris, he made up a threequarter line that was three-quarters Australian when Leeds beat Swinton 11–8 in the final of the Challenge Cup. That final was held at Wigan, the only one since 1929 not at Wembley, because of the need to play it before the tour party for Australia departed. In that same year, he scored both tries from what was now his regular position in the centres, as Leeds beat Wakefield Trinity 8–0 to give him his third Yorkshire Cup-winners' medal.

If he had done nothing else but persuade Eric Harris to join Leeds, Jeff Moores would still have done enough to be remembered by. As it was, his own contribution as a player was exceptional. Apart from all the tries he helped to set up for the men outside him, he scored ninety-eight himself in his 211 appearances for the club. His departure from Headingley, however, was acrimonious: he had broken his nose badly in a Challenge Cup tie against Hull in March 1933 and had paid for his own treatment at a local nursing home. Moores believed that the club should compensate him for that expense, but the directors adamantly refused to do so. When the second of his three-year contracts with Leeds expired soon afterwards, Moores, equally adamantly, refused to sign another and went instead to York.

There were further highlights in his career at Wiggington Road. He captained York to victory in the Yorkshire Cup final in 1933–34, his first season with his new club and, in 1935, he led a pioneering Rugby League XIII, which also included his old wing partner Harris, to Paris for a game against the French. He played his last game in 1939 and lived the last years of his life in Scarborough, where he died in 1989 at the age of 83.

The streak of fierce determination that made Moores such an

effective player, and which also led to him severing his links with Leeds, seems to have survived well into old age. Ken Dalby, in his paean to the greatest players of Leeds's history, *Nothing But the Best*, recalls the story of a would-be thief armed with a knife who broke into the newsagents and tobacconists shop in Scarborough run by the elderly Mr Moores. Jeff, then 75, sent him fleeing for his life.

*

In the initial impact of Mills, Moores and O'Rourke, Australian administrators could see the start of a potential talent drain which would impoverish their domestic game. As always, they would be most vulnerable to losing players in numbers immediately after a Kangaroo tour to Britain, and it was to try to protect them from that danger that a moratorium was declared on signing any of the 1929–30 tourists. The idea was that no approach could be made by British clubs to Australian tourists and that no transfer would be allowed until a year after the party returned home.

It is debatable whether the restriction achieved its aim. At best, it merely delayed British clubs doing what came naturally for twelve months. Exactly a year to the day from getting back to Australia, Joe 'Chimpy' Busch, the Eastern Suburbs scrum-half who had won six caps for his country, including all four Tests on the 1929–30 tour to Britain, signed for Leeds. It was in the third of those Tests at Swinton that he had become the most famous non-scorer the game has ever known. A win in that match would have given Australia the Ashes, and it was still scoreless two minutes from time when they won what was to be the last scrum. Busch picked up the ball and dashed diagonally for the corner; a tackle came in, and he was carried into touch, but Busch insisted that he had already planted the ball down for what should have been a fair try and was in the process of getting to his feet. Naturally, all Australia agreed with him; but the try was disallowed and Britain retained the Ashes, regardless of the result of the fourth Test, the status of which is still disputed.

The one-year rule meant that Busch missed registration for the Championship final in 1931 by a single day. It was an unfortunate start, and rather set the tone for his stay in England. Although he was a dazzling individual player and had some good matches during his four years with the club, he spent rather too much time in the shadow of Les Adams, who frequently kept him out of the team. The experiment of playing Adams at scrum-half with Busch at stand-off failed, and the Aussie could only be fully confident of holding his place in the side after Adams was transferred to Huddersfield in 1933. Joe 'Chimpy' Busch's greatest claim to fame – at home or abroad – remained that celebrated 'no try' at Swinton.

Others from the 1929–30 Kangaroo squad who joined British clubs were Cec Fifield, Vic Armbruster and Bill Spencer. Fifield was a centre from Western Suburbs in Sydney who joined Hull and went on to score eighty tries for them in 224 games. Known for some obscure reason as Cecil in Australia but Dick in England, he formed a famous midfield partnership for Hull with Joe Oliver, and shared in the club's Championship victory in 1936. Later that same year, another Australian, Frank Hurley, joined Hull and played there until the outbreak of war. Armbruster was one of the great back-row forwards of his generation, a stalwart of the formidable Toowoomba sides of the 1920s who later played in Brisbane. Along with Spencer, a winger for Bundaberg whose four Test caps all came on that 1929–30 tour, he joined Rochdale Hornets.

The most successful signing from that supposedly sacrosanct tour, however, and one of the most remarkable Australian sportsmen ever to cross the world to earn his living in Britain, was Bill Shankland. He was another who played in all four Tests – on the opposite wing to Spencer – but he was already well known in Australia as a centre or stand-off of rare promise; at the age of 18, he had played for Eastern Suburbs and Glebe in Sydney and had worn the No. 6 shirt for New South Wales. He had a marvellous tour, scoring twenty-four tries in twenty-three appearances; it would have taken more than legislation to keep British clubs off his trail. In the summer of 1931, he and his team-mate from Easts, Nelson 'Bill' Hardy, arrived at Wilderspool. Bill Shankland never left England and retired to Poole in Dorset, and his reminiscences of his life and times in British sport are revealing. 'There were heaps of clubs after me – Leeds, Wigan, Oldham – but I fancied Warrington,' he says. 'Their secretary, Bob Anderton, was one of the big men in the English League and he treated us very well while we were there on tour.'

If Shankland's case is any guide, nobody should feel too sorry for the Australian players of that era when it comes to financial reward. The deal that Warrington offered him was very lucrative for its time: 'I got £1000, plus £6 a match and £8 a week wages. They also built me a house on Chester Road for £675. I signed three two-year contracts in all. The others were for £1500 and £2000.' It was excellent money, but it brought its own problems with it. 'You can imagine what miners earning fifty bob a week thought of me getting £14 just for playing rugby,' he says. There was, to be sure, a measure of hostility from some of his team-mates; they would have known, as team-mates always do, the sort of deal that he was on. More than once, he was told in training: 'We'll give you some clog. What are you doing over here pinching our jobs?' There was one player in particular who was always reluctant to pass to Shankland. 'He used to throw it over my head all the time. All I could do was get him on one side and try to tell him that he'd get a lot more winning pay if he'd give it to me properly.' He was not to be the last player to find an equivocal reaction to his highly-paid presence in Britain.

Shankland overcame all that to become an outstanding servant to the club. His first season was a mediocre one for the club, and he was sent off in the home game against Barrow, but his own form was splendid, unlike that of the disappointing Hardy. The following year, he was appointed captain and started to exert a powerful influence on the fortunes of the club. Warrington won the Lancashire Cup, finished well up in the League and went to Wembley to play Huddersfield in the aforementioned Challenge Cup final of 1933. Shankland's play in the centre and his captaincy were both crucial factors. Perhaps unlike the 1980s, when the role of many Australian players was to introduce more pattern and organisation to British teams, Shankland's recollections of the 1930s are that the imports' effect was to open the game up. 'It was good for the game here that the Australian players came out. We opened the game out quite a lot because of our style of play. On the '29 tour, for instance, we weren't allowed to kick. I was an attacking player, and the thing I liked about the game at the time was that nobody told you what to do. It was all instinct. The game is too highly coached now, but it was every bit as hard in those days. Christ, they tackled hard! I trained hard, too, but it was mainly running round the park and chopping wood.'

Warrington's players were given some guidance on royal etiquette before the 1933 Cup final – very much along the lines of 'Yes, sir, no, sir' – so there was some surprise when Shankland and the Prince of Wales launched into an obviously friendly and animated conversation. In fact, the two had met before, on the 1929–30 tour, and shared a passion for golf. In the middle of Wembley Stadium, they stood comparing notes about the current state of their games.

Warrington lost to Huddersfield 17–21 that day, as Ernie Mills broke the game with that crucial try, but Shankland believes that the performance of their respective kickers was the only difference between the two sides. 'Billy Holding was one of the best kickers in the world, but he couldn't kick them that day,' he recalls. 'That made it especially hard to take.'

Shankland took Warrington back to Wembley in 1936. It was largely his own work, in fact, because a magnificent goal from him in his occasional role as place-kicker salvaged a draw in the second round against Halifax, when all had seemed lost. Warrington won the replay and again went all the way to the final. It was a disappointing final, however, in which Warrington, disconcerted by a controversial early try, lost 2–18 to Leeds. Their only points came from a penalty by Shankland, who played at full-back.

By this stage, Bill Shankland's other sport was starting to take over. He had always been a talented golfer, and one of the reasons, apart from £1000 and £14 a week, that he had been keen to accept Warrington's offer in 1931 was that he felt that Britain would offer a better chance of his launching a second career as a professional golfer. He went on to achieve as much success on the fairways as he had on the rugby field, making him one of the greatest of all-rounders in two wildly contrasting sports. Three times he came third in the British Open; on the middle occasion, at Hoylake in 1947, he should have won, but was bunkered on the sixteenth hole of his final round, took a 6 and slipped out of the lead.

Even after he retired from tournament play, he continued to exert an influence on British golf as one of the most respected teachers of the game. As professional at Potters Bar, he moulded the early career of a cocky young Tony Jacklin, who later reckoned that it was the tough regime which Shankland imposed upon him that put him on his way to worldwide celebrity. Many, Shankland among them, believe that he would have made an equally successful Rugby League coach, although the only time he had the opportunity to test the theory was when he coached a British Army team. He prepared them the same way that he had captained Warrington and taught young golfers – by command and by example. 'I told them they'd win by 30. I was wrong; they won by 35.'

Shankland thought of going home to Australia when the war started but stayed in England, was called up by the British Army and never saw Australia again. He has few regrets about that. 'I brought up three sons here – all now golf pros – and I got to love the place.' Britain was good to him although, interestingly, the golf never paid as well as the rugby. However, he was to pay any sporting debt back in full after the war, when he was instrumental in bringing perhaps the most magical Australian of all into the English game. But all that was for the future. In the 1930s, Bill Shankland was haunted by a player who, in his day, made just as sensational an impact as Brian Bevan did almost twenty years later.

*

Eric Harris was almost caught by the determination of the Australian authorities to staunch the haemorrhage of their best players to Britain. When Leeds announced his signing in August 1930, the Australian Rugby League asked their British counterparts to suspend him on the grounds that he had been selected for, and had later withdrawn from, Queensland's tour to New Zealand. The British view was that the restrictions only applied to Kangaroo tourists, and the deal, much to Leeds's subsequent relief, was allowed to proceed.

Harris was another product of the Leeds network of personal recommendations. Jeff Moores had played with him – albeit only briefly before his own departure for Leeds – at Brisbane Wests in 1927. Harris had by then moved from Toowoomba, where he had learned his football, but 'The Brisbane Wests Ghost' hardly has the same ring to it as 'The Toowoomba Ghost', it has to be admitted. Moores wanted Leeds to sign a winger for the specific job of playing outside him, and he assured the club that Harris was the man. Rarely can a recommendation have been as deadly accurate.

At 21, Harris had already played for Queensland and might have made the Australian tour in 1929 but for his youth and apparent doubts about his defence. He was keen to expand his horizons, however, and was mulling over an offer from Rochdale Hornets – very active in Australia at this time and successful in attracting Test winger Cec Aynsley to Britain – before Moores convinced him that Headingley was an altogether more suitable stage.

Harris was a very substantial ghost, 6ft 2in tall and guardsman-straight; but his special quality was his acceleration, the extra gear which he could engage even when he appeared already to be travelling at full pace. Unlike some Australian imports – even some of the best – there was no initial settling-in period for Harris, no teething problems while he grew accustomed to new colleagues and conditions: he was sensational from the very start. In his first game against Featherstone Rovers on 27 September 1930, he scored two tries. By Christmas, and after just seventeen games, he had broken the club try-scoring record of thirty.

It obviously helped immeasurably to have a centre of Moores's ability and selflessness alongside him – 'I lost count of the number of tries Moores laid on for him against us,' recalls Shankland – but Harris was far more than merely an efficient finisher. He could score tries out of nothing, and he had a seemingly insatiable appetite for them. During his first season, he put eight past Bradford Northern, and finished the season with fifty-eight. His subsequent totals were forty-two, fifty-seven, twenty-four, forty-five, sixty-three, forty, forty-five and twenty-one and, in five of those seasons, he led the League's try-scoring charts. His sixty-three in 1935–36 remain a Leeds record. Perhaps his most remarkable and enduring record, and the one that best illustrates the inevitability of his try-scoring, was another that he established in that same season when he scored a total of thirty-six tries in seventeen consecutive matches. It is a scoring run which stands unchallenged to this day, although there was a flurry of excitement in 1985–86 when Steve Ella got to eleven with Wigan, and again two years later when Martin Offiah had a similar run with Widnes.

Harris also had the knack of producing something special on the big occasion. In the Challenge Cup final of 1932, the one played at Wigan because of scheduling problems, it was his try – and a brilliant one at that – that accounted for Swinton. Leeds's other two Australian threequarters were involved, Moores scooping up a loose ball and passing to O'Rourke. Harris seemed to be covered by Swinton full-back Scott when he took the ball, but he slipped past him in his inimitable style to stride away and score a vintage Eric Harris try. He figured as both try-scorer and try-maker, as cutting edge and as the foil for a team-mate, in the Wembley final of 1936. As early as the eighth minute, he outpaced the Warrington defence and put up a high cross-kick – very much part of his armoury and that of some other high-class wingers of his day; the ball sat up neatly for loose forward Ike Isaac to take it in his stride and, although the Warrington defence was convinced that he had come from an offside position, the try stood. Jeff Moores had left for York by this time but, after one season of missing his old partner – hence the mere twenty-four tries in 1933–34 – Eric had found one just as compatible in his namesake, Fred Harris, who was signed from Leigh specifically to give the great man the right sort of service. The Harrises were famous for their scissors moves, a variation on which – Fred dummying his pass to Eric and then dashing down the wing himself – brought the second Leeds try. The third was pure Eric Harris: after beating three men in his initial burst he kicked, picked up, beat two more and scored by the sticks.

Harris was just turned 30 when the war ended his career; his last game for Leeds was the first of the 1939–40 season, and he naturally signed off with a try against Bramley. He continued to be involved in the game as one of the leading sports administrators in Queensland, but he played very few games after his return to Australia. When he returned to Leeds on a visit in 1965, Eddie Waring asked him why that had been; Harris's reply was illuminating and seemed to confirm the nature of his special gift. 'When I was at Leeds I could control my speed exactly as I wanted,' he told him. 'I returned to Australia and I could still run as fast as I did in Yorkshire, but I could not control my speed.' Harris understood the science of his speed better than any wingman; for him, it was not just a matter of running as fast as you could – it was a far more subtle art than that. Some with long memories now see something of the same quality in Martin Offiah; but athletes of such precision are great rarities.

Thanks to the war, Harris fell just short of 400 tries for Leeds, but his appeal cannot be measured in mere statistics. Around the time of his 1965 return to the city and the rugby ground he called his second home, a Leeds fan wrote a much-quoted poem to set him in his true context among great wingmen. As poetry it would win few prizes – except perhaps for the worst ever penultimate line – but it sums up the enduring magic of Eric Harris.

(To the tune of *The British Grenadiers*)
Some talk of Vollenhoven,
And some of Ellaby,
Of Sullivan and Cooper,
And such great wings as these.
But of all the game's great wingmen,
The one Leeds fans like most,
With a too! ooo! ooo! ooo!
Was 'The Toowoomba Ghost'.

*

If Harris dominated the touchlines of the north of England during the 1930s, he did not have matters all his own way as a crowd-pleaser and prolific scorer. Huddersfield, despite being embarrassed by the Albert Carr and Sid Harris affair, were always in the market for something special from Down Under. Carr, a utility player who had represented New South Wales, and Harris, a centre from the same South Sydney club, joined Huddersfield in 1927, not long after Ernie Mills. Their stay was to be far shorter and their departure far more abrupt. After an argument over Carr's unwillingness to have an operation on a knee injury, the pair of them took off and were next heard of booking passages on a ship bound for Australia – no flying home on impulse in those days. In 1931, the club received a letter from their pre-war centre, Tommy Gleeson, who told them that Carr was now player-coach with a country side and that Harris was back with South Sydney.

In 1933, undeterred by that letdown, Huddersfield signed Ray Markham, a winger from Cessnock in New South Wales who had represented Newcastle against the British tourists the previous year. Markham made his debut against Leeds on 7 January, and was a virtual fixture on the left wing for the rest of the season and the six following it. Markham was another player the fans loved to watch; he had plenty of pace, but his trademarks were his jink and swerve. His try-scoring feats were numerous: he was the League's leading try-scorer with thirty-nine in the last season before the Second World War – his own final season – and he scored fifty-three three years earlier in 1935–36, which was only good enough to give him second place, ten behind Eric Harris. Markham also set a new record for tries in a match when he ran in nine against Featherstone in 1935. Like the great Australian wingmen before and after him, he had a talent for multiple try-scoring; he scored four, five and six in a match on a number of occasions, one of the quartets when he went with Moores, Harris and company to play for a Rugby League XIII against France in Paris in 1935.

Ray Markham played twice at Wembley, the first time at the end of his first season when Mills's try helped to beat Warrington and they became the first Aussies to taste victory at the Empire Stadium. He was back in 1935, but Castleford were 11–8 winners. After his retirement as a player, Markham was one of the Australians who put down deep roots in Britain. He worked as assistant superintendent of Huddersfield Corporation's markets department and later headed the equivalent department in Bradford, the very model of civil respectability in his bowler hat. When he died in Huddersfield in September 1988 at the age of 79, however, it was the 264 tries he scored in the claret and gold for which he was remembered.

*

The lure of Britain in the 1930s is demonstrated by the way that, from the middle of the decade, some of the very biggest stars in the Australian game were recruited; they did not come any bigger in those days than Dave Brown. He was the most prolific point-scorer Australian Rugby League had seen, sweeping away the records that Dally Messenger had established a quarter of a century before. Although Brown was a great goal-kicker he was also a devastating centre in general play, as his thirty-eight tries in a fourteen-game Sydney season in 1935 show. He had lost every vestige of hair through illness in 1931 and, with his brown leather headgear covering his bald head, he was the most instantly recognisable player in the game. His performances for Eastern Suburbs when he was still at school put him into the New South Wales side at the age of 18 and, by the time he was 23, he was captain of Australia. He had also been an irresistible force on the 1933–34 Kangaroo tour to Britain – his 285 points from that tour remain a record – and, in 1936, he agreed a four-year contract with Warrington.

His stay in Britain brought him no honours; the nearest was the Championship final in 1937, which Warrington lost to Salford. Indeed, there were many who felt that he never really settled in Britain; the climate, the lifestyle and the heavy grounds, none of them exactly suited him. He played some fine football, however, to justify his £1000 signing-on fee, and always gave it as his opinion that he kicked the best goal of the thousands that punctuated his career during his time with Warrington. It was against St Helens and was from three yards inside his own half.

At the end of the 1938–39 season, Dave Brown returned home a year ahead of schedule. Harry Sunderland, who was by that stage Wigan's secretary-manager, advised him to pay back part of his signing-on fee and that, this done, he would be free to play again in Australia. He retired completely, at the early age of 28, in 1941, leaving behind a host of records and going on to a distinguished career as a coach and administrator. Although disappointment would be too strong a term, he was not the same colossus in Britain that he had been in Australia.

Vic Hey was a team-mate of Brown's on the 1933–34 tour, having been called up at the last moment to replace the injured Ernie Norman, and he played another three Tests against the touring Lions in 1936. It was a short Test career, but most judges in Australia would placc him at lcast level with Bobby Fulton and Wally Lewis among the greatest stand-off halves the country has produced. Hey possessed a rare combination of brute strength and delicacy. Standing 5ft 9in, he weighed 13½ stones, was built like a small tank and played with tremendous physical commitment in both attack and defence; and yet he had all the subtleties of the game at his command as well. His side-step and his dummy were both mesmerising. In short, Vic Hey was a stand-off who had everything, including a father born in Dewsbury, which made the idea of playing in Britain all the more attractive. Leeds signed him in 1937, and he made his debut against Hunslet that August. Two months later, he captained the side to a 14–8 Yorkshire Cup final victory over Huddersfield, and his first two seasons at Headingley before the war turned out to be among the most memorable any player has produced for the club. His all-action style of play took a toll on his own body, however, and he frequently played at less than full fitness.

Hey claimed a distinction that is unlikely ever to be matched on Christmas Eve 1938, when he became the first man to score a try on the Test cricket ground next door to the Headingley rugby stadium. By some quirk of the Yorkshire weather, the cricket field was fit for play while the rugby pitch was frozen solid; so, for the only time in the history of the two sports' co-existence at Headingley, the winter action shifted to the other side of the grandstand. Hey's try was the one which beat Salford 5–0, and seems destined to stand alone for ever.

In 1944, he moved as player-coach to what was virtually his hometown club of Dewsbury and, in 1946–47, he steered them to success in the Yorkshire League and to a Championship final against Wigan before returning to Australia at the end of the season. The following year, he took over as player-coach with Parramatta, a club established only the previous season, and helped them to find their feet in the Sydney competition. In 1954, he coached the Australian side that regained the Ashes and, in due course, became very much the grand old man of Australian Rugby League.

By contrast with Leeds, Wigan had been a club which had always gone looking for overseas players in New Zealand and South Africa; in 1932, they broke with tradition by signing Hector Gee, from Ipswich on the outskirts of Brisbane. Gee had played for Australia in all three Tests against the 1932 British tourists, as scrum-half to the great Eric Weissel at stand-off. In the second of them, the only one which Australia had won, he had shone with two tries. Although he also appeared for them at stand-off and centre, Wigan used him primarily in his Test position; he was the regular scrum-half in the side that won the Championship in 1934, scoring eleven tries in thirty-five outings. He played with Wigan until 1943 before ending his career at Leeds. Gee had company during his early seasons at Central Park in the shape of 1932 Test winger Joe Wilson, another Ipswich player who also featured in Wigan's Championship season of 1933–34. Fred Neumann, who played one Test on the opposite wing to Wilson in 1932, was at Barrow at the same time.

During Gee's latter days at Central Park, there was another important Australian presence at the club – although not on the field. Harry Sunderland was a controversial figure; 'The Little Dictator' was one nickname applied to him for his tendency to ride roughshod over opposing opinion. But he was a driving force with a genuine vision for the game of Rugby League, both in Australia and worldwide. He had been coach and secretary to the Queensland Rugby League, and coached Australia in the second Test against Great Britain in 1932 – the one in which Gee scored two tries and which became known as the Battle of Brisbane. He also launched Rugby League in Victoria, managed three Kangaroo teams, helped to get the game started in France and wanted to do the same in America. In 1938, he moved to England to become secretary-manager of Wigan, and later he became one of the game's best-known journalists and broadcasters. He died in England in 1963 and has been commemorated in both Britain and Australia for his services to the game: the Australians inaugurated the Harry Sunderland Memorial Medal, awarded to the best Australian player in a Test series while, in Britain, the Harry Sunderland Trophy goes annually to the man-of-the-match in the Premiership final. It was particularly apt when Australians John Dorahy, Les Boyd and Greg Mackey received the latter honour in 1984, 1986 and 1991 respectively.

*

As far back as 1931, the Rugby Leagues of New South Wales, Queensland and New Zealand had appealed again for an end to the free-for-all in player movements. All they had got then, however, was a system under which British clubs had to pay £200 to the relevant League before registering a colonial player. That, they felt, was little compensation for the loss – often permanent – of some of the finest players in the game. There was a feeling, even in Britain, that more radical action was needed. Since the lifting of the international transfer ban in 1927, Australia had lost five Test series against Great Britain and were in the process of losing a sixth in 1937–38 when John Bapty wrote in the *Yorkshire Evening Post*: 'The time has come for the Rugby League authorities to give Australia a chance in Test football, and to do that they must put up the bar against importation again . . . I am convinced that, if action is not taken, the prediction made in 1934 that the Australians will never win the Ashes will be fulfilled.'

Subsequent history makes that prediction look a little far-fetched, but there was a better argument for a restriction in the 1930s than there was, for instance, in the 1970s and 1980s. In the 1930s, a move away from Australian Rugby League could often be irrevocable; the option for a player to participate in both countries only became a realistic one with the growth of air travel. Players of the sublime quality of Eric Harris, Jeff Moores and Ray Markham never played a Test for their country; others, such as Bill Shankland, Joe Busch and Vic Hey, would have played many more if they had remained in Australia. With players of that calibre available, it is doubtful whether Australia would have been beaten in every Ashes series – and both countries needed the Ashes to be a competitive event if the health of the game internationally was to be sound.

Late in 1937, after a decade of free movement, the barriers came down again with a prohibition which was to run for four years. Vic Hey had been the last major signing, but Huddersfield, true to type, managed to squeeze in a last couple of Australians – Ron Bailey and Tom Grahame – before the guillotine fell.

3
Boom and Ban

The years immediately after the end of the Second World War were a boom time for British sport, with Rugby League very much included. They were also years in which players captured from an Australia which simply did not believe that it could again lose large numbers of its best men played a vital part. Indeed, it is hard to imagine those golden years gleaming quite so brightly without the likes of Bevan, Bath and Clues, Cooper, Devery and Hunter on the scene. They represented a crippling loss for Australia, but that loss was largely self-inflicted.

The 1937 ban on international transfers had expired during the war, when most minds were on other things. Britain was quite prepared to renew the ban after the war and, during the 1946 Lions tour to Australia, the managers, Messrs Gabbatt and Popplewell, approached the Australian board of control on that very subject. As far as the Australians were concerned, however, the boot now seemed to be on the other foot. As Alfred Drewry wrote in *Rugby League Review* the following year: 'The question of the moment was how many of our players would succumb to the many tempting offers which were laid before them during their travels in Australia . . . I was in a position to know that most of the offers were generous and genuine. Australian clubs lack nothing in enterprise, and the period of unparalleled prosperity enjoyed during the war years gave them a scope hitherto denied them. Healthy bank balances, plus a dearth of talent in their own country, encouraged them to try to get one back on England for the losses in star players Australia suffered in the between-wars period.

'They made no secret of their opinion that they could succeed, too. When managers Popplewell and Gabbatt approached the Australian board of control for their views on the possible renewal of the transfer ban, they were told that Australia did not want one. They fully expected to see half a dozen members of Risman's team return to Australia.' This turned out to be a massive miscalculation by the Australians, although why that should have been the case remains something of a mystery. The offers were there, the money was good; the lifestyle, to say the very least, compared well with that in St Helens and Castleford. But none of the British players took the plunge. We have to put that down to innate British conservatism, and the fact that nobody had shown that it could be done by doing it in the past.

The other respect in which the Australian authorities were proved wrong was the continuing willingness of their own players to pack their bags and leave. Amid all the speculation over which of the 1946 Lions would be snared by the Aussies, British clubs were hard at work. Just how effectively they worked is demonstrated by the list of sixteen top-class Australians Drewry was able to produce a year after the end of the tour:

Barrow – Harry Bath (forward)
Bramley – Bob Bartlett (centre)
Huddersfield – Lionel Cooper (wing), John Hunter (full-back), Pat Devery (stand-off half)
Hull – Duncan Jackson (half-back), Bruce Ryan (wing), George Watt (hooker)
Hunslet – Don Graham (stand-off half)
Leeds – Arthur Clues (forward), Jack Niddrie and Len Kenny (wings), Frank Cottle and Ted Verrenkamp (centres)
Wakefield Trinity – Denis Boocker (centre)
Workington Town – John McGilvray (full-back).

The Australian Test team had again proved a happy hunting ground; Cooper, Devery, Watt and Clues had all played in the 1946 Test series, and Harry Bath would have done so had it not been for a leg injury. Drewry had little natural sympathy for Australia who, he wrote, 'has only got what she asked for. We were ready to put the ban on whenever Australia said the word. They misjudged the situation and therefore they have no right to squeal now.'

That did not mean that there would be no squealing; Australia was thoroughly shocked by the number of defections and decided belatedly that a ban was essential. In August 1947, a five-year prohibition on signing Australian and New Zealand Rugby League players was voted through by the Rugby League council. It did not apply to Rugby Union players from either country nor, despite appeals from Australia and even threats to cancel the 1948–49 Kangaroo tour, could it do anything about the players who had already signed with British clubs.

Australia's concern about the strength of its Test team was shared to some extent in Britain. In 1947, Alfred Drewry wrote that 'those who look upon Rugby League football from an international aspect cannot help being perturbed at the wholesale drain on Australian talent. It is not necessary for me to tell you that playing standards in Australia are at a low ebb; the record of Risman's team in going through the Test series unbeaten and scoring a record number of points speaks for itself.

'Australia has been trying in vain to win back the Ashes for twenty-five years. Don't forget that she is due to send a team over here next season, and that we are all looking forward to seeing a Test series worthy of the great teams which have battled for the Ashes in the past. But you can't expect Australia to send over a first-class team when half her potential Test side are already playing for English clubs . . . the 1948–49 series will not be real Tests at all. If we win, the victory will be a hollow one.'

Tom Longworth, also in *Rugby League Review*, concentrated instead on the benefits to the British domestic game when he wrote of the succeeding generations of imported Australians, 'Whether the remuneration they received was lavish or otherwise, they conferred on our game inestimable blessings . . . Had there been no Australian visits to England I dread to think what would have been the condition of Rugby League football today . . . It has been said that the introduction of colonials into our teams reduces the opportunities of our own youths. Possibly; but in spite of everything we have still produced our quota of "star" players. What puzzles me is that none of the members of our last touring team, although offered remunerative posts in Australia, decided to accept them. So far as I am aware, no British player has ever gone out to Australia to play. Why?'

*

What was clear in England in 1947 was that Australia had closed the stable door after the horse – and a thoroughbred at that – had bolted. And nobody had derived more benefit from the delay than those accomplished rustlers at Huddersfield.

Lionel Cooper had been a late-comer to Rugby League. Brought up in the New South Wales country town of Cowra, he had played more Australian Rules than any other code in his youth, and he did not play League seriously until he was called up for the Australian Army. Once he got a taste for the game, however, his aptitude for it was astounding. Within a year of picking up a ball in earnest for the first time, he was playing for Eastern Suburbs and New South Wales. Within two, he was in the Australian side to play the 1946 Lions. The old Leeds star Dinny Campbell tried to arrange for him to go to Headingley, but Cooper was insistent that he would only go to England if his Easts team-mate Johnny Hunter, a full-back who had not gained any representative honours, could go with him. Leeds liked the sound of Cooper, but hesitated over the prospect of signing a relatively unknown player with him. That was all the opportunity that Huddersfield, with their nose for a great Australian wingman, needed.

Eddie Waring, who covered the 1946 tour for the *Sunday Pictorial* and the BBC, had formed a high opinion of Cooper. Huddersfield asked him to open negotiations, and both Cooper and Hunter were signed in January 1947 for the bargain price of £1500. After nine days at sea, they arrived in West Yorkshire in late February and both made their debut at Hull KR on 15

March. It was Hunter who made the greater impression that day, although Cooper was soon enough into his stride. In the remaining twelve games of his first season he scored ten tries, including one at Wakefield for which 'he went fifty yards from the touchline to the post and beat half a dozen opponents with speed, swerve or hand-off,' according to the *Huddersfield Daily Examiner*.

For the following eight seasons at Fartown, he was to average well over a try in each game, topping the try-scoring lists in 1948–49 (sixty tries), 1951–52 (seventy-one tries) and 1954–55 (sixty-six tries). Only Rosenfeld and Bevan have ever bettered that tally of seventy-one, and not even they matched his performance in one match that season. On 17 November 1951, Cooper ran in ten tries against Keighley, 'every one a Cooper "special",' enthused the *Examiner*. 'One occasionally felt sorry for the Keighley defence which was hopelessly at sea. The Australian's powerful running seemed to mesmerise them and, from the first try to the last, they had no answer and no counter to the determination shown by Cooper.'

That same month, Cooper scored a hat-trick of tries for the revived Other Nationalities side against France at Hull. 'The 16,000 spectators were lucky to see three flashes of majesty by the incomparable Cooper. All his three tries were splendidly taken,' said the match report. 'The best, for which he beat four men in fifteen yards with his left foot no more than six inches inside the touchline, was sheer magic.'

Lionel Cooper scored 420 tries for Huddersfield, as well as playing and scoring for the Other Nationalities at every opportunity. In 1955, he became one of the very few overseas players to be granted a testimonial by his British club, and that provided a chance for his many admirers to assess his mighty contribution. Ben Gronow called him 'the strongest winger I have ever seen,' and Harry Sunderland stated confidently that he had 'shone as brightly as any of the Australians who preceded him.' Brian Bevan, with whom he enjoyed so many memorable duels, drew attention to another aspect of his play: 'A notable feature is his burst in from touch to make play for the right wing; surely the essence of a great and unselfish player.' Sidney Crowther, of the

Huddersfield Daily Examiner, summed up his style thus: 'He is not, as wingmen go, very fast. He hasn't the power of taking evasive action such as that possessed by Brian Bevan but, in a dash for the corner, he can beat as many men as Bevan.

'He does it differently, of course. He has a stronger physique that makes him more difficult to hold but, though some of his tries may seem to be the result of sheer power, it would be entirely wrong to put down his qualities as a wing merely to personal strength. He has a powerful and often precisely timed hand-off, he has at times an amazing way of disposing of a tackler, and he has a shake of his thigh from which the opponent who has gone for him bounces off like a man thrown from a horse. None of us, I imagine, have ever seen anything like that last attribute in football before.'

Nor would the likes of Lionel Cooper be seen very often in the future, although the dynamic energy of Eric Grothe in his prime revived some memories for those lucky enough to have seen both. Although he returned to Australia, Cooper was never forgotten in Huddersfield. When he died in Sydney, more than thirty years after his last try for the club, there was much talk of erecting a suitable memorial to him, possibly overlooking the area of the Fartown pitch which he made virtually his own domain – 'Cooper's Corner', where he scored so many of his tries.

Johnny Hunter, in his own different way, was as great a hero at Huddersfield as Cooper. When the two played their first game, he was the one who instantly caught the eye. 'The Rovers forwards gave him no rest, but he went down to their feet with pluck,' said the *Examiner*. 'It was a display of the greatest promise for the future.' Hunter's own memories of that match were vivid: 'It was so cold that even the goal-posts had goose pimples.' He adapted to British conditions by the simple expedient of ignoring the potential problems they presented, scooping up the ball one-handed from mud-bath pitches, for instance, to the horror of the purists of the time.

Hunter, as was observed of him early in his English career, was 'a full-back with ideas of his own . . . his very courage often got him into difficulties.' More often than not, he would get out of them with sheer exuberance. 'His skill in catching, kicking and running is blended with such evident enjoyment of his football,' said the report of a match at Halifax. 'I fully expect to see him jump over the cross-bar one of these days – just for the fun of it.' His unorthodoxy and vivacity made him a huge favourite at Fartown; Albert Rosenfeld, a regular spectator in those days, had a particularly soft spot for him, regarding him as the most entertaining player in the game.

It was an opinion which was widely shared. When he, like Cooper, was awarded a testimonial, Sidney Crowther again went to the heart of the player: 'He has a great capacity for doing the unexpected. Few players in recent times have so often made a crowd gasp because he has done the last thing anybody, either on the field of play or around the touchlines, expected . . . There never was anything of dull science about Johnny.'

Pat Devery arrived at Fartown after the other two Australians and did not stay for quite as long but he, too, made an important contribution. He had been Balmain's stand-off in their three Premiership-winning sides in 1944, 1946 and 1947, and had played the same role for Australia in the 1946 Test series. After the 1947 Sydney season, he followed the exodus to Britain, just beating the reimposition of the transfer ban. Devery captained Huddersfield's Championship-winning side in 1948–49, and his eighteen tries were second only to Cooper's customary swag. In 1953, he and his two fellow-countrymen were in the side that met St Helens at Wembley in the Challenge Cup final. Both Devery, playing in the centre, and Cooper kicked goals in a 15–10 Huddersfield victory, but Johnny Hunter knew little about the last seventeen minutes of a highly physical match. For once, his intelligent understanding with Cooper had rebounded on him. The big winger, who, perhaps surprisingly, failed, like Bevan, to score a try on his one Wembley appearance, dummied to pass to him; Saints' wingman bought it, carried on and clattered Hunter 'on suspicion', and the full-back was stretchered off.

Huddersfield's great Australian era – which had begun with the signing of Rosenfeld more than four decades before – was drawing to a close. But Cooper, Hunter and Devery rounded it off in style.

*

Although the major exoduses of the 1920s and 1940s threw up a number of other candidates, Harry Bath is widely regarded in Australia as the greatest forward never to win an Australian Test cap. His claim is a convincing one. As a young player immediately after the end of the war, he had already shown his home country that he was a second-row forward of exceptional talents; strong, mobile and tactically aware, he was, almost by way of a bonus, one of the best goal-kickers of his time. By 1946, he had played for both Queensland and New South Wales, the latter after moving south to play alongside Devery in the Balmain side that won the Sydney Premiership. For his new state, he formed a superior second-row partnership with Arthur Clues and was in line to step up to the Test side that year when he injured a leg muscle in the first half of New South Wales's game against the tourists. His decision to continue after half-time aggravated the problem and cost him his cap, and he was never to get another chance.

After the 1947 season, he accepted an offer from Barrow. Bath never settled in the ship-building town and, in March 1948, Warrington paid £1400 for his transfer; it was to be the making of him. He arrived too late to play in the top four play-offs that season but featured prominently in all Warrington's other achievements over the next nine years. Pride of place must go to the club's two Challenge Cup victories. In 1950, Harry Bath became the first overseas captain to lift the Cup at Wembley after the Wire beat Widnes 19–0; he played in that final despite a pain-killing injection and scored the first try. By 1954, he was also Warrington's regular goal-kicker, and his two second-half penalties salvaged a 4–4 draw with Halifax at Wembley – the first draw the stadium had seen – and set the stage for one of the most momentous matches in the history of the game. The official attendance for the replay at Odsal Stadium, Bradford, was 102,569, but many more than that actually saw the game, or part of it, after the staff gave up the uneven struggle of trying to regulate the crowds pressing to get in. Then there were the thousands of people who set off to see the match and never got there; traffic jams are said to have stretched back across the Pennines as far as Oldham. Never was the appeal of the game in the post-war years more graphically illustrated, and Bath was still moved, thirty years later, to have been part of the occasion. He again kicked a penalty as Warrington won 8–4.

Bath was also a key figure in Warrington's two Championship triumphs of the mid-1950s. He provided a prelude to that success in 1952–53 when he topped the League's goal-kicking charts with 170 and scored a club-record 363 points. Then, in the 1953–54 season, he scored 246 Championship points, including 117 goals, and his boot steered his side to an 8–7 win in the final, against Halifax at Maine Road. It was an unforgettable season for Warrington, with the Lancashire Cup also joining the Challenge Cup and the Championship at Wilderspool. In 1955, Warrington won the Championship again, with Bath landing 110 goals and totalling 244 points.

In March 1957, almost ten years after he had arrived in England, Harry Bath went home. St George took the calculated risk of signing him for that season, when many suspected that he might be over the hill. His success over the next three years in Sydney is a shining example of the way Britain could sometimes put something back into the Australian game, via the players it had borrowed. Bath had always been a skilful, crafty forward, more interested in finding a gap for himself or a player in support than in running headlong into a defensive wall. Forward play at the time was far more sophisticated in Britain than in Australia, and Bath thrived in that environment. When he got back to his home country, his clever ball-handling set him apart from the crowd even though, at 33, he was positively ancient by Sydney standards. That constructive influence was to spread through Sydney football, first during his three seasons as a player with St George and then through his coaching career with Balmain, St George, New South Wales and Australia. Bath believed that the English style of forward play was the best way, and popularised that view in Australia, which was greatly to the benefit of the game. In a more just world, he would have finally worn the green and gold jersey that he had missed in 1946, but there was still a simmering resentment over his defection to England as a young player. Bath himself believed that his strong claims were ignored because some in Australia regarded him as having deserted the ship after the war.

Powerful influence as Harry Bath was during Warrington's boom years, another name is even more closely associated with that era – a name that did not even seem worth including in Alfred Drewry's 1947 list of rich pickings from Australia. Unlike the players who figured in that roll-call, Brian Bevan was a 'no-name', a player with no pedigree to speak of in his home country whose signing had gone virtually unnoticed. By a splendid irony, his was to become the first name that Rugby League enthusiasts would always think of when Australian players in Britain were the subject of the conversation.

Never has a player looked less like the popular British conception of an Australian sportsman. Pale, spindly, bald and cadaverous; Bill Shankland recalls that 'he looked like he needed a good meal,' and he had little form on the board in Australia to belie that unathletic appearance. Born into a Rugby League family in Bondi on 24 June 1924, Bevan had been wild about the game as a boy and remembered going to the Sydney Cricket Ground to watch heroes of the day such as Dave Brown. The folktale that he perfected his side-step by weaving past telegraph poles on his way home is perfectly true; sometimes he varied it by stepping around people walking along the pavement – it must have been a disconcerting sight. At 17, he was in the Eastern Suburbs third-grade team, but there was little clue to the try-scoring phenomenon that he was to become; he played a handful of first-grade games in 1942, without scoring a try. The war intervened at this point, and Bevan joined the Australian Navy; in 1945, he landed in Britain as a stoker on HMAS *Australia*, armed with a letter of introduction to Shankland from his father, Eric, who had played alongside him at Eastern Suburbs in the 1920s.

Shankland was by that time a golf professional in Leeds, and he takes up the story. 'He just came and knocked on the door and said, "Can you fix me up with a game of football?" If I hadn't known his father, I might have turned him away, but I told him I thought I could.' He went first to Leeds, but was told that their teams for the weekend were already picked and that they had no room for an unknown Australian triallist. It is another notable irony that Leeds, who benefited so greatly from the shrewd acquisition of Australian talent, should have turned away perhaps the greatest of them all. Hunslet showed a similar lack of interest, so Shankland decided to contact his old club, Warrington. On 10 November 1945, Bevan played as an unnamed triallist in an 'A' team game against Widnes, scored a try and caught the eye with his obvious speed and elusiveness. He played in the first team the following Saturday and was signed on for the laughable sum of £300. 'But he was so pleased to have got a contract that he went out and had a few drinks – something he rarely did – and made himself ill,' recalls Shankland. Bevan promised to return to the club after his discharge from the navy the following season.

That was to be the start of an incredible sixteen-year career, marked by freakish try-scoring, at Warrington. In his first season, he was the leading scorer in the League with forty-six tries. In four other seasons he also led the way, and his seventy-two tries in 1952–53 have only ever been bettered by Albert Rosenfeld. His career total of 796 tries – including 740 for Warrington and twenty-six for the Other Nationalities, for whom he and Lionel Cooper formed a devastating wing pairing – leaves all other try-scorers far behind and still sits in the record books with an air of permanence. Twice he scored seven tries in a match and four times he garnered six; his hat-tricks were so common as to be hardly worth a headline.

The exciting quality of many of those tries gave him a status that transcended their mere quantity. He could leave defenders flat on their back with a side-step or a body-swerve, and many of his greatest tries were scored without a hand being laid upon him. He remembered one against Wigan which he rated as his best. 'I started off on my own line on one touchline and scored in the opposite corner, after beating quite a few Wigan players on the way. It was a good try,' he said. Eye-witnesses who are not inhibited by modesty reckon that Bevan beat *every* Wigan player on a weaving run which must have covered 150 yards. Newsreels of him in action have a Chaplinesque quality; Bevan with his bony legs and baggy shorts flitting across the screen as the unlikely hero of some jerky, speeded-up slapstick comedy. He never looked any more like a footballer than he had when he first arrived; indeed, he seemed to wear an extra layer of bandages every couple of seasons, and Warrington had a trainer whose main responsibility was to see that Bevan was properly strapped up before a match. He kept his unprepossessing physique in a superb state of repair, however, training and practising with a single-minded dedication and spending many hours treating any knocks and injuries.

Warrington fans could hardly believe their luck; they took Bevan to their hearts in a way that few players, British or Australian, have been revered. The question of how and when Bevan would score was almost a game within a game, and his tally sometimes seems to have been regarded as more important than the result. Bill Garvin, in his centenary history of the club, recalls a game against Bramley in 1954; Warrington were leading by 40 points, but the crowd was restive because Bevan, astonishingly, had failed to score. 'Give it to Bev,' they demanded. They did, he scored a hat-trick in the final quarter, and everybody went home happy.

Brian Bevan played his last game for Warrington on Easter Monday 1962. The Wire beat Leigh 29–17 at Wilderspool, he scored his last try for them and, after the match, the crowd gathered in front of the stand and chanted 'We want Bev'. Bevan overcame his natural reticence to climb up into the grandstand and wave to the adoring throng while they sang *Waltzing Matilda.* Yet that emotional farewell was not quite the end of Bevan as a player in Britain. He was persuaded in the August of that year to join Blackpool Borough, and scored on his debut for them against Wigan at Central Park. During his two seasons by the seaside, he played forty-two games and added seventeen tries to his peerless collection before finally retiring a couple of months short of his 40th birthday.

Australia did get one tantalising glimpse of the player they had lost. In 1962, Bevan accepted an invitation to play in a seven-a-side competition which was being held in Sydney as part of the testimonial for Australian scrum-half Keith Holman: he scored tries from all over the field. He was also invited back in 1983 to present the Rothman's Medal to the outstanding player of the Sydney season. Like his election to British Rugby League's new Hall of Fame in 1988, the honour touched him deeply.

After bowing out of the game, he worked for many years as a naval policeman in Portland, Dorset, just a few miles from the home of Bill Shankland, the man who had introduced him to Warrington. On his retirement, Bevan moved back to Blackpool and, even in his 60s, he could be seen running on the beach and sandhills near his house.

There are a lot of ifs and maybes about Brian Bevan. What would he have achieved if he had stayed in Australia? Would he have been as prolific a try-scorer and would he have won Test caps – the lack of which he described as 'my only regret'? And would he have been as staggering a try-scorer if he had come into the game forty years later? He would certainly have been a good deal richer; it was a matter of some bafflement, and occasional bitterness, for him and his Cheshire-born wife, Doreen, that he made so little money out of the game compared with later and lesser players. I was with him once when the subject of Ellery Hanley and Martin Offiah's wages came up; he found the figures being mentioned quite incomprehensible. 'I was born too early,' was all he could say. But, if Harry Bath was the greatest forward never to play for Australia, then Brian Bevan was, beyond any argument, the greatest back. He had the consolation of becoming a legend in a country that hardly saw him play as well as in a land that witnessed his unprecedented feats.

The esteem in which Bevan was held in Britain was obvious when he died in June 1991, at the age of 66. He had been taken ill during a visit to his daughter in Southport, and his funeral at the town's crematorium was attended by scores of former team-mates and opponents. Billy Boston, second to him in the all-time try-scoring lists, was there and had no hesitation in describing him as 'the best there has ever been. Nobody since has been able to hold a candle to him.' Arthur Clues, an opponent for Leeds and a colleague with the Other Nationalities side, recalled the trips away, sharing a hotel room with the chain-smoking, wheezing Bev. 'There are wingers,' he said. 'Then there are great wingers and, way out beyond them, is Brian Bevan.' But perhaps the most poignant sight, among the floral tributes in the shape of the Australian flag and the sober suits, were the little knots of Warrington fans in their primrose and blue scarves. Many of them were too young to have seen Bevan play, but they too felt bereaved that day.

*

Leeds, like the record label that rejected the Beatles, were never to be allowed to forget their blunder in letting Bevan slip through their fingers. What they could say in their defence was that there continued to be many decisions involving the possibility of signing Australian players which they got absolutely right. The best example of that in the immediate post-war years was Arthur Clues, the Western Suburbs second-row forward who played for Australia in all three Tests in 1946. Clues was, and remains, a boisterous, larger-than-life character who enjoys the many good stories about his turbulent and colourful career as much as anyone. His original game was Rugby Union, from which he was banned for life when, as a touch-judge, he threw down his flag and joined in a fight which had broken out on the pitch. As a Rugby League second row, he looked set for a long Test career after playing in his first series at the age of 22.

There were two factors, however, which made Clues susceptible to an approach from Leeds's long-serving secret agent in Australia, Dinny Campbell. The first, he freely admits, was the money; he had quickly realised that his combined earnings as a policeman and a Rugby League player in Sydney were not going to make him wealthy, and Leeds were willing to offer a deal that could set him up for life. The second was the birth of the new Parramatta club; as a junior from that district, Clues would have been obliged to forsake Wests and play for them, a new side with few players and little money, and he did not fancy that at all.

It was with relief, therefore, that he left for Leeds in January 1947, and it did not take him long to become a firm favourite with fans who warmed to his fearless style. He took over as captain for the 1947–48 season, after the disappointment of losing the Challenge Cup final to Bradford Northern the previous May. Clues, in fact, was only on the winning side in a major competition once during his seven and a half years at Headingley – in the Yorkshire League in 1951 – but that bald record fails to do justice to his stature in the British game. He was a tower of strength in the great Other Nationalities side of the time, resuming his old New South Wales partnership with Harry Bath while less wholesomely engaging in a recurring battle with France's equally uncompromising Edouard Poncinet. Even at the age of 30, it was a surprise when Leeds let Clues go to Hunslet in October 1954, and he gave three years' good service to the club across the city before retiring.

Arthur Clues is one of those players who become even more vivid as personalities after they hang up their boots for the last time. Whereas some ex-players become grey and anonymous, others, like Clues, seem to grow more impressive with the years. For many years, he ran a sports shop in Leeds, but his main function has been as a sort of unofficial Australian sporting High Commissioner. Generations of Australian footballers and cricketers – like Johnny Hunter and several other expatriate Aussie League players, he was almost as good at the summer game – have sought him out when they have made their way to England. He has remained a mighty presence around Headingley, lives in some style overlooking Roundhay Park and calls that decision to come to Leeds in 1947 'the best I ever made'.

Others made similar decisions, although not as irreversibly as Clues. Of the four other players who arrived at Headingley in 1946–47, the only one to make a significant contribution was Teddy Verrenkamp. Primarily a centre, he suffered to some extent for his versatility and found himself used in a variety of positions. He finished, however, with a handsome haul of sixty-eight tries in 165 games for Leeds, and was another whose links with the club were to yield a long-term dividend. He became a leading administrator in Queensland, accompanied the state team on its influential tour to England in 1983 and helped to send a number of young Queenslanders to Headingley when the ban on transfers was lifted in that same year.

Leeds also did well out of two forwards who arrived in 1949 from Rugby Union, to whom the transfer ban did not, of course, apply. Bob McMaster stayed for five years, making 179 appearances at prop, before embarking on a world wrestling tour. Ken Kearney was a young hooker who played at Headingley for three years before returning home to make twenty-five Test appearances for Australia as well as player-coaching the mighty St George side that was to dominate the Sydney scene for more than a decade. Kearney attributed his subsequent success in Australia to the lessons in ruthlessness he had learnt from British hookers such as Joe Egan of Wigan.

The only club to rival Leeds for numbers of Australians signed in the seasons following the end of the war was Hull. In the first season after the end of hostilities, Drewry's list included a high-calibre trio bound for the Boulevard: Test hooker George Watt, a dashing wingman in Bruce Ryan, and half-back Duncan Jackson. Watt was appointed captain in 1948 and settled permanently on Humberside. Ryan was a regular try-scorer without being in the Bevan or Cooper class, and scored twenty-four in his first season and fifty-nine in eighty-four games overall before being transferred to Leeds in 1951 for a then record fee of £4750. He ran into an unusual problem with Hull during the 1949–50 season, when he was suspended for two matches for failing to make sufficient effort to catch the train carrying the team to an away match at St Helens; a compromise of sorts was reached when Ryan volunteered to play in the next two games without pay. Jackson earned the privilege of playing five times for the crack Other Nationalities side. Keith Gittoes, later to become a top administrator in Australia, and John Payne brought Hull's Australian contingent to five in 1948–49 and, although Payne's stay was brief, Gittoes proved the most durable of Hull's post-war imports, playing 143 games.

Of the other Australians in that wave, none performed better than Denis 'Dinny' Boocker, a winger or centre from Kurri Kurri in New South Wales who had also played for Newtown in the Sydney competition. Boocker arrived in 1947 and played in Trinity's Yorkshire Cup-winning side that year and again in 1951. The first Australian ever to be signed by a reticent Wakefield, he was a regular try-scorer from the wing, crossing 127 times in 221 matches. His last season was his best; he scored thirty-two tries in as many matches, a club record at the time. Boocker also had the distinction of playing for Wales; he had been born in the principality and, although his family had emigrated to Australia when he was 18 months old, he therefore qualified to wear the red shirt. He did so five times, including playing against the 1948 Australian tourists. A promotion by the club and the local *Wakefield Express* newspaper in 1991 revealed Dinny Boocker to be one of the most popular players to turn out for Wakefield since the war. Efforts were made to trace him, but Trinity were told that he had died in Newcastle, New South Wales, a few years earlier.

Others worthy of a footnote to this period include Brian Bevan's brother, Owen, who played briefly for Warrington before moving to Leigh; Len Horton, who made a brief but impressive contribution on the wing for Warrington in 1953–54 – four tries in five games – and played in the side that won the Championship final the following season; and Max Garbler, who played both wing and loose forward for St Helens in 1950 and 1951.

*

From 1947 onwards, the only Australians that British clubs could sign without clearance from the Australian board of control were Rugby Union players, who did not come under the terms of the new ban. Two sides did particularly well out of the enforced change of tactics, one of whom was Workington Town, only admitted to the Rugby Football League in 1945. Three years later, they imported two leading Rugby Union players, centre Tony Paskins and second-rower John Mudge, and both played important roles in Town's exhilarating early successes. They were virtual ever-presents as Workington, captained and coached by the great veteran Gus Risman, won the Championship in 1951, Paskins scoring eighteen tries over the season.

The following season, Workington were at Wembley, and Mudge and Paskins, along with a third Australian, Bevan Wilson, did more than their share to bring the Challenge Cup to West Cumberland. Mudge scored the try that broke a 7–7 deadlock with equally unfashionable Featherstone Rovers, taking a pass from loose forward Bill Ivison and galloping sixty yards to score. 'It felt like two miles,' he said later, but he got there. Brilliant play in midfield by Paskins set up the try that clinched it beyond any doubt for Town, and they ran out winners by 18–10. Three years later they were back again, but this time Barrow beat them 21–12, Paskins kicking two goals. Workington's enterprise in signing the two eventually benefited Australian Rugby League as well: both played for Eastern Suburbs when they returned to Sydney, Paskins captaining both them and New South Wales and being a little unlucky not to crown his career by playing for Australia.

Aside of Workington, Leigh also thrived on the restriction to Rugby Union players, even though they had been quiet in the Australian market since Mick Bolewski of the first Kangaroos. They now showed a considerable flair for finding Union players who would do well in English League. Their first venture was Jeff Burke, a forward from the Randwick club in Sydney, who arrived in 1949 and played seventy-four times over the next four years. The masterstroke, however, was the signing in 1950 of Trevor Allan, the Wallaby centre with fifteen caps to his credit. Allan cost Leigh a signing-on fee of £5000, and he only stayed for three seasons before persistent injuries forced him back to Sydney; but it was still considered money well spent. Allan emerged as a marvellous Rugby League centre, a rare combination of excellence in both attack and defence. He scored fifty-four tries in ninety-seven games and left a lasting impression; he remains the benchmark by which older Leigh supporters judge a player, and the way he caught the imagination in the town is underlined by the number of them who, during the early 1950s, christened their offspring Trevor. He played for North Sydney after his return to Australia, but never quite recaptured the form that had made him such a hero in Leigh. He later became a leading commentator on Rugby Union which had, by that time, forgiven him for his defection.

Leigh made another illustrious capture from Rugby Union in Rex Mossop, the Manly RFC and Australia second-rower, who arrived late in 1951 after agreeing a similar £5000 deal with Leigh. He played ninety-eight times for them over the next three years, before a nagging back problem forced him to call it a day in England. Unlike Allan, however, his League career continued to thrive in Australia: he played for several seasons at Manly and represented Australia nine times as a Rugby League international. There must have been something in the water in Leigh, for he, too, went on to pursue a high-profile career in broadcasting. 'Moose' Mossop was Sydney's best-known League commentator for more than a decade – relished by some, loathed by others, but never ignored, and very much an Eddie Waring figure in that respect.

A further notable recruit was Keith McLellan who, in 1957, became the first Australian to captain a Challenge Cup-winning side at Wembley, when Leeds beat Barrow 9–7. McLellan, a distinguished Rugby Union player but never a Wallaby, played a round century of games in the centres for Leeds, scoring thirty-two tries. Less prominent, but more unusual in Rugby League terms, was Wally McArthur, a rare signing from Australian Rules territory in Adelaide. He joined Rochdale Hornets in November 1953, spent three seasons with the newly-formed Blackpool Borough and later moved to Leigh. McArthur, one of the first aboriginal players to come to Britain, was a goal-kicking winger who enjoyed a degree of success with all three of his English clubs.

The fact that Rugby Union players such as Allan and Mossop could command large fees in England while Australian Rugby League stars could not struck both players and administrators in Australia as unsatisfactory and inconsistent. The players' answer was to try to break down the ban, and Clive Churchill, one of the greatest players of his day and perhaps Australia's best ever full-back, was the test case. In January 1949, Workington Town announced that they had signed him for a world-record £12,500 and applied to the Australian board of control for his release. The request was turned down, despite Town's argument that Churchill would have come to England in order to advance his non-playing career as well as to play football. In 1951, five Australians were allowed to play for Rochdale until the Australian board of control protested that they were League players who had switched to Union in order to circumvent the ban – a recurring dodge, this one!

The whole matter was to be resolved in a manner that suited the Australian administrator, with his abiding fear about the cupboard being left bare, rather than the Australian player. In December 1951, the ban on League players from New Zealand was extended to cover Union men as well; the following year, Australia succeeded in having the same change made to the restrictions governing their players. The barriers came up for discussion again in 1954 but, with Australia and New Zealand both still in favour of the ban, it remained in force, and English clubs looked instead to South Africa and Fiji for the overseas players who could enliven the game in Lancashire, Yorkshire and Cumbria.

4
The Lean Years

The flow of Australian players into British Rugby League never dried up completely, but there were times during the 1960s and 1970s when it slowed to the thinnest trickle. They were not quite the dark ages, but they were undeniably lean years as far as Australian imports were concerned. While South Africans of the quality of Tom Van Vollenhoven, Len Killeen, Fred Griffiths, Trevor Lake, Alan Skene, Colin Greenwood and Gert Coetzer were illuminating the scene, and the Fijian adventures of Rochdale and Huddersfield provided an entertaining sideshow, most Australians attracted to this country and given clearance to play by their board of control were little-known players who had short and unremarkable English careers.

There were exceptions, none more startling than the case of Ken Thornett. A Rugby Union centre with the illustrious Sydney club Randwick that later produced, among others, the Ella brothers, Thornett had been unlucky to miss out on international selection for a couple of Wallaby tours. Disillusioned, he decided to try his luck at Rugby League, a game he had played as a schoolboy, in Britain. Once more, the Leeds 'old boy' network operated to their benefit: letters from Australia tipped off Arthur

Clues about Thornett's imminent arrival, and he was able to alert the club. After a trial at full-back in the 'A' team, Leeds signed him on a three-year contract.

Thornett played his first senior game at home to Batley on 19 March 1960, scoring his first try for the club. It was too late to salvage anything from a depressing Leeds season but, the following year, he was a vital component in the club's first-ever Championship win. He was outstanding in the final, a 25–10 victory over a Warrington side including Brian Bevan, and displayed all the qualities that Leeds had come to expect of him: exemplary tackling, total certainty under all manner of kicks and vigorous counter-attacking ability. The disquiet over his late start to the same season, when he had gone to watch his brother, Dick, play for the Australian water polo team at the Rome Olympics, was all forgotten.

Thornett played two further seasons at Headingley, his complete reliability establishing him as one of the best full-backs Leeds have ever had. The rest of his story shows how surviving links with Britain, even at this low point in contacts, could do Rugby League in Australia a great deal of good. Stories of his prowess in Britain meant that there was no shortage of Sydney clubs eager to offer him the chance to continue the Rugby League career he had begun with Leeds. The official history of the Parramatta club notes that, in England, 'bookmakers used to lay odds, not on the result of the game, but on whether Thornett would drop the ball. Legend has it that they never paid out.' Thornett had already played a handful of games for the Eels whilst on holiday from England in 1962; in 1963, he joined them permanently, along with brother Dick, and made such an immediate impression in Sydney that he toured with the Kangaroos the same year. So did Dick, making them the first pair of brothers since Oldham's Farnsworths to play together for their country.

Even in an era of great Australian full-backs, Ken Thornett was one of the very best, and Australia owed him to Leeds. A tower of strength to his Sydney club, just as he had been at Headingley, he became known as 'The Mayor of Parramatta'. In 1965, he agreed to make a short return to Leeds to fill a pressing need for a reassuring full-back, and played another dozen games for the club, the last of them in January 1966. He retired from his role with Parramatta in 1968, making a one-season comeback in 1971, after playing twelve Tests for Australia, one more than his second-rower brother.

Another exception to the general rule was Bob Hagan, who was already a Test player when he joined Huddersfield in the 1964–65 season. A crew-cut centre from Townsville in Queensland, he had played for Australia in one Test against Great Britain in 1962 and another against New Zealand the following year. He made his debut against Salford on 9 January 1965, and topped thirty appearances in both of the next two seasons. Hagan also became a leading Sydney player, with Canterbury, and he played in their first Grand Final in 1967. He also provides a link with what was to come in West Yorkshire a decade and a half later; Michael Hagan, one of Halifax's first signings in their all-Australian phase in the mid-1980s, was his younger brother.

Bradford Northern also bucked the trend, bringing over stand-off Garth Budge and full-back Errol Stock for the 1964–65 season. Stock stayed for just the one season, but Budge settled down in Britain and played for a number of other Yorkshire clubs, including Dewsbury. He eventually became an important figure in the National Coaching Scheme, wherein he was responsible for introducing a number of Australian ideas before they became fashionable.

That same 1964–65 season, winger Lionel Williamson, from Innisfail, the North Queensland cane-cutting town that later produced Kerry Boustead, played for Halifax. Bradford grabbed him for the following campaign, during which his natural pace and long stride brought him fifteen tries in thirty-five appearances. A shorter stay the next season brought him ten from thirteen, but the highlight of his Northern career was the Yorkshire Cup final victory over Hunslet in October 1965. Williamson scored two tries in Bradford's 17–8 win, which was an outstanding achievement by a club which had been out of business little more than a year earlier.

Williamson, like Thornett, was an international in the making. He was in the Australian squads for the 1968 and 1970 World

Cup matches, and afterwards played five Tests, including two on the 1973 Kangaroo tour. His successor at Odsal, another great favourite with the crowd, was George Ambrum, a stocky and powerful wingman who scored fifteen tries in twenty-six matches in 1967–68. He, too, went on to become an Australian international, playing twice against New Zealand in 1972.

These were notable characters, but they were put in the shade – quite literally, if the sun was behind him – by a player who joined Hull KR in 1968. Arthur Beetson had already played for Australia – a famous forty minutes in the third Test in 1966 which destroyed the British defence and earned him the indestructible nickname 'Half-a-Game Artie', and then again in the 1968 World Cup series. There was something very English about his brand of forward play; the way in which he was constantly looking to squeeze the ball out of a tackle to a man in support had little to do with current Australian fashions. Yet Beetson had size and power as well as technique; at his peak, he represented the best of both worlds. Colin Hutton of Hull KR, who coached the Great Britain World Cup squad in 1968, was certainly impressed. 'It was Colin who fixed me up at Rovers after he went home from the World Cup tour,' says Beetson. 'In those days, you had to have smallpox injections but, when I got to England, they found mine hadn't taken. They gave me one there and then in my other arm, so neither arm was much good when I arrived at Rovers. Mind you, I hadn't missed a meal on the way over; they damn near had to put me over a weighbridge.'

Despite that, Beetson found himself pressed into immediate service. 'The first thing they said to me was, "Can you play tonight?" I thought, "This is nice," but I couldn't really say no.' He got through half a game.

By December, Beetson was well into his stride. 'I was man-of-the-match in two out of three games, and I remember playing against a young bloke called Malcolm Reilly who quite impressed me.' It was all to end on Christmas Day, however, when Rovers played their traditional morning derby fixture against Hull. 'We were winning 33–30 or something, and it was the simplest thing in the world. I ran on the blind side, fended off a couple of tackles and, as I half-turned, the leg just went. Colin Hutton came running on and said, "Come on, Arthur, this is no time to be messing about",' he laughs to recall. 'I got up to play the ball, but I couldn't move, and that was it for me in England. I still made it to the Christmas dinner, though!'

Beetson still talks with warmth about the way Rovers looked after him, and he has always maintained his links with the club. His subsequent career brought him a total of fourteen Test caps, plus appearances in three World Cups; he was Queensland's first captain and inspiration in the State of Origin matches against New South Wales, and he also coached the state and, briefly, Australia. 'But my one big regret is that I never went back to play in England again,' he says.

*

Warrington were a club that never quite lost the Australian thread during the 1960s and 1970s. In 1968, they had John Grant, a centre from Brisbane Souths, guesting with them. Grant went on to play for Queensland and to make the Australian squad for the 1972 World Cup, playing on the wing against Great Britain in the final at Lyon. The following season, Warrington brought back home the greatest player the club never had.

It always seems ironic that such a prototypal Australian competitor as Bobby Fulton should have been born a Pom, but it was in Warrington in 1947 that he first opened his lungs – whether it was by way of complaint is not recorded. His parents emigrated to Wollongong when he was still a toddler, so Britain can claim little part in his subsequent development into one of Australia's finest ever footballers. At the age of 18, he was plucked from the obscurity of Wollongong Wests to play a key role in the rise of Manly; at 20, he was playing for Australia in the 1968 World Cup and was already being compared with the very best backs his adopted country had produced.

Fulton joined Warrington for a short but sweet thirteen-match stint in October 1969. It is often stated that Warrington won all those games, but that is not the case; they lost two and drew one, but Fulton, who started in the centres only to be quickly moved to what was to become his established position of stand-off, did not disappoint. His stay was a great success in playing terms, and it was also particularly poignant for him to return to what would have been his hometown, but for the intervention of the assisted passage to Australia. He was to return again several times: as a try-scorer in Australia's series-clinching third Test victory at Wilderspool in 1973; as captain of the 1978 Kangaroos who were beaten by Warrington; and as coach of the 1990 team which beat the Wire as they did all other British club sides. He always retained a soft spot for the place, which was more than was apparent in his attitude to the country as a whole. As one Australian assessment of his playing career puts it: 'It seemed Fulton always reserved his best for the age-old enemy, "Mother England". Although born in England, Fulton competed against the Englishmen with a fierceness that bordered on hatred. He was involved in some of the most violent and bitterly contested international games ever played.'

What he would have developed into if he had remained a Pom and a Warringtonian is anybody's guess. The natural ability would still have been there, but that was only part of the story. The ruthless professionalism that went with those gifts was a product of a particular time and place, of Australian Rugby League in the 1960s and 1970s when it was breeding an intensity that was new to the game. A Bob Fulton growing up in northern England would not have been the same player. Australia deserves all the credit for him.

Alongside Fulton in the 1973 Kangaroo side was a player who owed his sudden emergence as an international footballer to a year spent in one of the backwaters of Rugby League with small-time British club Blackpool Borough. Tim Pickup came to Britain on holiday in early 1970 and thought, just for the hell of it, that he would try his luck at St Helens. He made little impression there but, when Allan Bishop, the lesser-known younger brother of Tommy, was transferred to Blackpool in March of that year, he took Pickup along with him for trials. Pickup played the rest of the season with the Borough, but it was only the following term, when he was switched to full-back, that he reached his true potential. It was a time of one-division Rugby League in Britain, so Pickup had the chance to shine against all the top sides. Despite – or possibly because of – some uncertain defence in front of him, he managed to shine very brightly indeed and was a virtually unanimous choice as Blackpool's player-of-the-season.

More significantly, word of his exploits had filtered back to Australia and, when he decided to return there in 1972, there was a queue of clubs keen to sign a player who had left the country as a complete unknown eighteen months earlier. Blackpool were frustrated by the fact that, even though seven of the twelve clubs then playing in the Sydney Premiership were interested in recruiting him, they could collect no fee for him. Pickup had played for them as an amateur, in order to keep all his options open. Back in Australia, he opted to join North Sydney, later moving to Canterbury and playing a total of seven Tests for his country as a stand-off before knee problems ended his career prematurely. Along with Ken Thornett, he later became one of the first Australian League players to be reinstated by the Rugby Union, which allowed him to play some undemanding social rugby without undue risk of injury.

Another of that 1973 Kangaroo squad, Newcastle scrum-half Dennis Ward, who had been in Manly's first Grand Final-winning side the previous year, also played in Britain with Widnes; and Bob Landers, a full-back whose point-scoring record for Penrith stood for twenty seasons, was with Leeds for a time. By this stage, however, most of the significant movement was, for the first time, in the opposite direction. The 1960s saw top British players finally start to work their way into the Australian game, with Dick Huddart (St George) and Dave Bolton (Balmain) the most prominent of the early signings. Even a Sydney second-division club like Wentworthville – and second division in Sydney is a long, long way from the Premiership – could attract a British star like Lewis Jones as their player-coach. In some cases, the desire to play for an Australian club might have been mingled with the wish to emigrate, but many others followed the trail of those first two or three.

After Great Britain's Ashes win in 1970, for instance, Cronulla snared Cliff Watson while Malcolm Reilly and Phil Lowe joined Manly. Although the restrictions on international transfers had never been lifted, they amounted to a 'no poaching' ban rather than an actual transfer ban; thus, if an Australian club could negotiate the transfer of a British player from his club, they were free to do so. The trend continued thereafter, with Mike Stephenson and Bill Ashurst joining Penrith and Brian Lockwood going to Canterbury and later Balmain. There was nothing in the rule-book to stop British clubs reversing the situation by attracting Australian players of similar stature, but they failed to do so. One reason was that British Rugby League, after a boom which had continued through the 1950s, was at a low ebb. Crowds were down sharply, and most clubs lacked the cash as well as the enterprise. There was also the illusion – fuelled by occasional blips on the radar screen like the 1970 Ashes series and the 1972 World Cup – that Britain enjoyed, if not a monopoly of the best players, then at least more than her fair share of them. And so British clubs signed no dominant figures from Australia in this period; instead, they borrowed players from friendly Australian clubs and they provided short-term havens for Australians who were, essentially, just passing through.

In that process of passing through, however, a surprisingly large number of them took home something to remind them of their stay, not least from the BBC2 Floodlit Trophy competition. A rare Australian medallist in the mid-1960s, for instance, was David Wood, who played inside the great Vollenhoven in the 1965–66 final, which St Helens lost 0–4 to Castleford. Seven years later, two Australians were instrumental in Leigh winning the same, now defunct, competition: in the 1972–73 season, Leigh had brought over three young players from Eastern Suburbs in Sydney – Frank Paulger, John Atkin and Graeme Lawson – and Atkin and Lawson both played in the floodlit final of that year against Widnes as an Antipodean right-wing partnership. Lawson, a former beach sprint champion in Australia, scored the only try in Leigh's 5–0 victory, using his pace to chase a kick and score. Four years later, Paul Khan was in the Castleford side that beat Leigh 12–4 to bring the trophy to Wheldon Road. Khan was a prop forward who had a long and distinguished career in Australia, playing regularly for Queensland, touring with them to England in 1983 and coming close to Kangaroo selection. His year with Cas also brought him a winners' medal in the Player's No. 6 Trophy, when the Glassblowers beat Blackpool 25–15 at Salford.

Bob Smithies, Balmain's full-back in the 1969 Grand Final, spent longer in Britain than any other Australian player in the 1970s. He spent several seasons with Hull KR, and his stay was highlighted by his appearance in the side that won the Yorkshire Cup in 1974. Along with his colleague from the Illawarra club Dapto, Allan Fitzgibbon – later to become a leading Sydney coach – and South Sydney centre Ross Birrell, Smithies played for Rovers against the touring Australians in 1973. Leigh's team against the same tourists included not only a young John Dorahy, getting his first taste of British club football, but also his brother Tony. Following on from the trio of 1972–73, Leigh had five Australian players in all in 1973–74, although the other three played only one game each. Hull had also had five in 1972–73, of whom Brisbane Brothers forward Len Dittmar was the most effective, as well as two Britons returning from stints playing in Australia, Mervyn Hicks and Graham Williams.

Smithies's association with Hull KR coincided with the revival – to date, the last revival – of the Other Nationalities side. In the first season of its resuscitation, he was the one Australian selected. The following season, 1975–76, he was emulated by a whole clutch of Aussies: Richard Moncrieff of Keighley, Tom Sheppard of Castleford, Neville Elwin and Bruce Gibbs of Workington Town, Ron Pomering of Bramley, a very young Steve Martin, enjoying his first British season at Barrow, and Gary Souter of New Hunslet. Not a Cooper, a Bevan or a Bath among them, perhaps, but they were enough to give the Other Nationalities side a distinct Australian flavour again. Martin, Souter, Pomering and Gibbs – a big prop from Oberon in New South Wales who went on to be the cornerstone of the pack at Western Suburbs in Sydney – all played in the team that achieved the Other Nationalities' one satisfying result of the County Championship, a 16–16 draw with Yorkshire. Martin also won a second-division Championship medal when Barrow ended the season at the top of the table.

Other Australians of some note who appeared for British clubs in the mid-1970s included Steve Edmonds and Barry Andrews, who played for Halifax and York respectively during the 1974–75 season; both played for Cronulla in the Grand Final in 1978, as did Paul Khan. Also at Halifax that same year was Allan Thomson, a forward from Newcastle who played three times for Australia in 1967 and 1968 and also in a winning Manly side in a Grand Final. Les Mara, a good half-back from Balmain, played for St Helens, while Warrington maintained their Australian connection by bringing over forward Peter Connell, from Valleys in Brisbane, for part of the 1975–76 season.

*

The mid-1970s, however, really belong to two players who broke a long Australian drought at the occasion which has always meant the most to imports from overseas. For seventeen years – the longest gap since the game was first taken to Wembley – Keith McLellan, Leeds's captain in 1957, remained the last Australian to play in the Challenge Cup final. Then came Warrington and David Wright. A second-rower from Brothers in Brisbane, Wright joined Warrington in the autumn of 1973 and quickly established himself in the club's fearsome pack. He was there at the right time because, although performances in the League were patchy, it proved a notable season for the Wire in other respects. Wright scored a try in the Challenge Cup first round against Huddersfield and shared in the subsequent victories over Huyton, Wigan and Dewsbury. The final, against strong favourites Featherstone Rovers, was no classic, even by the rather depressed standards of the time; but Warrington, guided by player-coach Alex Murphy, were convincing 24–9 winners. Wright, apart from a typically heavy tackling stint, caught the eye with a number of ground-gaining runs from the short passes provided by the Wire's ball-playing prop, Dave Chisnall. He fully earned the right to climb up to the royal box to receive his medal from, appropriately, the Australian High Commissioner, John Armstrong.

Wright had returned to Australia by the time Warrington played in and won what was then the Club Championship final against St Helens, but he already had another winners' medal in his pocket from his appearance earlier in the season in the Warrington side which beat Rochdale Hornets 27–16 in the final of the Player's No. 6 Trophy. For good measure, he was also in the side that won the short-lived Captain Morgan Trophy in its one and only year of competition, packing down in his customary second-row position for the Wire as they beat Featherstone 4–0. It had been a long time since an Australian player had enjoyed such a haul from a British season, and Wright continued the good work when he returned to Brisbane. He won a place in Australia's 1975 World Championship squad and played, along with British-connected players Anderson, Fulton, Pickup and Strudwick, in the side that beat New Zealand 36–8 in Brisbane.

By the time Chris Anderson represented his country for the first time in 1975, he had already become another Australian to do a lap of honour at Wembley. Recognised as one of Sydney's most promising wingers when he joined Widnes in 1974, everything he did – or almost everything he did – in Britain went to confirm that view. His Canterbury team-mate, the solid forward John Peek, accompanied him and played only six games for the Chemics, but Anderson became an important member of the side, enjoying the best try-scoring sequence of his whole career with eighteen in as many games.

It wasn't all plain sailing for Anderson. Had it not been for Wembley, he could have been remembered merely as the player who cost Widnes another major trophy. Anderson had scored five tries to help Widnes to the 1975 final of the Player's No. 6 Trophy, including a hat-trick in the second round against Wakefield Trinity. The final itself was a dour affair against Bradford Northern, but Anderson had a golden opportunity to score a freak try that would have won it for his side. The chance came when a violent gust of wind blew a penalty-kick by Ray Dutton backwards and virtually straight into Anderson's arms. Bradford, not surprisingly, were caught unawares, but Anderson fumbled the ball as he crossed the try-line, and Northern survived to win 3–2. Peek was a Widnes substitute that day.

Anderson and Peek both scored tries in the first-round victory over Swinton in the Challenge Cup, but both were long gone by the time that Widnes won their way through to Wembley at the semi-final expense of Wakefield Trinity by 13–7. Coach Vince Karalius's decision to fly Anderson back for the final was a controversial one: but when, apart perhaps from John Ferguson ten years later, are they not? Widnes had earned their trip to the capital with locals like Jimmy O'Neill and Terry Karalius in the threequarters, but Vinty was adamant: 'Anderson is, in my opinion, the best winger in the world.' Canterbury agreed to let him travel – no Australian club, for all their mumblings and rumblings, has yet had the nerve to deny a player a Wembley appearance – and Widnes cheerfully paid out the £1000 for his return air-fare. However, that investment almost proved a complete write-off because, as soon as he landed at Heathrow, Anderson was arrested for an unresolved motoring offence committed during his previous visit. Widnes managed to sort out the legal problem, and Anderson was free to take his place in the final against Warrington, who were defending the trophy that they and David Wright had won the previous year.

The kicking of Widnes full-back Ray Dutton and a powerful display by a pack that subdued Warrington's normally rugged forwards were the crucial factors in Widnes's 14–7 triumph. Anderson had few running chances but, from one of them, he was a likely try-scorer until tripped by Warrington's Alan Whittle: the resulting penalty edged Widnes further towards their goal and, for a second consecutive year, an Australian collected his winners' medal shortly after 4:30.

It was just the start of an eventful career for Anderson. After the 1975 World Championship, he went on to win eight Test caps for Australia and toured with the Kangaroos in 1978 and 1982. For his club, Canterbury, he played and scored in their first-ever Grand Final victory in 1980, and he became one of the most durable of Australian club players before returning to Britain ten years after his Wembley visit to be the mover and shaker behind Halifax's rise to the top of the heap. Time alone will tell whether his return to Canterbury as coach in 1990 will be the final twist in the tale of his transcontinental Rugby League career.

*

By 1975, clouds were gathering around the whole question of international transfers, be they sales, loans or swaps. Despite sporadic Australian successes in Britain, the bulk of the traffic was still travelling in the opposite direction: Gary Stephens and

Steve Norton had followed Reilly and Lowe to Manly, Roger Millward had gone to Cronulla, and David Topliss had joined Balmain. Topliss was just one of a fistful of British players whose Australian commitments made them unavailable for the 1977 World Cup; the concept of an international transfer that left a player free to represent his country had still not surfaced. The forwards were particularly hard hit: Lockwood, John Gray, Ashurst, Paul Rose, Jeff Grayshon and Norton were all missing from their country's colours while playing for Australian clubs, and Great Britain lost the final to Australia by a single point. The irony of the Lions fielding what amounted to a second-team pack while world-class forwards went through their paces for Sydney clubs was bound to bring matters to a head.

At the meeting of the International Board in Sydney at the end of the World Cup, the British delegates went in with a shopping list and came out with what they wanted: the scrapping of World Cup tournaments in favour of a return to a four-year cycle of tours . . . and an international transfer ban that would actually hold water. No more transfers were to be permitted, even if British and Australian clubs agreed them, although English players already in Australia could not be dragged off home against their will. Thus, for instance, John Gray, the former England Rugby Union and Wigan hooker or prop, continued to play in the Sydney Premiership until 1983, transferring from North Sydney to Manly and back to Norths.

Nor was it quite the death-knell that it appeared for Australians in Britain. Take the case of little Blackpool Borough, for instance. Their appearance in the final of the Player's No. 6 Trophy in 1977 brought another Australian a British medal, albeit a losing one, when Queenslander Ken Groves lined up in their pack opposite Paul Khan and Castleford. That should, in theory, have been the end of the road for him; but Groves was still around the following season, when he was transferred to Workington Town and, but for injury, would have played for them in their Lancashire Cup final victory over Wigan. Barry Geary, another forward from the same Queensland town of Gympie, was still at Blackpool for the 1977–78 season and, as late as 1979–80, there were three Australians on Borough's books, one of whom, Steve York, made seven first-team appearances. I do not doubt that the same thing happened at other clubs and that small pockets of obscure Australians lingered on for some time. But, by the time they were all weeded out, the international transfer ban had fallen into disrepute, and it was time for a new wave of Australians to pick up the baton.

5
Beating the Ban

Darryl Pierce was an unlikely revolutionary. In 1981, as a veteran of ten seasons with his local club, Manly, he should have been looking to wind up his career, not send it off on a whole new path which was to open up startling possibilities for a subsequent generation of Australian players.

Pierce was the catalyst for the scrapping of the international transfer ban, and yet his role is largely forgotten. Perhaps that is because he was never a particularly high-profile player, either in his native Sydney or in Britain, when he won the right to play there. Pierce had played 110 first-grade games for Manly, initially replacing Peter Peters – later to become better known as a broadcaster than he had ever been as a player – in the Sea Eagles' pack. He had not, however, played in any of the club's Grand Finals during his decade with them; by a splendid irony, places in the back row of the pack in the 1972, 1973 and 1976 Grand Finals had been occupied variously by Malcolm Reilly, Phil Lowe and Steve Norton – British players whose moves to Sydney had been the rationale behind the imposition of the ban on international transfers in 1977.

It was another Englishman who provided the link that

eventually brought Pierce to Britain, with all the consequences which were to flow from that. Graham Williams was a scrum-half from Swinton who had emigrated to Australia to play with Manly and had settled in the area. When Pierce's career at the club began to fade, the two discussed the possibility of his playing in Britain. Williams tipped off his old club and, when Pierce landed at Heathrow in July 1981, Swinton secretary Steve Moyse was there to meet him. At this stage, the club was more sanguine than the player about the prospects of him being able to play in Britain: he was armed with a clearance from Manly but knew that he would need one from the Australian Rugby League as well. 'Swinton told me that they would make the arrangements to get me a clearance,' recalls Pierce. 'I told them they might have some trouble.'

Undeterred, Swinton registered Darryl Pierce, making no attempt to disguise his Australian origins, on 14 July – the first Australian player to be signed by a British club since the ban was imposed. Needless to say, it was not to be that simple; Pierce's own predictions of 'trouble' turned out to be perfectly accurate. 'Swinton wanted to play me in a trial match against Huyton. But they got a telegram from David Oxley [then secretary-general] at the English Rugby League, saying that I wouldn't be permitted to play. We pressed them, we threatened to take them to court on the grounds that it was a restriction of trade, but they stood firm: I couldn't play unless I'd got a clearance from Australia. There were dozens of phone calls and telexes going back to Australia.'

There was also a good deal of buck-passing going on between the British and Australian Rugby Leagues, with each claiming that it was the other's responsibility to clear Pierce to play in Britain, if that was to be the outcome. Pierce, Swinton and Oxley all complained of being unable to get a straight answer from the ARL; ARL president Kevin Humphreys, later to resign from his all-powerful position in Australian Rugby League over allegations of malpractice, told a different story. His version was that the ARL had made its standpoint clear: 'Manly issued a clearance for Pierce. Both Pierce and the Swinton club have been informed that the ball was in the court of the English Rugby League. If they wanted to clear Pierce, then it was up to them,' he said.

That still was not the Rugby Football League's interpretation of the case; they believed that Australia could give the 'yea or nay' on the matter, and it was Australia's failure to do so that drove Britain to make a unilateral decision. In January 1982, after sending off one last telegram inviting Australia to speak now or forever told its peace, the Rugby Football League finally gave Swinton permission to play Darryl Pierce. In fact, Pierce had been playing for the previous three months, without fanfare or international incident, for local amateurs Eccles in the North-West Counties League. But he was fit, eager and anxious for a chance to play professionally again, which was why he was prepared to wait and fight for the opportunity. His case had become something of a *cause célèbre*; via the Member of Parliament for Eccles, Lewis Carter-Jones, Swinton had succeeded in having the matter aired in the House of Commons, and two Ministers, Norman Tebbit and Neil MacFarlane, had given replies encouraging the belief that Pierce was entitled to play in Britain if he so desired.

On 19 January, Pierce made his debut for Swinton in their home second-division fixture against Batley. The breakthrough had been made, and there was never the slightest chance of the breach in the ban stopping there. The Rugby Football League continued to insist that Pierce was an exception to a general rule that still held good. As David Oxley said at the time, the ARL 'have had their chance. Even if they object now, we will not go back on what we have decided for Pierce.' But that, they still believed, did not mean that the ban as a whole was doomed. Pierce himself could see the position a little more clearly. 'The decision to let one in was all that Australia was waiting for,' he says. 'They just wanted Britain to make the first move.' Leeds players Tim Wilby and Roy Dickinson had already flouted the ban by playing in Perth under assumed names the previous season; now Pierce had shown that there was a way through the barriers in the opposite direction.

'The thing he had in his favour was that he was prepared to take the risk of coming to England,' says Steve Moyse, the man who, on Graham Williams's recommendation, had gone to Heathrow Airport to claim Pierce for Swinton. 'Graham told us that Darryl was the player who had done Phil Lowe's tackling for him while he was at Manly, and he was a very strong defensive player who became a big favourite at Swinton. I had a shock when I saw him at Heathrow, though. I was expecting someone about 6ft 8in and carrying a boomerang, and he was nothing like that at all. He had no size, but he was a tremendously hard worker.'

As it turned out, Pierce played only a modest thirty first-team games for Swinton in his three seasons in Britain, largely because he had some dreadful luck with injuries. Moyse recalls one particularly nasty one. 'He was playing in the 'A' team, on his way back from another injury, against Wigan 'A'. They had a big prop whose reputation was well known, but Darryl went in to tackle him around the legs. He just stamped in Darryl's face. You often hear injuries called "horrific", but this one really was. It turned his cheek inside-out and split his lip in two.'

Credit for wanting to play again after an injury like that goes to Pierce; but Moyse gives a lot of the credit for keeping his resolve firm during the months when he was battling for the right to play professional League in Britain to his own mother, with whom the player was lodging. 'It was something she got her teeth into. I think she was tired of having him around the house like a bear with a sore head. Still, it's funny, really, that it should have been Swinton who forced the issue, because we were never in a position to benefit from the changes that it brought about.'

Swinton, a faded shadow of their great eras in the 1920s and the 1960s, were assuredly never equipped to exploit the breakthrough that they and Darryl Pierce achieved. The only Australian player of note that they signed over the succeeding seven years was former Test forward Ian Thomson – yet another Manly player – but injury prevented him ever making an impact at Station Road. Indeed, it is possible to argue that the lifting of the international transfer ban was another in the string of circumstances that polarised the prosperous and the not-so-prosperous clubs in the British Rugby League. The ability of their bigger neighbours to go out and recruit world-class players from Australia has done clubs like Swinton no good at all; it has led to a draining away of support and made it harder for them to compete on level terms with clubs with both the cash and the imagination to spend it on the right imported players. But those were consequences which were, at best, uncertain as Swinton fought their corner alongside Pierce.

The player himself needed to cultivate a philosophical approach to his own role in the scheme of things as his early trail-blazing was soon obscured under the thundering hooves of hordes of imports with bigger names and better contracts. As his fellow-countrymen started to arrive in numbers, he showed that he could do just that. I wrote in the winter of 1983, as each Qantas flight seemed to be bringing in new Antipodean stars, that 'the man who started it all could be excused for being bemused and even a touch bitter. But Darryl Pierce is neither. The first Australian to bust the ban is well into his third season with second-division Swinton, earning a few cents as opposed to the big-dollar contracts commanded by the stars heading north now. "But good luck to them," he says. "The only thing that would spoil it now is if you get some Australians coming out here for a holiday. That would be a shame because, now this has started, we want it to kick on."

'Pierce claims no credit for what he has triggered. His belief is that it would have happened anyway. "If I deserve credit for anything," he says, "it's for what I'm doing now." In his job as a full-time employee with the Salford Recreation Department, he spends his days in the local schools enthusing the kids with the appeal of Rugby League – a job that no one had tackled until he decided to settle in the area.'

Pierce established a valuable precedent for the new wave of Australian players by putting something back into the host country with coaching and development work. In his case, at any rate, the benefit was mutual: during his time in Britain, he qualified as a Grade 1 coach, something which stood him in good stead when he returned to Australia. He became similarly well-qualified there and, in 1990, was the coach of the successful Eastern Suburbs reserve-grade side, at a time when the first team was having a disastrous season.

When he had arrived in Britain, Pierce had had what might be termed a typically Australian reaction to some of the casual and *ad hoc* arrangements for match preparation. 'I remember one training session at Station Road when it was snowing,' he says. 'We couldn't go on the pitch so we had a game of touch on the car park, and that was it. On the other hand, I liked the way the players all used to get together after training or a match. In Australia, they tend to get changed and go their own way. That's a form of Australian professionalism I don't agree with and which I would like to change.'

Whether he will convince them in Sydney that the Swinton way is best in this regard is open to doubt; but Darryl Pierce has already instigated more change in his Rugby League lifetime than scores of players who have achieved far more in terms of recognition and honours. There is a good Australian epigram about those who drink the water remembering those who dug the well; when the hundreds of players who followed Pierce to Britain and did very nicely thank-you check their bank balances and revive the good memories by leafing through their scrap-books and photograph albums, a nod of thanks in his direction would be in order.

*

In the early spring of 1983, while the world's Rugby League administrators wondered what they were going to do about the ban and Darryl Pierce was being routinely referred to as the only Australian to have found a way through it, the telephone rang one morning, and an unmistakably Australian voice began to take me to task. 'You keep writing that there's only the one Australian here,' it said. 'But there isn't: there's me as well.' The voice belonged to one Peter Donkin and, as he said, he had found a way round the restriction as well.

Donkin was playing for Cardiff, who were then just getting into their stride in the best spell they were ever to have in the second division. It was their second season in the Rugby Football League and, with this mysterious man Donkin in the pack alongside all the big-name but, in League terms, terribly raw recruits from Union, they were going well. Donkin had arrived there by the most circuitous of routes. Coincidentally, he, like Pierce, was from Manly but he had not achieved a great deal with his hometown club; a few appearances as a substitute in the first team were the most that he could boast of. He had, however, had a wide-ranging career in country competitions, notably in Wollongong. Wanderlust had afflicted him early in his career, and he had sampled British League as a teenager, before the ban was put in place, by playing briefly for Castleford and Halifax. 'I was very young, and it was only a short stay; but it gave me a taste for it,' he says.

When gaps had started to appear in the ban, Donkin, never a player to stay anywhere for very long, had been keenly interested in trying his luck again in Britain. His first port of call was Dewsbury, with whom he trained for a while, hoping to get a run in the team. 'But the coach didn't seem very interested, so I thought I'd try elsewhere.' Elsewhere was Cardiff, a club which appeared at the time to have quite bright prospects; the Welsh club registered him, omitting any reference to a previous Australian club, on 16 December 1982.

Donkin had been rather crafty. After a period out of Rugby League with injury, he had applied for, and been granted, reinstatement as a Rugby Union player – a game he had dabbled with in his youth. Whether this was enough to place him outside the scope of the international transfer ban was a moot point, but it allowed him to argue that a British club was on safe ground in signing him. At any rate, Cardiff were persuaded and were happy to have him around alongside the likes of Tommy David, Paul Ringer, Brynmor Williams and Steve Fenwick. Perhaps his finest hour was in Cardiff's 20–14 victory over Fulham, at Chelsea's cavernous Stamford Bridge ground on the eve of the 1983 Challenge Cup final.

'I was playing well and I played particularly well that night, so much so that Fulham wanted to sign me. I wanted to go as well, but Cardiff – with whom I'd fallen out by this stage – managed to block the move,' he remembers. That was the end of his second venture in Britain; he had looked a good, workmanlike loose forward but, more importantly, he had knocked another small hole in the wall separating Britain from Australia. 'Britain badly needed to re-establish its links with Australia,' he says. 'Nobody had any idea how far behind they had fallen.'

Donkin's subsequent career saw him play and coach in Western Australia and New South Wales before embarking on another adventure by coaching a club side in Wellington, New Zealand. He later returned to Perth and, when last heard of, he was looking for an opportunity to coach in Britain. He deserves his share of the praise for the dramatic change in circumstances that made Britain an option once more for Australian players and coaches. It was, after all, hard to insist that Darryl Pierce was a unique exception to the rule at Swinton while there was another exception playing for Cardiff.

*

Colin Penola found a different way around the potential problem of his Australian nationality: he kept very quiet about it. A full-back from the Carltons club in Mackay, northern Queensland, he arrived in Britain in the spring of 1983, intending to take an extended working holiday. He knew players Kevin Dick and Sean Miller from their travels to Queensland, where they had played a spot of social rugby, and so he headed for Leeds. By this time, Miller had moved from Headingley to Carlisle; after the euphoria of promotion in their inaugural season in the Rugby Football League, Carlisle were now bottom of the first division and glad of any reinforcements they could get, without enquiring too deeply into their origins. Penola played three games for them towards the end of that doomed campaign and, in two of them – heavy defeats at the hands of Castleford and Warrington – he scored tries, and was hoping for a contract for the following season. When that failed to materialise, he became one of the first signings made by newly-formed Kent Invicta, who found him a job in the building trade in Maidstone.

I tracked him down there in August 1983, intrigued by rumours that another Australian had inflicted further damage on the credibility of the ban. 'I've been keeping pretty quiet about being an Australian,' he told me. 'But there just doesn't seem to be any problem.' He was, I wrote, 'the latest Australian player to laugh in the face of the international transfer ban . . . As in the cases of Darryl Pierce and Peter Donkin, there have been no attempts to prevent him being registered.'

That season, Kent seemed momentarily to have achieved a much bigger Australian coup when news agencies put out the story that they had signed the legendary Wallaby Rugby Union star, Mark Ella. However, it transpired that a gremlin had crept into someone's typewriter, and that Invicta had in fact secured the services of New Zealander Mark Elia – no mean player, as his later success with St Helens, Canterbury, Halifax and New Zealand proved, but not quite the sensational capture that his near-namesake would have been.

The Australian who *was* at Maidstone was able to get away with it because he looked exactly as though he came from somewhere else. Penola was the fourth-generation offspring of Solomon Islanders who had come to Queensland to cut cane and, to the uneducated eye, looked as though he could be related to many of the islanders from New Zealand who were already making an impact in British Rugby League. People assumed he was 'from somewhere that way on', and Penola said nothing to disillusion them.

Penola faced a struggle for his favourite full-back position during his first full season in Britain, because Invicta had spent £25,000 on a goal-kicking No. 1 from Workington Town, Lynn Hopkins. With his ability to play in the centres as well, however, Penola was a regular member of the side in its first and, as far as Kent was concerned, only season. What is more, he was destined to become one of the most durable of all Australian imports; in his own quiet way, he made the most lasting impression of any of the original pioneers who restarted the flood of Aussies into Britain. Indeed, he was the only one of the newcomers to settle in Britain, marrying an English nurse, and he enjoyed a long and eventful playing career.

He was one of the Kent players who agreed to move to Southend in the ill-fated 'flit' of 1984, and was one of the mainstays of the side during a catastrophic season that finally saw Invicta go out of business altogether. He and a random assortment of team-mates – including, for the latter part of the season, the colourful Western Suburbs and Australia prop, John 'Dallas' Donnelly – played in front of some of the smallest crowds that even a traditionally poorly-supported second division has ever seen. There were eighty-six people at Roots Hall, Southend, when they played Blackpool Borough in January 1985. Things couldn't get much worse; but they did, slightly, with an official attendance of eighty-five for the home fixture against Huddersfield in April. Southend Invicta finished next to bottom – only Bridgend, as Cardiff had now become, were below them – and they folded in the close-season.

That would have been quite enough for most people. But Penola stuck around the following season, signing for Oldham on a month-by-month basis without ever making the first team. The next phase of his English career was altogether more satisfactory, however; in January 1986, he joined Hunslet and was a member of the side which was promoted as second-division champions at the end of the following season, 1986–87. Terry Webb, one of the first Australians to clamber over the rubble when the wall that Pierce, Donkin and Penola had undermined came tumbling down, was the captain of that side, and Graeme Jennings, later to be player-coach at the club, was another stalwart. To nobody's great surprise, Hunslet came straight back down the following season, but Penola played on with them in division two and celebrated five years with the club early in 1991. An extended working holiday it certainly did turn out to be!

*

If the ability of three players to bypass the ban had raised obvious questions about its feasibility, then two other events put it under pressure which was, ultimately, to render it indefensible. The first was the Australian tour of 1982, which showed even the most blinkered and parochial elements within the British game just how far they had been left behind. It was no longer possible to argue convincingly that British League was thriving in isolation from Australia; it clearly was not. Even the old, faithful theory that 'they might be fitter, but we've got the skills' was getting badly frayed around the edges.

The second event was the rise of a new voice arguing the case for scrapping the ban. In December 1981, the Rugby League Professional Players' Association was formed, as a branch of the white-collar trade union, APEX. From the very start, one of its main objectives was the lifting of the ban – largely, it must be said, for the increased opportunities that it was felt would then be available to British players in Australia. The RLPPA set up a working party on the ban, which included British players who had played in Australia – David Topliss, Gary Stephens and Brian Lockwood – and that body drew up a detailed policy statement, some of which reads now as rather quaint. Under the heading of 'Benefits to the Australian professional player', for instance, the working party argued: 'The financial rewards would probably be considerably less than the Australian norm . . . Having recognised that the Australians are more physical, they do lack the ball skills and general expertise of our players. It would surely follow that, by playing in this country, they would be taught skills . . . that are all too often missing in the Australian game, thereby improving their own game immensely. Perhaps a classic example currently in Australia are the giant Kleel [*sic*] brothers, two extremely powerful players who feel that the only way they will improve is to play in this country.'

The working party was perhaps more sound on the subject of the effect that Australian players could have on the fortunes of British clubs. The feeling was that 'the inclusion of Australian players can transform any side.' The paper concluded: 'As there is a great desire by players on both sides of the Atlantic [*sic*] to have the ban lifted, and also a great many clubs, the intransigence would appear to be with the game's administration. Recently, the Australian press accused the English Rugby League of relaxing the ban to suit themselves, i.e. to avoid litigation in the case of D. Pierce (Swinton) . . . The working party feels that agreement should be reached to lift the ban in a constructive, co-ordinated manner, ensuring that the game is protected. Otherwise, it may be that the floodgates will be forced open with little or no control.'

The RLPPA's chairman, Gary Hetherington, wrote in February 1982 of the need for 'an organised exchange system which would give all players the opportunity to gain experience abroad and similarly encourage overseas players to our game.' With the Australian players' association – a far better established body and one with a very good record in court-room battles – making similar noises, and the impact of the undefeated

Kangaroos there for all to see, the RLPPA believed that the meeting of the game's International Board in Wakefield in November 1982 would lift the ban. When the British delegation voted for its retention, there were accusations of betrayal.

The association claimed that it had been 'led up the garden path' and said that it would support any member who challenged the ban in court. *Open Rugby* magazine called it 'this awful, awful decision' and said: 'The failure to lift the international transfer ban has to be one of the most misguided decisions ever taken in the history of Rugby League. Why? Why? Why?' The RLPPA's own newspaper, *In Touch*, searched for answers: 'We understand that the Australians would not have opposed the lifting of the ban . . . We also understand that the Rugby League council was seriously split over the issue, with clubs such as Hull, Oldham and Barrow arguing the folly of the ban. But narrow-mindedness prevailed, and the British Rugby League delegation at the International Board meeting in Wakefield was mandated to support the ban.

'So British players are banned from playing Down Under, and Aussies can't come over here, although the ban does not involve France, New Zealand or Papua New Guinea. The decision is crazy in every respect. It is unfair and it displays a reluctance to learn any lessons, either from the positive effect the Kiwis have had over here, or from what the Aussies could do for the game by playing in our league and boosting interest . . . But the ban will be lifted, we shall ensure that. Already we are consulting leading lawyers to obtain a legal opinion and, if the League is not persuaded by that, then we shall pursue the matter through the courts. The ban is an issue on which the RLPPA is determined, and we shall win.'

That prediction was to come true at the 1983 International Board meeting in Auckland, by which time the players' associations on both sides of the world were warning of concerted legal action. Some individuals were already making ominous moves. Hull KR, whose chairman, the Great Britain manager Colin Hutton, was a strong supporter of lifting the ban, had been first out of the starting stalls; they had reached agreement with the Illawarra and former Western Suburbs, Manly and Australia back, John Dorahy – a highly experienced, top-flight player who had spent a short time with Leigh before the international ban had been imposed and who was desperately eager to return to Britain. Dorahy now took the Australian Rugby League to the Equity Court in Sydney, arguing that he had signed a contract with Rovers which the ARL's failure to grant him a clearance to play in Britain was preventing him from fulfilling, which was therefore losing him money.

Evidence in the case made fascinating reading, both for players contemplating similar moves themselves and for administrators wondering whether there was anything they could or should do to stop them. It was revealed in court that Dorahy had been promised a signing-on fee of £10,000 [around A$17,000 at the time] which he doubted whether he would receive in full because of his delayed departure. 'We have already booked two plane flights to London and had to cancel them both. All the delaying is costing me a mint, and every day I stay here I lose money. Hull KR gave me a deadline that passed a couple of weeks ago and are now likely to cut my sign-on fee . . . I've also missed out on more than A$1500 [around £900] in match payments.'

So much for the RLPPA's expectation that there would not be the sort of money floating around that would attract top Australian players. Those were the type of figures, widely reported as they were, to make even the best-paid Australians wonder whether Britain was such an unattractive place after all. They caused some interest in Britain as well, where they formed an ironic contrast with the rewards that the original ban-buster, Darryl Pierce, was getting at Swinton. But, as Pierce said, referring to Dorahy by his universal nickname of 'Joe Cool': 'Joe's always been a good businessman; he's got a good deal, and good luck to him.'

And good luck to anyone trying to keep him away from that good deal for very long. Dorahy lost his Equity Court case, Chief Justice Helsham saying that, although he was sympathetic towards the player, he could find no legal grounds on which he could help him. But Dorahy was confident that his action, and the threat of plenty more like it, would force the hand of the International Board and effectively consign the ban to the dustbin of history. 'Frankly, I don't think they have any option,' he said. 'It's obviously a restraint of trade, and keeping it in force would only result in more court action.'

Hull KR had also shown interest in signing Les Boyd, the Australian Test forward who was under a twelve-month suspension in Sydney after breaking Darryl Brohman's jaw in a State of Origin match – the most infamous victim of the determined effort to clean up the game in New South Wales. Rovers' initiative was to founder on the obvious grounds that suspensions should apply right across the League-playing world, but it was an indication of how busy Rovers were at the time, and how confident they were that the ban would be lifted. Neighbours Hull FC were also active, announcing the signing of Peter Sterling before the International Board meeting in 1983. A less famous name, that of forward Terry Webb, from the Redcliffe club in Brisbane, was bracketed with Leeds in another deal which just needed the sanction of the Board to make it official. In the event, there were some alarums: the NSW Rugby League and then the Australian Rugby League were both quoted as saying that they would vote to retain the ban. But, when the delegates of the League-playing nations gathered in Auckland on 29 September 1983, they finally did the deed that was being demanded of them; they voted to scrap the ban and end the six-year 'dark age' of artificial barriers between Britain and Australia. There were no restrictions, no quotas, no checks and no balances of the sort that had been talked of by the RLPPA. It was a free-for-all – or, as the Australians might say, 'open slather'. When walls come down, they often do so with an almighty crash.

6
The Invasion Begins

The best advertisement in Australia for the whole idea of 'playing away' – crossing the world to play Rugby League – was that those who had done it once were so keen to do it again. The first wave of Aussies to sweep into Britain when the defences came down consisted of confirmed wanderers. John Dorahy, with memories of his time at Leigh, was on his way; but he was beaten to the punch by a trio of players, all of whom had also tasted football life in the northern hemisphere. Terry Webb, Steve Martin and Kerry Hemsley were all trail-blazers who at least had some idea of what the trail looked like.

Webb and Hemsley had both played the previous season, 1982–83, in France. 'I'd wanted to go to England, but I couldn't, because of the ban,' Webb says. 'So Greg Oliphant, who was at Redcliffe with us at the time, tried to get me and Wally Fullerton-Smith fixed up with a club in France. One day, he just said, "Pack your bags, you're off".' So Webb and Fullerton-Smith, who were later to link up together again at Leeds, spent a pleasurable four months with Tonneins. 'The football was no good, but the rest was,' is how Webb remembers it.

Meanwhile, down the road at Le Pontet, on the outskirts of

Avignon, Hemsley was passing a season in an enjoyable haze of wine, women and motorcycles. A Harley-Davidson rider, with the beard and hair of General Custer, Hemsley loved France as an antidote to the conformity and discipline of the Sydney scene, something which had always chafed on him. At Le Pontet, he could sleep till noon, party till dawn, train when he felt like it and still do the business on the field.

Steve Martin – 'The Wizz', as he was known in Australia – was a veteran of British League in the pre-ban era: as an 18-year-old, fresh out of the scrum-half factory in the outback town of Wagga Wagga, he had come to Britain in autumn 1975 and played in the Barrow side that won the second-division Championship that season. He signed for Manly on his return to Australia, made the Kangaroo tour in 1978, winning his one Test cap against France, and later moved on to Balmain.

The link that brought both Martin and Webb to Leeds was Frank Stanton, the coach of the 1982 Kangaroos. He had made a deep impression in Britain during that squad's undefeated progress through the country, and the state of British Rugby League had also made a deep impression on him. He was of the opinion that the arrival of Australian players, and with them the revelation of what was going on in Rugby League on the other side of the world, could not come quickly enough. Although Australia has had no more determined or meticulous coach, Stanton was completely sincere in his belief that Britain needed to be helped to raise standards if international League was ever to mean much again. He had already backed that conviction with actions, taking the remarkable step of allowing the British director of coaching, Phil Larder, to study and absorb his methods. That was a piece of enlightened self-interest which was, indeed, to lead to a British revival over the following decade, and with it a revival in the appeal of international matches.

On that 1982 tour, Stanton had also cemented a friendship with Leeds chairman Harry Jepson; for years it seemed inevitable that the man they called 'Cranky Franky' or, less obviously, 'Biscuits' would eventually coach Leeds. That fascinating prospect never materialised, but Stanton still made a major contribution towards turning Headingley into what, at one stage, amounted to a little bit of Australia abroad.

Stanton had coached both Martin and Webb – Martin at Balmain and Manly and with the 1978 Kangaroos, Webb at the Redcliffe club in Brisbane which he had left in order to go to Balmain – and he was the go-between who brought Leeds and the players together. They arrived, first Martin from Sydney and then Webb from Brisbane, in early October 1983. 'We've obviously arrived at a difficult time,' said Martin, quickly getting the lie of the land, and he was not wrong. Leeds had been coached for the previous two years by their former player, Robin Dewhurst. 'But, on the day we arrived, he resigned,' Webb said. 'Nothing to do with us; it was just that things had been going bad, with a few heavy defeats.' The final straw had been a 4–54 defeat, one of the worst in Leeds's history, at Castleford the previous week. It was a bad time to make your debut.

Martin and Webb duly became the first players to appear for a British club following the official lifting of the ban when they played for their new team against Hull at Headingley on 9 October. The match programme that day noted that: 'Remarkably for Leeds and our long association with overseas players, they become the first Australians to wear our colours for sixteen years, since that popular hooker from Queanbeyan, Peter Moscatt, whose last match for Leeds was in early 1967. The legendary Ken Thornett's final appearance had been exactly one year earlier.' Yet the day was a disaster. Leeds went down 12–40 to deepen the gloom around the place; a difficult time indeed, but at least the two newcomers provided a couple of pinpricks of light and hope.

After all the furore over the ban, the appearance of the first official immigrants was something of an international event in itself and was widely reported in Australia as well as in Britain. It was no use pretending that it had all gone smoothly or that the two Aussies were very happy about what they had walked into. As I wrote in *Rugby League Week*: 'After ninety minutes and a sound thrashing at the hands of Hull, the Balmain half-back and the Redcliffe second-rower were wondering whether the months of negotiation and the 20,000 km flight had been worth it.' The

1 & 2. *above* Ernie Mills, third from right on the front row, was the first Australian to score a try in a Wembley Cup final, in Huddersfield's magnificent 21–17 victory over Warrington in 1933. *below* Bill Shankland introduces his old golfing chum the Prince of Wales to his Warrington team before that same final.

3. *top left* Eric Harris, 'The Toowoomba Ghost', whose try-scoring run of seventeen consecutive matches in 1935–36 may never be equalled.

4. *top right* Johnny Hunter, Huddersfield's full-back from 1947, about whom 'there was never anything of dull science.'

5. *left* Vic Hey, a tank-like stand-off signed by Leeds in 1937, who is the only man to have scored a try on Headingley's cricket ground.

6 & 7. *left* Lionel Cooper's 420 tries for Huddersfield, and the ten he scored in one match in 1951, are still a club record. *right* 'Pale, spindly, bald and cadaverous,' Warrington's Brian Bevan was perhaps the greatest winger the game has ever seen.

8. Warrington's Harry Bath is held aloft by his team after becoming the first Australian to captain a Challenge Cup-winning side at Wembley in 1950; the Wire beat Widnes 19–0.

9 & 10. *left* The uncompromising Arthur Clues, who came to Leeds in 1949 and stayed to become a sort of Australian sporting High Commissioner. *right* Current Australian coach Bobby Fulton, a Warringtonian who had to fly 12,000 miles to represent his hometown club in 1969.

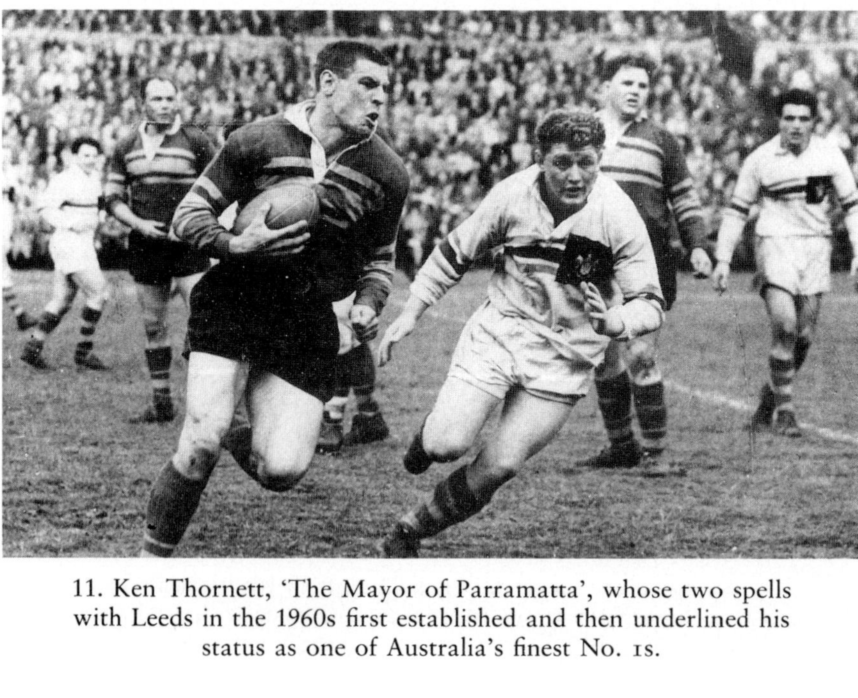

11. Ken Thornett, 'The Mayor of Parramatta', whose two spells with Leeds in the 1960s first established and then underlined his status as one of Australia's finest No. 1s.

12 & 13. Two of the ban-busting pioneers in 1983: *left* John Dorahy, whose court case against the ARL did much to force the hand of the International Board; and *right* Terry Webb, who was one of the first over the collapsing wall.

14. Steve Martin (No. 6), 'The Wizz', needed all of his magic to help restore a Leeds side in serious disarray on his arrival at Headingley in October 1983.

15 & 16. *left*. Kerry Hemsley's initial enthusiasm for Wigan knew no bounds, although his experience at Wembley in May 1984 soured his overall impression of his time at Central Park. *below* Wally Lewis, seen here evading Peter Sterling on his Wakefield debut against Hull in December 1983, could not save Trinity from relegation, but his stint at Belle Vue was in no sense a failure.

17 & 18. *above* Peter Sterling launches another Hull attack during their gruelling Challenge Cup semi-final against Castleford in 1985. Sterling's determination saw his team through to a classic final against Wigan and his great friend Brett Kenny *below*, seen here in the form that just shaded Sterling for the Lance Todd Trophy.

19. John Ferguson, the chain-smoking aboriginal winger, scores at Wembley for Wigan in 1985, in the greatest Challenge Cup final of modern times; Wigan beat Hull 28–24.

20 & 21. Mal Meninga *left* and Phil Veivers *right* joined St Helens from Brisbane Souths in October 1984. Meninga's one season at Knowsley Road was a huge success, while Veivers has given outstanding service now for eight years.

two players 'admitted to being in a state of mild shock after sampling Leeds's state of health.' Martin had played the full game at stand-off, scoring a try, tackling strongly and winning the Leeds man-of-the-match award. 'But all his professional instincts, honed through his career with Manly, Balmain and Australia, were outraged. "There was no organisation out there at all," he said. "I've been here three days and I felt I knew more about what was going on than anyone – and that is just ridiculous."

'Already, [Martin] feels a load of responsibility on his jet-lagged shoulders, with him inevitably being expected to revive an ailing team, rather than settle smoothly into an established pattern.' Webb, who had barely slept since leaving Brisbane four days earlier, was used as a second-half substitute and immediately showed an ability to use the ball shrewdly to put men through gaps. He was slightly more optimistic than Martin about the prospects of tidying up the ragged outfit they had joined. 'I'm sure I can do some good,' he told me, 'because one thing they have here is plenty of hard, straight runners. But there's a lot of hard work to be done, especially in defence, which was very lax, with too much high tackling.'

It said everything about the state of British Rugby League at the time that Webb was in no doubt that he had stepped down in class from a Brisbane competition which, despite the presence of players like Wally Lewis, Mal Meninga and Gene Miles, was unquestionably a poor second to the Winfield Cup in Sydney. For his part, Martin could find no evidence of any improvement since his last visit with the 1978 Kangaroos. 'It's about the same,' he said. 'Hull . . . try to do some of the things you find in a Sydney side. They don't always do them particularly well, in my opinion, but it's good enough to get results here.'

*

Later that week, I found Kerry Hemsley in a very different mood; upbeat, assertive and pro-England to an extent which was to land him in considerable trouble back home. Never one to mince his words, he compared and contrasted the footballing ways of the two countries in a way that earned him the nickname 'Buckets' –

as in 'tipping the bucket' or criticising outspokenly. Just five days after arriving, he announced that he wanted to move to Britain, and Wigan in particular, permanently when his contract with Balmain finished the following season. 'After that, I want to come back to England where I can enjoy my football and have a good time,' he told me. 'The money's comparable with Sydney, and the clubs seem a lot friendlier. It's a "town" thing, with everyone in the place associating with the club.' His one reservation, like most Australians when they arrive in Britain, was the weather. 'When the club offered me a motorbike, I turned it down and asked for a raincoat,' he said. But he had no doubt that others would be similarly impressed. 'I think Australia has made a big mistake letting the ban come off,' he confided. 'Too many players are going to come over here, like what they see and want to stay.'

One reason for Hemsley's ambition was his disappointment at being ignored by the state selectors in New South Wales. 'As far as I'm concerned, the dog-eat-dog world of Sydney football is only worth it if you can play rep football. But all the prizes seem to go to two clubs; if you don't play for them, you're out.' Hemsley was getting into his stride now and getting into the area of how the game in Australia was run. 'A million-dollar game with a ten-cent administration,' he called it. 'It's still run by blokes who were running chook [chicken] raffles in the 1940s. Balmain went on an end-of-season trip to Perth, and I thought the League out there was better run than in Sydney.'

There was talk in Australia of bringing a charge of disrepute against Hemsley over those comments. Although he was never officially censured, it was made clear to him when he returned that he had stepped badly out of line. Looking back on it five years later, however, he stuck to his guns. 'I told the truth, but it didn't go down too well,' he said. His team-mate in Balmain's reserve-grade side in 1988, Paul Clarke, chimed in significantly: 'He's still paying for it; they've never forgiven him.' Doing the unthinkable and calling the Sydney administration as he saw it made certain that Hemsley would never achieve any of his remaining ambitions in Australia – even if he had been a more consistent performer than he was.

Hemsley had arrived at Wigan at an interesting juncture – at the start of the climb that was to make them the dominant side in British Rugby League. Alex Murphy had been there as coach for rather more than a year; whatever his merits or failings on the training pitch, he had already succeeded in his first declared objective of putting Wigan Rugby League club on the back, and sometimes even on the front, page of the local evening paper every night, pushing the upstarts of the town's soccer team back where they belonged. Quality players such as Graeme West, Henderson Gill and Brian Case had already arrived; New Zealand Test hooker Howie Tamati landed in the same week as Hemsley, and youngsters such as Mike Ford, Steve Hampson and Shaun Edwards were in their first season at Central Park. An early run of four consecutive League defeats undermined their hopes in the first division, but Wigan still looked a good bet in the cup competitions.

In the first major trophy competition after the lifting of the ban, however, it was Leeds who pulled themselves together to take their first prize for five years. There had been major changes at Headingley since Webb and Martin had arrived: Maurice Bamford, Murphy's predecessor at Wigan, had been appointed coach and, in November, a second wave of Australians had arrived. Two Richards, Lulham and Laurie, both came from the Wauchope club up the eastern seaboard from Sydney and, although neither of them made much of an impression that season, Richard Laurie's brother Mark most certainly did.

Leeds had just embarked on what was to be an eighteen-game unbeaten run, and Terry Webb, for one, was feeling much happier with life. 'We'd gradually got things right on the field,' he says. Off the field, things were starting to look pretty good as well. 'The club put me and "The Wizz" in a big old mansion in Roundhay, just by the park. What a good part of town that was, up with all the rich people, and plenty of pubs and bars. We had a bit of money in our pockets, too, and we had a great time. We were over there, and everyone knew about us. Everybody looked after us and wanted to know about Australia and the football.'

The football was starting to become worth talking about. In among the early stages of the undefeated sequence were wins in the John Player Special Trophy over Hull KR and Swinton, and then an 18–11 semi-final victory over Leigh, to set up a final against Widnes, who had beaten Wigan in the third round.

The day of the final at Central Park was one to support Hemsley's misgivings about the Wigan weather. It had been so windy that the goal-posts had blown down and had to be replaced and, at kick-off time, there was still an icy gale howling around the ground. Steve Martin had a hamstring strain and was out of the Leeds side, allowing his English rival, Kevin Dick, to reclaim his position; but Terry Webb was at loose forward, and Mark Laurie, just a couple of months after appearing as a substitute for Parramatta in the Sydney Grand Final, was in front of him in the second row. The match was to be a triumph for Laurie. Widnes took an early 6–0 lead, but it was Laurie's penetrative run and pass to Dean Bell that enabled John Holmes to score the try which, along with two David Creasser goals, put Leeds ahead. Laurie did it again to help set up Dick for a further try, although Widnes hit back with one from Joe Lydon to trail 10–14 at half-time. Leeds had to survive heavy pressure after the break, with Laurie's indefatigable tackling always an outstanding feature, but they picked up two penalty-goals from Widnes indiscretions to win the trophy 18–10. Laurie's first-rate display won him the man-of-the-match award, making him the first Australian to win such an honour after the raising of the ban.

Despite his Grand Final appearance, Laurie had been virtually unknown when he arrived at Leeds; yet his display in the John Player Special final and his overall form during his relatively short stay of seventeen matches wrote him into Headingley folklore and made him the yardstick by which Australian forwards have been judged at Leeds ever since. Paul Fitzpatrick of the *Guardian* made Laurie one of the five players of the season in the *Rugby League Review* of 1983–84, and wrote of him: 'His attitude, commitment and discipline were first-class. Some British players are reluctant to train two days a week. Laurie trained every day and, although in appearance he is fairly slight, his tireless performances in the Leeds second row helped to stiffen the side's defences immensely.'

It was a hard act to follow and, even when Laurie returned to Leeds as a recognised Sydney first-grader in 1989, he could not quite scale the same heights again. In the aftermath of the John Player final, however, he was beyond criticism, and Terry Webb remembers the reception Leeds got when they went home with the trophy. 'It was a great thrill for me, because it was the first major medal I'd ever won. I got a sore back from people slapping it all the time. I remember having my picture taken with the Lord Mayor of Leeds and Arthur Clues – and I still can't work out who was the more important.' Clues, as was his accepted role with visiting Australian sportsmen, had been busy making Leeds's imports feel at home. 'Cluesy helped us a lot with settling in,' Webb says. 'He was always checking whether anyone was putting any shit on us, and taking us to play golf.'

It wasn't all fun, however; there was always the potentially tricky question of relations with their British team-mates lurking in the background. 'When the ban first came off,' says Martin, 'nobody really knew what was going on. But we were on contract money, which the English players weren't.' Just as in Bill Shankland's day, that, and hometown players losing first-team places, were possible sources of conflict. 'I can honestly say that everyone got on pretty well,' says Webb. 'Obviously, a few players might have got the shits when they were dropped, and there might have been quite a bit of complaining behind the scenes. There was a story that went round that "The Wizz" and Kevin Dick had a "blue" before the semi-final. But it wasn't true; it never happened.'

Maurice Bamford's theory was that mischievous rumours of friction – including one story about a stand-up fight between British and Australian players after a defeat the following season – were put about by one British player who was particularly disgruntled at losing his place. Yet the general attitude, Martin says, was that 'if a few outside players were brought in, we might win a few matches.' As always, then, the popularity of Australian players in Britain was in direct proportion to the amount of winning pay that they helped to bring in.

Martin returned to Balmain after the 1983–84 season, his second English adventure over. But Webb was to become something of a fixture in the British game. Towards the end of his first season, he signed a new three-year contract, but a change of coach before the 1985–86 season was to prevent him seeing it through. The new incumbent was Peter Fox, a man who, at various stages of his long coaching career, has been a trenchant critic of the Australian influence on British League. 'I was disappointed to leave Leeds at the end of the 1985–86 season, because I didn't think my form was too bad, and the players around me thought I was playing well,' Webb says. 'I put it down to Peter Fox. A lot of people rate him very highly, but I have to say that I've played under better coaches. And when a bloke stands up and says that he doesn't want Aussies in the side, that he'd rather have home-produced players, it's not very encouraging; it's not the best confidence-boost. So when the chairman called me into the office and told me, "You don't figure in Peter's plans," I knew it was coming. I had a year to go on my contract, but they paid me up and I was all set to go home.'

Leeds's city neighbours Hunslet had different ideas. When their then coach, Peter Jarvis, phoned Webb and asked him if he was interested in a challenge, he answered in the only way a red-blooded Aussie footballer could: 'I told him I wasn't. I'd had three very good and enjoyable years, and it was time for me to go home. My fiancée Lesley and I were off to Australia; she'd got permission to emigrate.'

What changed Webb's mind was the appointment of his former Leeds team-mate, David Ward, as Hunslet coach for the 1986–87 season. 'He convinced me that we could do things there; and we did do things. We had a great season, winning promotion as second-division champions. The only bad thing was that I missed the Premiership final at Old Trafford because I'd damaged tendons in my foot in the semi-final. It was heart-breaking, really, to miss playing at a famous old ground like Old Trafford. Everyone in the world knows the place, but I had to sit on the sideline, powerless to do anything about it.' Despite the presence of Webb's fellow-countrymen Penola and Jennings in the line-up, Hunslet went down 10–27 to Swinton.

Webb played one more season with Hunslet, the season of their virtually inevitable relegation back into the second division, before going back to Redcliffe. He left with few regrets for the five years he had spent away, and he expressed his satisfaction in a typically vivid way: 'I'm financially better off. I've seen half the world for free – going to Europe and stopping off at different places on my way home. And the people in Yorkshire couldn't have been more friendly and hospitable – although I've been to London and I wasn't real struck with that joint. The way I feel now is that I've done something a lot of people have never done. I've got stories to tell for the rest of my life. Most people never get out of their own backyard. I look back on what I've done and I'm as happy as a pig in shit.'

At 28, Terry Webb went home still hoping that he might yet play in Sydney – possibly as a hooker, as he felt that the continuing trend towards big, powerful back-rowers would rule him out of those positions. It was not to be; but his partner in pioneering, Steve Martin, continued to make his mark. His success as reserve-grade coach with North Sydney won him the top job there in 1990, and it is his belief that his two spells in Britain made a significant contribution towards preparing him for the task.

*

If the arrival of Mark Laurie gave Leeds a crucial mid-season boost, then the same applied, in a slightly more delayed way, to Mark Cannon at Wigan. Cannon was from the St George club in Sydney, where he had been in and out of the first grade without fully establishing himself. He paid his own way to Britain and simply knocked on the door at Central Park, describing himself as a second-row forward, rather than his normal Australian position of stand-off, because he believed that he had more chance of being taken on as a potential pack-man. Wigan, however, had serious problems at stand-off; they had been trying for years to find someone to fill the position on a long-term basis. After a couple of moderately successful games in the forwards, Cannon came clean. He admitted to being a stand-off and, with few other options, coach Murphy tried him there.

Neither Wigan nor Cannon looked back. He scored nine tries in his first nine games at stand-off. 'More than that,' I wrote at the time, 'he has shown the organisational ability to bring the best out of a Wigan back-line that has frequently failed to produce the goods in the past. Players like the erratic wingman, Henderson Gill, and schoolboy prodigy Shaun Edwards are profiting enormously from Cannon's promptings. He has only been on the losing side once since moving to midfield, and his pace and eye for a gap have made him a local hero amongst some of the most League-daft supporters in the world.'

Wayne Elvin was an even more unlikely success story. A complete 'no-name' from the League backwater of Campbelltown City, he too had arrived in Wigan hoping to make his reputation. 'Elvin's is a classic *Boy's Own Paper* story of a young hopeful who has made the grade against the odds,' I was able to tell the Australian readers of *Rugby League Week*. 'When he and team-mates Bruce Gaynor and Peter Cole [the latter two destined for Blackpool Borough] arrived in Wigan, the club already had four expensive Antipodeans on its books and was not desperately interested in acquiring any more. Humbler teams were interested in trialling them, and Elvin looked set to be sent up the road until he was given a run in the reserve side. He was dynamic, and Alex Murphy was so impressed that he scrapped plans to hive him off and catapulted him straight into the first-team squad.'

Elvin made the loose forward position his own and earned himself a contract for the rest of the season plus the following one. Short and squat – barrel-shaped was the polite way to put it – he looked nothing like a sportsman, but he was an all-action player who quickly became highly regarded.

It was Elvin and Cannon, rather than Hemsley, who had already gone home to fulfil the remaining year of his contract with Balmain, who helped to steer Wigan to Wembley in 1984 for the first time in fourteen years – an unconscionable length of time for a club which had made its second home there in the 1950s and 1960s. After almost going out at the first hurdle to second-division Bramley, Cannon had scored twice and Elvin once in the replay. Cannon also got two against Oldham in the second round, and one in the third at St Helens. A 14–8 win over York in the semi-final, with Cannon unusually missing from the score-sheet, clinched a Wembley meeting with Widnes.

The question of whether to bring back Hemsley, a man who had played no part in the Cup run, caused considerable controversy in Wigan. Murphy, whose opinion of him had gone from high to low and back to high again during his twelve-match stint at Central Park earlier in the season, decided that he wanted him. Yet, a few months earlier, he had been castigating him in public and threatening to kick him out unless he bucked his ideas up. At one stage, he dropped him to substitute, and that seemed to do the trick: when Hemsley came back on to the field in that match – the John Player Special Trophy tie against Widnes – he looked a revitalised player. 'He took the criticism like a man and did something about it,' said Murphy. 'You can't ask more than that.'

The debate went on in Wigan over whether it was the right thing to do, especially as it would mean dropping a player who had produced the goods in the previous rounds. 'Hemsley sometimes looked one of the world's best props at Wigan,' I wrote. 'On other days he looked anything but.' The player himself put his improvement late in his stay down to an interesting development at the club. 'The three Australians, the Kiwis . . . as well as one or two of the more highly motivated young English players like Shaun Edwards, started getting together at Central Park on Saturday mornings to work out ball drills and moves that they felt were being neglected in Wigan's regular sessions.'

However, it was one of the regulars at those sessions, Wayne Elvin, who lost his place in a pack reshuffle to accommodate Hemsley. That played its part in what was to be a disastrous Wembley for the Australians. 'Right from the start,' I had to report, 'that looked a questionable move. Wigan could certainly have benefited from [Elvin's] no-nonsense approach early on and might then have settled down to a more organised pattern.' Instead, Wigan were an unmitigated mess, with both Cannon and Hemsley failing to produce the goods. It was Cannon, 'having probably his worst game in Wigan colours', who tried a misconceived kick to present Joe Lydon with the first of the long-range tries that brought him the Lance Todd Trophy and Widnes a 19–6 victory. As for Hemsley, Murphy was scathing after the match, saying that he 'didn't compete at all' in the first half. He did have the small consolation of scoring Wigan's only try in the dying minutes. 'I suppose I may value that when I think about it later on,' he said, as he steamed gloomily in the bath.

Murphy's criticism of Hemsley – and also of Cannon and Howie Tamati – after the final was to establish a pattern for the future. When St Helens lost 18–19 to Halifax in 1987, New Zealander Mark Elia took much of the blame. After their 0–27 defeat by Wigan two years later, Murphy expressed his dissatisfaction with the performances of his two Australian Test players, Michael O'Connor and Paul Vautin, and vowed that he would 'never again' fly players back from the other side of the world for a final.

Hemsley, as you might expect, is an unwilling scapegoat. 'The problem was,' he says, 'that we didn't go in with any sort of cohesive plan.' Like all Australians, he cherishes the memory of the atmosphere of the day, if not the result. 'We went there the day before, and I saw all the rusting girders and wondered what the fuss was all about. But it was so different on the day.' What happened on the field that day, however, meant that Kerry Hemsley would not be back at Wigan; nor, as it turned out, would that most committed of early Anglophiles ever play in Britain again.

Wembley had further repercussions when Wayne Elvin, who had come on for the last half-hour but was bitterly upset at having been left out of the starting line-up, simply failed to turn up the following season. Mark Cannon did return, but lost his place to the big Australian signing, Brett Kenny, and finished the season with Barrow; back in Sydney, he wound up as a reserve-grader with Norths. That spring of 1984 in Wigan was to have been his golden time, even if it had ended unhappily at Wembley.

*

For John Dorahy, by contrast, the final weeks of the 1983–84 season could hardly have been better. If Laurie and Cannon were heroes of their sides' knock-out successes, then 'Joe Cool' was the man who ultimately looked the biggest success of all. He was joining a strong club, one which had been regularly among the honours since the late 1970s, and one which knew the value of a judicious import policy. They had already struck gold in the form of New Zealand international scrum-half Gordon Smith and his Kiwi team-mate, the prolific centre Gary Prohm. The 1983–84 season saw them add not only Dorahy, but also a third Kiwi, prop forward Mark Broadhurst, who had played alongside him at Manly and Illawarra. They put the finishing touches to a formidable side.

Broadhurst was as hard as they came and, like so many prop forwards arriving from Sydney, revelled in the extra freedom of expression that the British game gave him. If anything, though, Dorahy's impact was even greater. He was a strategist and a skilled distributor of the ball, a good defensive organiser and, although he had never been blindingly fast, his eye for a gap gave him the ability to make telling breaks. Much of his football in Australia had been played at centre and at full-back, but Rovers saw him as a stand-off, the ideal man to orchestrate the whole back-line. When Dorahy also turned out to be just about the most reliable goal-kicker in the first division that season, it was a considerable bonus.

Rovers always looked likely champions and tied up the title with a run of seven successive victories, six of them away from home, between mid-March and mid-April. They beat Widnes, Salford, Featherstone, Wakefield, Wigan and Salford again, before clinching the Championship with a 44–16 victory at Leigh. Dorahy's importance is hinted at by his record of five tries, twenty-five goals and a drop-goal during that run-in, including a try and six goals in the decider at Hilton Park. Statistically, he was far and away the most productive of that first post-ban season's Australian signings, but his finest hour was yet to come.

It coincided with the Premiership play-offs at the fag-end of the season. In the first round against a woeful Leeds, badly weakened by injury, he scored 22 points from two tries and seven goals in a 54–0 massacre. Dorahy had a quieter game in the semi-final, but his four goals were still a major factor in a hard-fought 21–16 win over St Helens. The final was unquestionably his. The match was a stirring one, with Rovers beating Castleford 18–10 after trailing 0–8 at half-time. It was the sort of game in which any number of players could be said to have played outstandingly well, which made it all the more remarkable that Dorahy won the

Harry Sunderland Trophy as man-of-the-match by a unanimous vote from a large number of pressmen, total agreement among whom is usually hard to come by. In the event, though, there was no disputing his right to become the first overseas player to take an individual award named in memory of the most illustrious of all Australian administrators. The *Rothmans Rugby League Yearbook* said that he had 'combined direct running with subtle touches and vast experience to outplay completely his opposite number, young fellow-countryman Steve Robinson.' Dorahy set to work overturning Cas's lead within a minute of the restart, making a devastating break and sending Prohm in unopposed with a sweetly-timed pass. His conversion was his only success from six kicks in a rare off-day with the boot, but Dorahy continued to torment Castleford with the ball in his hands, and he scored a try himself with another dashing break.

Dorahy stayed away the following season but returned to Rovers in 1985. His long and fruitful relationship with Britain eventually came to an unhappy conclusion at Halifax in 1989–90; that first season on Humberside, however, was close to perfect.

The other Australians to pick up medals, albeit losers' ones, during that first season after the demise of the ban were on the wrong end of Dorahy's virtuoso display that day at Headingley. Steve Robinson might have found himself decisively outgunned in the Premiership final, but he had enjoyed an excellent half-season with Castleford after arriving from Penrith in January. Cas coach Malcolm Reilly was so impressed by him that he called him 'one of the best stand-offs in the world' and predicted a big future for him when he returned to Australia; somehow, that promise was never quite fulfilled. Nor did Manly second-rower Brett Atkins ever have quite so productive a phase again as the twelve tries in fourteen games that he achieved that season for Castleford. He was the first of a series of long-striding forwards from Australia to be imported to Wheldon Road, but he ended his Sydney career as a winger – a huge one, even by Australian standards – with Parramatta.

*

The most publicised Australian signing of all, however, won no gongs; not even so much as a losers' medal. In fact, at the end of the season, his club was relegated. And yet Wakefield Trinity's bold move to bring Wally Lewis, the man regarded as the world's number one Rugby League player, cannot be dismissed as a failure. Lewis captained Queensland on a short tour of Britain in the autumn of 1983, during which they played against Hull KR (including John Dorahy), Wigan (with Kerry Hemsley in their side), and Leeds (with Steve Martin). He was in extraordinary form during that tour, confirming his status as the most sought-after player in the game; so it was no surprise when Leeds, so alert to the international possibilities now that the barriers were down, sought after him. They were prepared to offer him an awful lot of money for a three-month stint in Britain – £500 a game for twelve games: Lewis said no. But Wakefield, with nothing like Leeds's financial clout, managed to dangle wages two-and-a-half times as high, and that was the proverbial offer he couldn't refuse.

Trinity, desperate to avoid the drop into division two, had already recruited three Australians: Allan Burns, a compact but determined loose forward in the Terry Webb mould from North Sydney; his team-mate, Glen Worne, a big threequarter; and the experienced Penrith prop, Brad Waugh. But Lewis was to be the key to the escape. The revelation of what he was being paid, however, shocked many people in British Rugby League, some of the Wakefield players among them. Trinity were able to reply that they were not spending their own money; the cost of bringing Lewis to the club was being borne by two local firms. That, at least, was the theory; one of the companies never paid up.

Wally and his younger brother, Scott, arrived at the start of December and went straight into the side to play Hull, one of the pace-setters in the first division. It was to be one of the most dramatic illustrations of the effect a real star from Australia could have at the turnstiles: there were 8179 at Belle Vue that day, more than three times the previous home gate. Wakefield were unfortunate that Lewis only played four home games during his brief stay, but the average attendance for those four was over 5600, more than twice the average before his arrival. That means more than 10,000 extra spectators paying an average of, say, £3 a time. It all adds up to just about twice what Wakefield were paying Lewis; it would have been a gilt-edged investment even if it had been exclusively their own money involved.

In playing terms, the bold move of bringing the world's most famous player to Wakefield was less of a success, although largely for reasons beyond Lewis's control. That first game was just a day after he flew in and, although he played superbly in the first half, making a try for Scott in the process, he admitted to feeling exhausted in the second half. Hull, inspired by Peter Sterling, also making his debut, won 32–16.

Wakefield won at an ice-bound Whitehaven – one of those trips that invariably convinces Australian players that they have made a terrible mistake coming to Britain when they could be on the beach at home – and at home to Oldham, after trailing at half-time. Talking to Adrian McGregor in his biography *King Wally*, Lewis reckoned that the Oldham game marked a turn-around in his relationship with his English team-mates; after blasting them and accusing them of being 'gutless' at half-time, he was pleasantly surprised when they dived in to help him after he was flattened by a high tackle. Lewis was undoubtedly a target for some particularly ruthless treatment. Big-name newcomers from anywhere – Rugby Union, Australia or wherever – invariably attract special attention in the tackle; Lewis got extra-special attention, but that was hardly a new experience for the player whose conspicuous skills had made him a marked man from his schooldays. The difference, as he saw it, was that British referees allowed the aggressor to get away with more.

Defeats followed at Castleford and Leigh. In the latter of those games, Lewis was jeered by the Leigh crowd, so poor was his performance. In fact, he was playing on one leg; incapable of running at all, he tried to get through by just standing and distributing, much as Gavin Miller tried to do when he played for Hull KR at Wembley with a hamstring injury in 1986. Any other player would have taken the afternoon off but, as Lewis told me after the game, at £1300 a match he felt obliged to play come what may – on one leg if necessary or, like something out of *Monty Python and the Holy Grail*, with no arms or legs. Crazy money brings its own pressures.

Restored to health, Lewis enjoyed his best game in Britain against St Helens, scoring a hat-trick of tries in a memorable 31–22 win at Belle Vue. Trinity then lost at Warrington, but the real disaster came in the next match, against Leeds at Headingley. Lewis had always been a 'talker' on the pitch, and there was a feeling in some quarters in Britain that he was exploiting his stature as a player to put referees under undue pressure. For sheer volubility and querulousness on the field, Lewis was not remotely in the same class as some home-bred chatterers, such as Ellery Hanley or Andy Gregory, but there was an undercurrent of thought which believed that he was getting away with verbal murder. Lewis himself believes that Salford referee Peter Massey, who had charge of the Leeds match, was out to prove a point.

He had already been penalised for talking, but the flashpoint in the game came when forward Lindsay Gill, newly arrived from Wests in Brisbane, was sent off for a tackle on Leeds's Australian, Steve Martin. Lewis reckoned Martin had taken a dive and told him so, and Mr Massey promptly sent him off. Foul and abusive language was the charge; Lewis says he merely called Martin a 'wimp', which was not the worst thing he would have ever heard. Mr Massey's report told a very different story – what McGregor calls 'row upon row of alleged abuse that would have taken thirty seconds speed-talking if Wally had said it all.' The late Mr Massey is not able to reiterate his version, but the League's disciplinary committee accepted it and suspended Lewis for two matches. The time lapse between the offence and the judgement meant that he had already played his last two games for Wakefield (victories over Featherstone and Halifax) before it came into effect. In a classic case of British compromise – or fudge, as it is sometimes known – it was decided to avoid an international incident by ruling that Lewis would only have to serve the ban if he returned to play for a British club, something which obviously ran counter to the principle of suspensions applying across national boundaries.

Wakefield had won five of their ten matches during Lewis's guest spot with them, a modest revival which gave them a chance of avoiding the drop. The trouble was that they won no more; a run of nine defeats consigned them to the outer darkness of division two. Thereafter, Trinity never seemed to throw off the dream of bringing him back again. It all became something of a local joke; so much so that, when Trinity enthusiasts launched their own fanzine, they called it *Wally Lewis is Coming*. Other clubs shared the same dream, and approaches to him continued to be too numerous to keep track of; in the 1990–91 season, for instance, both Featherstone Rovers and Fulham reckoned he was joining them, while Bradford Northern had been equally convinced of the same thing six years earlier. No season was complete without its quota of 'Wally Lewis is Coming' stories.

Once it very nearly happened. Wigan had first approached Lewis during the 1983 Queensland tour; by 1986, they were being coached by a confirmed Lewis fan, Graham Lowe, and they were able to announce that he was, indeed, coming. The various estimates of how much he would be paid for half a season at Central Park caused, to put it mildly, a good deal of interest among his future team-mates. Reports that a players' meeting had voted that he was not wanted were denied, but it would be true to say that opinion was split on the subject; Ellery Hanley put in a transfer request. In December, Lewis finally announced in Brisbane that a shoulder injury would prevent him coming to Wigan; there has to be a suspicion that there was a diplomatic element to that injury.

In all, thirty-four Australians played in Britain in that first season following the lifting of the ban. Others of note included the 1978 Kangaroo full-back, Allan McMahon, who played for Featherstone, and Penrith forward Bob Jackson, who began what was to prove a long British career at Fulham. Gary Hambly was a prop from South Sydney whose ferocious appearance and adventurous lifestyle made Kerry Hemsley look positively conservative: his idea of a satisfactory close-season included rafting down crocodile-infested rivers, sailing single-handed across the Pacific or climbing a few mountains. Not surprisingly, playing Rugby League for York seemed a little tame by comparison, and he stayed for just four games before hitting the road. And then there was the considerably less ferocious-looking Peter Sterling, who was to play one or two useful games in the north of England . . .

7
Wembley's Wizards of Oz

For Australian players, Wembley has always been special. When Bill Shankland captained Warrington in the 1933 Challenge Cup final – only the fourth to be played at the Empire Stadium – he considered it the proudest day of his eventful life. Fifty-six years later, Ray Price, one of the greatest Australian players of the modern era, risked ridicule and embarrassment by coming out of retirement at the age of 36 to try to get there with Wakefield Trinity. In between, dozens of Aussies have found Cup final day at Wembley the most unforgettable of their whole careers.

Part of the mystique is to do with sheer numbers. Only at Wembley have crowds approaching 100,000 regularly gathered to watch games of Rugby League. Unlike Melbourne, neither Sydney nor Brisbane have stadia which can hold anything like that figure. The Sydney Cricket Ground held a record 78,056 when St George beat South Sydney in the Grand Final of 1965; but, due to the erection of grandstands, its capacity had shrunk to just over 50,000 by the time that Manly took the last lap of honour around the old ground in 1987. Its replacement, the controversial Sydney Football Stadium, holds a mere 40,000. Wembley has shrunk as well – from its Rugby League record of

98,536 for St Helens and Wigan in 1966, to 78,000 in 1989 – and, with the relentless march of the all-seater stadium, it will lose even more capacity. But the Cup final at Wembley is still the best-attended match in the Rugby League world, year after year.

Then there is the different nature of the crowd, compared with that at a Grand Final in Sydney. The Grand Final is almost exclusively an event for the supporters of the two teams which have battled through several months of league competition and survived Sydney's convoluted play-off system. Yet the Challenge Cup final is a tribal occasion, for which fans of teams like Doncaster and Carlisle, which never have appeared at Wembley and quite possibly never will, buy their tickets every year regardless. Yorkshiremen, Lancastrians and Cumbrians virtually take over the capital for the weekend, and the whole thing has become an annual affirmation of what it is to be a northerner – and a Rugby League person to boot – as opposed to an effete southerner. The only equivalent in Australia would be for Rugby League's Grand Final to be played at the Melbourne Cricket Ground or VFL Park, and the city to be occupied by an army of fans from New South Wales.

British crowds also behave differently. Players from Sydney never cease to marvel at the noise an English crowd can make at a big match – at Wembley more than anywhere. Despite its size, Wembley is a very enclosed stadium; the roar of the crowd bounces back from the roof above the stands and terraces and seems to become amplified into what, at times, can be a truly fearsome racket. Players who have experienced the torrent of sound at a State of Origin match at Lang Park in Brisbane still say that the noise as you come out of the tunnel at Wembley is of a different order of decibels altogether. Quite a few knees have turned to jelly under its impact.

Wembley is also invested with an extra significance by the fact that it is the climax of a competition unique to British Rugby League. For all its twenty years of supremacy in the game, Australia has never mastered the formula of knock-out football. The Sydney Premiership has elements of a knock-out in its latter stages, but it is not a *pure* knock-out, a one-chance, lap-of-the-gods affair. The Australian midweek cup competition, under all its various names and formats, has also lacked this clear-cut quality. It has become extremely lucrative, and clubs no longer routinely field reserve-standard sides to give their stars a rest. But no Australian footballer would ever seriously suggest that winning the Amco, Tooth or Panasonic Cup was in any way comparable with the 'real' business of the Premiership.

In Britain, the situation has often been exactly the reverse. Going to Wembley traditionally makes up for whatever other disappointments a club might suffer in a season. Fans have always been more interested in knock-out football than in the state of the League table. The media devotes more attention to the road to Wembley than to any other aspect of the game. The success or failure of a player's career is often measured in terms of how many times he played at Wembley.

It has become customary for the Australian coaches who are now commonplace in the British game to deplore these attitudes. One of the problems with the game in Britain, a coach like Castleford's Darryl Van de Velde will argue, is that too much emphasis is put on cup football and that what really deserves the greatest recognition is the consistency required to win the long and gruelling slog for the first-division Championship. Yet the record suggests that the actual scent of Wembley in the nostrils often changes that point of view. Chris Anderson had already led Halifax to the Championship in 1986 and had even played at Wembley for Widnes in 1975 but, until Halifax went to Wembley in 1987, he regarded the first division as the big prize. But, in 1987, unlike 1975 when Widnes flew him back from Australia shortly before the match, he was in town for the build-up to the day. 'I didn't realise just how much it meant to people,' he said.

Part of the continuing hold that Wembley has upon the imagination is illogical. The ground may have been a showpiece once; now it seems increasingly outdated. Its facilities are primitive, it is not particularly well-run and, short of being located in the highlands of Scotland, it is as inconveniently situated for the majority of Rugby League followers as it is possible to be. It is stuck out in the middle of the stultifyingly dull suburbs of north London, and it doesn't even offer a very good view of the action to a lot of the paying customers. But, as

Anderson found out after Halifax won their semi-final in 1987, the magic of the place and the event transcend petty considerations such as these.

That magic was at its most potent on 4 May 1985 for a match which has become one of the milestones of Rugby League. Not only was it, by virtually unanimous acclaim, the best final ever; it was also the game which epitomised the contribution of Australians to the recent evolution of the game in Britain. Englishmen and New Zealanders played notable roles for Wigan and Hull that day, but it was, overwhelmingly, the hour of the Aussie. And, more than anyone, it was the hour of Brett Kenny and Peter Sterling.

*

British enthusiasts had first become aware of Kenny and Sterling, bracketed together at stand-off and scrum-half, during the epoch-making Kangaroo tour of 1982. But their joint playing history went back further than that. It was in 1978 that Terry Fearnley, then coach of Parramatta, brought a schoolboy from Wagga Wagga, the New South Wales country town with an apparent production line for great scrum-halves – Tommy Raudonikis and Steve Mortimer have been others – to the big city. He was a blond, straggly-haired youth, not particularly strong to look at, and he fancied himself as a stand-off. In fact, it was as an emergency full-back that Peter Sterling made his nervous first-grade debut, in a semi-final replay against Manly in 1978. He still recalls it vividly – as something of a disaster. But, when Sterling got hold of the No. 7 jersey the following season, there was no holding him back. Right from the start, he had not only all the skills that make a great half-back, but also a precocious ability to organise players who had been established stars while he was in short pants.

Parramatta were starting to build the side that would dominate Sydney in the early 1980s. Ray Price had fully integrated into the League code; players like Steve Ella and Eric Grothe had already made their first-grade debuts. But, most significantly, midway through the 1980 season, Sterling got a new half-back partner. Brett Kenny was another who looked far less impressive than he was to prove. Gangly, almost skinny, and with such a casual, laid-back air that he seemed likely simply to wander off the pitch if he tired of proceedings, Kenny soon proved that, like Sterling, he was a young player of the very highest calibre. It immediately looked like a half-back marriage made in heaven. If there was one quality in which Sterling might have been slightly lacking, it was blinding pace; Kenny had that in abundance, and with it the ability to switch from the ambling shuffle of a man in thongs on his way back from a hard day on the beach to the taut stride of the sprinter in a fraction of a second. Kenny had no kicking game to speak of, but Sterling had that in trumps. And they balanced each other in other ways, too. Sterling thrived on – indeed, demanded – constant involvement in every aspect of play; Kenny flitted in and out of the action, and was all the more dangerous for that. Sterling was a talker, a genuinely articulate man on and off the pitch; Kenny said little, but merely smiled or, just occasionally, yawned.

There were other players who did a great deal to bring the Parramatta club its first ever Sydney Premiership in 1981, but Kenny and Sterling were at the heart of the triumph. In the final, against the turn-up team of the season, Newtown, who had one John Ferguson on the wing, Kenny was the match-winner, scoring one try from Price's break from the scrum and a late clincher with a characteristic dummy. The partnership with Sterling was fully mature now. Neither player had to stop and think very often about what the other might do, and that deep understanding helped Parramatta to a second Premiership in 1982, with Kenny again scoring two tries in the final.

It was no surprise when both men were named in the Kangaroo squad to tour Great Britain and France in the same year; Kenny, in fact, made his Test debut in Papua New Guinea when half of the party called in on a promotional visit on their way to Europe. Both players, however, travelled to the northern hemisphere as clear second choices for their positions: Sterling was understudy to that other Wagga-bred half-back, Steve Mortimer, and Kenny had the even tougher – some would have said hopeless – task of dislodging Australia's vice-captain and arguably their most gifted player, Wally Lewis. But on this, as on most things, Kangaroo coach Frank Stanton had his own ideas. He preferred the approach of the Parramatta pair to training and he liked the concept of an established and proven club partnership. So Kenny and Sterling played in the first tour game, a stormy affair at Hull KR, and they instantly looked the part together in the green and gold. The argument about who would be Australia's first-choice half-backs was over before Lewis and Mortimer had even had a chance to state their case.

It was the 1982 tour that made it inevitable that the ban on importing players from Australia would have to be lifted; the massive gulf in class and effectiveness between the Kangaroos and their British opponents saw to that. On the one hand, British fans and administrators could see all too plainly how far they had fallen behind during the period of isolation and stagnation that had followed the imposition of the ban in 1977. On the other, followers of the game saw what they had been missing in the shape of players like Kenny, Sterling, Mal Meninga, Eric Grothe and Steve Rogers. On both counts, to say nothing of players' organisations on both sides of the world making ominous noises about restraint of trade and court action, the ban had to go. When it was lifted, in September 1983, it was equally inevitable that the players who had captured the imagination on the tour the previous year would be the most keenly sought-after. Although it tended to be players less well-known to the British public who arrived in the first wave, clubs were well aware of who the really big prizes would be.

*

Hull FC had already earned a reputation as the most far-sighted of clubs in their recruitment policy. After the 1980 New Zealand tour had, in a smaller way, proved an eye-opener for the parochial British game two years before Stanton's Kangaroos, Hull had signed Gary Kemble, Dane O'Hara and James Leuluai from that party and had later added their team-mate, Fred Ah Kuoi. They were always certain to be among the front-runners for the best Australian talent as well and, in December, they duly announced the signing of Peter Sterling on a short-term contract.

Less predictable was Wakefield Trinity's capture of the only other current Australian Test player to come to Britain for 1983–84, Wally Lewis. The remarkable deal that brought Lewis to struggling Trinity is described above, and there is no doubt that, of the two, it was his arrival that was the more eagerly awaited. The signing of Sterling was a one-phone-call affair, and he returned to Britain with considerably less fanfare than Lewis. 'The offer came right out of the blue,' he said. 'I was sitting in Wagga when my accountant phoned and asked me if I wanted to go to England for two months.'

Unlike some of his Kangaroo colleagues, Sterling had fallen in love with England the previous year and had been particularly impressed by the passionate support that Rugby League attracted on Humberside, and he was immediately receptive to the idea. He and Lewis made their first appearances, by a coincidence which almost looked stage-managed, against each other on 12 December 1983. Lewis, just eighteen hours after getting off the plane, had a marvellous first half, but Sterling outplayed him completely in the second as Hull pulled away to win 32–16. He turned out just eight times for Hull on this first visit to the club – only one of which was lost, 12–14 at Wigan – but plans were in place from the start for him to return for a longer stay the following season.

In 1984–85, Sterling produced one of the finest sustained efforts ever seen from an individual player in a British season. Just two weeks after he arrived, and with problems over his work permit making it uncertain how long he was going to be able to stay, he inspired Hull to a Yorkshire Cup final win over their local rivals, Hull KR. That was after Rovers had taken a 12–0 lead, while Sterling and his brother-in-law and Parramatta team-mate, John Muggleton, were still adjusting to being back in Britain. But Sterling then took the game by the scruff of the neck. Phil Larder, Britain's director of coaching, was in the stand at Boothferry Park, home of the Hull City soccer club and scene of the first Test two years earlier, and he summed up the way Sterling turned the game around. 'I saw Hull crucified by Rovers a few weeks ago, and they started the final in the same way. It took Sterling twenty minutes to work out how they were playing, and then he just took over. He was everywhere, getting Hull moving. It was an outstanding tactician's game.'

Hull won 29–12, and there was no doubt who they had to thank. Sterling maintained that sort of form, as well. In December, I wrote of him: 'Don't try to convince anyone in England that Sterling is not the best half-back in the world. Every time he steps on to an English paddock, he is the ideal advertisement for his country and his code of football. Two and a half years of playing without a proper rest, but Sterling's standards show no sign of slipping. The man is a phenomenon and England, even more than the Sydney Premiership, is his natural stage.'

It was a long way from being an easy ride for the two Australians, however. In only his second game, Muggleton, a 1982 Kangaroo who had lost form alarmingly in Sydney the following season, suffered another setback when his nose was badly broken by a Warrington forward; he was hit by an elbow and then, for good measure, by a boot after he was down. Sterling described a John Player Special Trophy tie at Fulham soon after that as 'probably the most spiteful match I've ever been involved in.' He was up against a young half-back called Michael Davis who had, for a time, understudied him at Parramatta and who, in English parlance, 'got stuck right into him' from the first whistle.

'They started out with the intention of fouling us out of the game, and then we started getting drawn into doing some uncharacteristic things – and that includes me,' he said. Hull eventually won 36–14, and ultimately reached the final of the competition, but it was a warning of the sort of treatment Sterling could expect. In the semi-final, he had another dominant game in an 18–6 win over Leeds but, in the final, another clash with local rivals Hull KR, he was overshadowed for one of the very few times on British soil. In a match kept in doubt by a week of frosts and snow, Sterling's opposite number, Paul Harkin, emerged as the hero, constantly pinning Hull back with his kicking game. Another crucial factor was the way Rovers' Australian import Gavin Miller policed Sterling throughout the game and then showed his own handling skills as his side surged to a 12–0 win. It was the first hard evidence of what a towering figure Miller was to become in Britain.

Hull swallowed their disappointment and set off in pursuit of the Challenge Cup; the first-division Championship had effectively got away from them during an erratic spell of form before Sterling's arrival. Despite two post-war periods in which they had been one of the country's top clubs, Hull had never won at Wembley; they had lost in 1959, 1960, 1980 and 1983 and, although they had won the Cup in 1982, it was in a replay at Elland Road, Leeds, after drawing with Widnes at Wembley.

Their campaign in 1985 began smoothly enough: a 52–6 win over Carlisle in the first round was followed by a 22–6 victory at Halifax, where John Muggleton, fit again and making up for lost time, scored two tries in his best game for the club so far. From that point, it became a lot tougher, and the quarter-final tie against Widnes emphasised just how much Hull relied on Sterling; he missed the first match, and Hull struggled to a 6–6 draw. Although he was fit for the replay, Widnes took an early lead – but then the little man seized the initiative. He laid on a try for Steve Evans to put his side level and, even though he had to go off to have a bad head gash bandaged, he returned to lead them to a 19–12 win.

Hull were doing it the hard way, and their semi-final against Castleford was another gruelling double-header. Hull were 4–10 down to a side including Canberra players Ron Sigsworth and Nigel Wilson when Sterling produced a remarkable piece of play to snatch a draw. He put up a high kick, followed it up to flick it on to Muggleton, and then took the return pass from his brother-in-law to score. It was a difficult kick from wide out, but Lee Crooks managed it, and the game finished at 10–10. If that was a dramatic match, though, the replay was even more stirring. An early break by Wilson set up a try to put Cas ahead, then Sterling helped to create an equaliser for Dane O'Hara. And then, as I wrote at the time: '. . . Sterling, whose kicking game has never looked sharper than it does now, hoisted a bomb and snatched it himself to score. Cas levelled matters again with a try from full-back David Roockley, goaled by Gary Hyde. But some quite brilliant Hull football, with Sterling at the centre of it, yielded tries for Kevin James and James Leuluai, the second converted by Crooks, before half-time.

'It was dazzling stuff, although there was an ugly streak

running side by side with it. Cas, especially after the shock arrival of player-coach Mal Reilly – aged 36 and playing on one good leg – as a replacement for the concussed Wilson, started to pursue a "get Sterling" policy. That triggered off a real boots-and-all stoush in the in-goal area on the stroke of half-time . . . Sterlo, despite finishing virtually blind in one eye, turned in a display to rank with the very greatest. Everyone longs to go to Wembley; but I doubt whether anybody has ever wanted it with the fierce passion that burns inside Sterling.'

Hull's match-winner finished the match in a dreadful state. His right eye, covered with cotton wool and strapping in the latter stages of the game, was completely closed; his allegation that he had been deliberately gouged in an attempt to remove his crucial influence led to legal action by Reilly. He was also in tears – partly through exhaustion, partly through pain, and partly through disgust at his treatment by Cas. Most of all, though, it was an overflowing of emotion at clinching his appearance at Wembley. For Sterling already knew who Hull's opponents would be, because Wigan had qualified seventeen days before, without any complications like replays. He also knew that he would be playing against probably his closest friend in the game: Brett Kenny.

*

Kenny's arrival at Wigan had been delayed by his wedding in Australia, but he was such a home-bird that he would not have come to Britain at all if it had not been for his new wife Julie's desire to see a bit of the world. That was quite an irony, because Julie Kenny never took to life in Britain – and in Wigan in particular – and the club had to devote a lot of time and effort to smoothing that potentially damaging situation. Fortunately, Kenny was able to pine for home and concentrate on his rugby at the same time. He admitted to me two months into his stay that he had 'been looking forward to going home almost since the day I arrived.' But none of that showed on the pitch. Kenny might have been an easy-going character, but he was just as thorough a professional as Sterling, or Ray Price, or Wayne Pearce, or any of the other outstanding Aussies of the mid-1980s. He might have strolled along to sessions like a man intent on preserving his energy, but that didn't stop him training with a ferocity that amazed Wigan's joint-coach at the time, Colin Clarke. He might have loped lazily on to the field before matches, but that didn't prevent him electrifying British crowds with his personal brilliance and, equally significantly, by the way he drew better and better performances from the players around him.

Wigan fans were doubly blessed that season, because the club had also imported another player from Sydney; not one with a massive reputation like Kenny's, but one destined to become just as big a favourite – a player, in fact, more *loved* by the crowd than any for twenty years.

John Ferguson was a winger already into his 30s; some would say a lot older, because he has never been able to convince everybody that his passport birth-date of 1954 is necessarily the whole story. Ferguson had come into Sydney football late, via Glen Innes in New South Wales country football. In his first season in the big league, he had reached the Grand Final with Newtown – indeed, his elusive wing-play had a lot to do with getting them there – and he had appeared at the SCG in 1981 opposite Kenny and Sterling. 'Chicka', as he was known, had moved to Eastern Suburbs by the time Wigan recruited him in 1984 and, as soon as the Central Park crowd saw him, they knew they were on to a winner. Ferguson scored twenty-four tries in twenty-five games for Wigan that season, but those figures fail to capture the impact that he made.

It had long been an article of faith among Wiganers that there never had been, and never would be, a winger to compare with the legendary Billy Boston; Ferguson, however, was soon being mentioned in the same breath. Not that the two had much in common, outside of basic pace; Boston's strong suit had been his power, while Ferguson tended to beat men by sudden, explosive changes of direction. Boston, at any rate, was soon among the new man's biggest fans. 'He's the best thing since hamburgers,' Boston told me. 'For his size, his power is fantastic, and I've never seen anyone to touch him from acting half-back. Dummy-half is the hardest place on the field to run from, but I've seen Ferguson score some fantastic tries from there. I'd put him right up there with the best I've seen. His defence is very strong as well. Take Brian Bevan, for instance; he was the best attacking winger I've ever seen, but his defence was terrible.'

Ferguson's feats are all the more remarkable when you consider that he suffered dreadfully from the cold throughout a particularly bleak British winter. When the first cold snap struck the north-west, Fergie knew that he would not be coming back again, thank you very much. But, while he was here, he might as well try to keep warm by running the ball as often and as fast as he could. The juxtaposition that year of the talents of Kenny and Ferguson, neither of whom was ever likely to play club football in Britain again, gave Wigan a unique opportunity to break a twenty-year drought without a Challenge Cup win. There was a feeling of 'now or never'.

Ferguson scored two tries in the first-round win over Batley, and he and Kenny were Wigan's heroes in a tricky second-round tie at Warrington. Kenny was in superb form, scoring one try and having a hand in the other two, but it was Ferguson's sixty-yard effort that really sent the Wigan fans into raptures. The only man who could stay with him as he broke from his own half was the ineluctable Kenny, who created one of the most memorable images of the sporting year by running virtually alongside him, gesturing to him to get as near to the posts as possible. Because of his commitments at Easts, that 24–14 victory was to be Ferguson's last before returning to Sydney. At the end of it, I reported in *Rugby League Week*, 'his team-mates carried him shoulder-high to the Wigan fans at one end of the ground – a gesture which left him slightly embarrassed and not a little moved. "If it had been up to me, I would have been straight down that tunnel," he admitted. "But those fans are something else".' Although there were still two more rounds of the Cup to go before the final, Wigan put in an immediate request to Eastern Suburbs for Ferguson to be released for the big day – when, rather than if, they qualified.

Those intervening rounds almost proved Wigan's undoing. In the quarter-final, they trailed at Bradford into the second half and only scraped home 7–6 on the strength of a controversial try from their other charismatic wingman, Henderson Gill. Gill was a fine, early example of a British player who blossomed under the influence of the Australian invasion of the domestic game. An exciting but wayward talent, he seemed to settle down during Ferguson's time at the club and become a more reliable, if still unpredictable, player. The then Great Britain coach, Maurice Bamford, restored him to the national squad and credited Ferguson's influence for what he saw as a transformation in Gill's attitude. Wigan could also have lost their semi-final against Hull KR – and it would have been largely Brett Kenny's fault. He had his poorest game so far in Britain; a match, he said, which he just couldn't 'get into'. Wigan were nevertheless leading 12–11 with ten minutes to go, when Kenny made a break on his own 22-metre line which almost ruined his Wembley ambitions for ever. A terrible pass gave the ball to Rovers, and Kenny was only rescued by one of his least-known team-mates.

'I tried to pass to Steve Donlan, but he was further back than I thought,' Kenny explained. 'The ball hit the deck, Rovers winger Garry Clark picked it up, and I thought – that's it, that's the ball game.' Just at that moment, it certainly looked that way. But, as I described at the time, 'that was when Mick Scott wrote himself permanently on to the Kenny family's Christmas-card list. On the field as a second-half replacement, Scott is an honest toiler who is not exactly regarded as world Rugby League's fastest player. But, in an instinctive movement, he whipped around and grabbed Clark by the waistband of his shorts. In that moment, the game – and one very red Australian face – were saved. "It's certainly the most relieved I've ever felt in my career," Kenny admitted.

'Brett Kenny is on his way to Wembley. But, if he played Rugby League for 1000 years, he could never repay his debt to a little-known English second-rower.'

*

There were echoes of the long Australian passion for Wembley in a unique prelude to the 1985 final. It was the fiftieth time that the match had been played at the stadium, and the Rugby Football League decided to mark the occasion by staging a parade of representatives from each of the previous forty-nine finals. Ray Markham was there, reliving his appearance at Wembley with

Huddersfield in 1933; and one of the biggest cheers of the afternoon was for Brian Bevan, the player invited from the 1950 final.

As far as League followers in Britain and Australia were concerned, however, it was a match that needed no extra build-up; certainly, no clash between Australians at Wembley had ever been anticipated as keenly as that between Kenny and Sterling. Both of them spoke before the game about how they saw each other's likely role. 'I hope that Brett enjoys himself and that he has a good game,' said Sterling. 'But I wouldn't want him to have one of his great games.' The way to prevent that, he reasoned, was to cut off his lines of supply, particularly from Wigan's captain Graeme West, a 6ft 5in New Zealand international who was adept at getting the ball out of the tackle to a man in support. 'Brett has struck up a great understanding with West, and does a lot of damaging running off him,' Sterling said. 'The key to it for us is stopping West getting the ball away in the tackle.'

While Sterling analysed and worried, Kenny, typically, was just planning to take it as it came. 'Obviously, Sterlo's got to be one of their main dangermen, but I don't see us coming into direct contact with each other too often,' he told me. 'When we played each other in a League match recently, we hardly had to tackle each other. I expect it to be that way again; he'll be working closer to the rucks while I'll be out wider.'

Kenny's nerveless, apparently casual approach to the whole occasion offended many people. Ian Heads, of *Rugby League Week* – one of a number of Australian pressmen who flew across the world for the final – described it this way: 'The Parramatta star riled English fans, particularly TV watchers, with his ultra-casual attitude before the Wembley final. Kenny slouched around with his hands in his jacket-top pockets, and stood that way when the national anthem was played. When he was introduced to the Earl of Derby [the president of the Rugby Football League] he took one hand out of his pocket, and then replaced it.' Television commentator Alex Murphy also talked disapprovingly of Kenny 'sulking' and 'slouching around', and former Great Britain international Brian Briggs called it 'an insult to the occasion. I thought he showed arrogance of the worst kind . . . it was bloody disgusting.'

Kenny only found out later that his attitude had struck a raw nerve. 'I was shocked by the reaction,' he now says. 'I always put my hands in my pockets if I'm wearing a jacket with pockets in it. I know now that some of those aristocratic people there thought it was wrong, but I never did it to make trouble or out of disrespect for the person involved – even though I'd no idea who he was. I'd said before that I wouldn't mind being introduced to Lady Di, so perhaps they thought I was being funny because of that.'

Heads, who heard complaints from a wide spectrum of people involved with the game, attempted to put it all into context. 'Frankly, the super-cool Kenny did virtually nothing different from what he does in Sydney on Grand Final day. Kenny "switches off", never runs on to the field, but walks around seemingly engrossed in his own thoughts. But English fans claim the occasion of Wembley deserves better.' Whatever they thought of his demeanour, Kenny was about to give them something better.

There was no place in Wigan's squad for the man who had saved his bacon in the semi-final, Mick Scott. Arthur Bunting, the Hull coach, created a bigger surprise by only finding places as substitutes for two of his most talented young players, Garry Schofield and Gary Divorty. John Ferguson flew back to Britain five days before the final, after some of the usual conjecture about whether Wigan should send for him or stick with the players who had helped them through the quarter- and semi-finals, and whether Easts would let him miss a round of the Sydney competition. The two teams that lined up on 4 May were as follows:

Hull: Gary Kemble; Kevin James, Steve Evans, James Leuluai, Dane O'Hara; Fred Ah Kuoi, Peter Sterling; Lee Crooks (capt), Shaun Patrick, Neil Puckering, John Muggleton, Paul Rose, Steve Norton
Subs: Garry Schofield, Gary Divorty

Wigan: Shaun Edwards; John Ferguson, David Stephenson, Steve Donlan, Henderson Gill; Brett Kenny, Mike Ford; Neil Courtney, Nicky Kiss, Brian Case, Graeme West (capt), Brian Dunn, Ian Potter
Subs: Danny Campbell, Nick Du Toit
Referee: Ronnie Campbell (Widnes).

22 & 23. *above* Chris Anderson, pursued here by Hull KR's Paul Harkin, was the catalyst behind the most successful period in Halifax's history in the mid-late 1980s, player-coaching them to the Championship and the Challenge Cup. His biggest coup was to lure Graham Eadie *below* out of retirement and see him score this try and win the Lance Todd Trophy at Wembley in 1987, when Halifax beat St Helens 19–18.

24. *top left* Gavin Miller was a colossal influence in Hull KR's heady period of success from 1984–86, and was the first overseas player to be voted Man of Steel.

25. *top right* Noel Cleal's two spells in British football, with Widnes and Hull, perhaps never saw the best of him, and ended in anger when Hull sacked him as coach in April 1992.

26. *left* Eric 'Guru' Grothe, a monstrous presence on the touchline at Headingley during his sixteen games for Leeds in 1984–85.

27 & 28. *above* Although many thought the worst of Warrington's signing of the fiery Les Boyd in 1985, he repaid the club's faith by leading them to the Premiership the following year with a Harry Sunderland Trophy-winning performance against Halifax. When Boyd turned down the coaching position at Wilderspool, it went to Brian Johnson *below*, the former St George full-back, who won the Regal Trophy with the Wire in 1991.

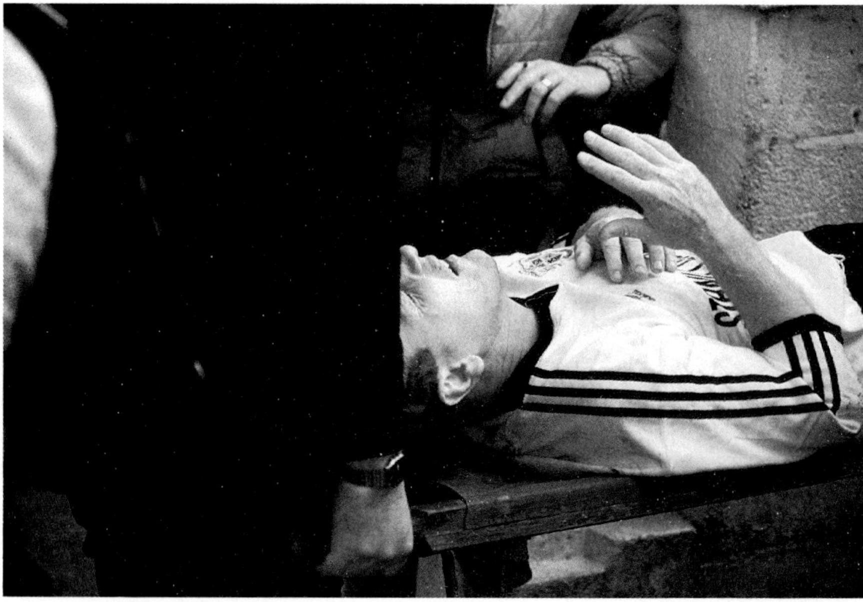

29 & 30. *above* The crock: Steve Rogers is carried off with a career-ending broken leg after just thirteen minutes of his Widnes debut at Wigan in 1985. *below* The flop: Sam Backo, the world's most fearsome prop at the time, seldom got much further than the bench during his stay with Leeds in 1988–89.

31 & 32. *left* Try-machine Greg Austin, unloaded by Hull KR to Halifax in 1990–91 when he found himself the spare man on the Robins' quota. *right* The greatest character of them all, Kerry Gibson, who trialled with both Springfield Borough and Runcorn Highfield even though he only had one arm.

33 & 34. Dale Shearer *left* and Garry Jack *right*, who guested for Widnes and Salford respectively during the 1987–88 season.

35, 36 & 37. Three hard men: Castleford's Ron Gibbs *top left*, whose two years at Wheldon Road from 1988–90 were never far from controversy over alleged violent conduct; Ray Price *top right*, who came out of retirement in 1989–90 and showed all his old fire with Wakefield Trinity; and Steve Roach *left*, in the Warrington colours he wore in 1988–89.

38 & 39. *above* Greg Mackey's move from Warrington to Hull in the middle of the 1989–90 season caused considerable acrimony, but led to his winning the Premiership with the Airlie Birds in 1991. *below* Gene Miles, an irresistible force in Wigan's march to Wembley in 1992, carries the ball into the heart of the Castleford defence in his side's 28–12 win in the Challenge Cup final.

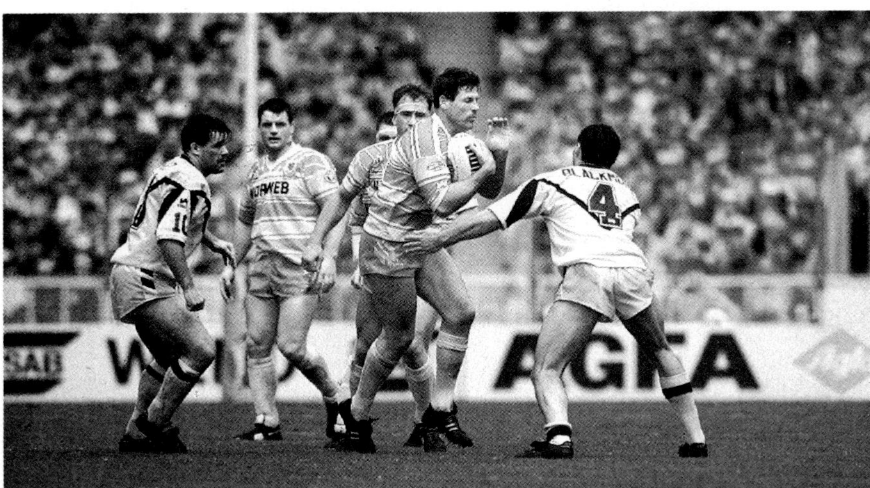

40. Phil McKenzie would have been the first Australian to represent Great Britain after a period of naturalisation, had it not been for selectorial prejudice and bad luck with injury.

Apart from the two Australians on each side, Kemble, Leuluai, O'Hara, Ah Kuoi, West and Campbell were all New Zealanders, and Wigan's other substitute, Du Toit, was from South Africa, making it the most cosmopolitan Wembley ever. The crowd, announced at the time as 97,801, was among the biggest for a Rugby League final at Wembley. Although public expectation is not as easy to quantify, there had never been a Wembley of which so much was anticipated. It would have been easy for the match itself to be an anti-climax; but it never looked, for a moment, like being that.

It was Hull who started the better, pressing Wigan back into their own 22 and getting a quick reward when Dunn was penalised for lying on in the tackle, and Crooks kicked the goal. On ten minutes, Sterling, reputedly the shortest-priced favourite ever for the Lance Todd Trophy as Wembley's man-of-the-match, drew first blood in what, despite Kenny's predictions, was going to develop into a personal battle with his Parramatta club-mate.

Sterling received the ball ten yards from the try-line, with the Wigan defence on top of him; but he ducked his back into Donlan's tackle and showed his deceptive strength by maintaining his feet and, against all probability, keeping the ball moving. It went to Muggleton, then to Kemble, and Welsh winger James was over in the corner. Crooks missed the kick, but a 6–0 lead seemed more than useful – and still nothing had been seen of Kenny, perhaps still in his pre-match reverie. But then there was a sudden reminder of his threat, as he set Ferguson free with a perfectly timed pass, only to see the try saved by an equally good tackle from Kemble. Wigan switched their attack from right to left and then back to the centre, where Kenny's scything run took him to within a couple of yards of the line, with three tacklers – including Sterling around the ankles – clinging to him. Kenny showed a strength more often associated with prop forwards to stand in that tackle and get the ball out to Potter. The Wigan loose forward was not regarded as a great passer of the ball, but he had spotted Ferguson out of the corner of his eye, and he lofted the ball in his direction. Ferguson had read the situation, took the ball ideally balanced and left O'Hara embarrassingly flat-footed as he shimmied round him. Gill, the most inelegant of kickers but often an effective one, landed the goal to make it 6–6.

It was still uncertain which side would get on top when Kenny made his next telling intervention. Ford, who proved an ideal foil for him on the day, found him with an excellent pass, but the advancing Hull defensive line seemed to have matters under control until Kenny suddenly hit the accelerator. From forty-five yards out, he outpaced all attempts to cover-tackle him once he had found a chink in the line. Even Kemble, perfectly positioned, had no hope of getting to him; Stephenson, this time, kicked the extra points, and Wigan were 12–6 ahead.

An obstruction by Kiss as Hull pursued Sterling's bomb brought a penalty with which Crooks got his side's score moving again, but it was a brief respite. Kenny's demonstration of the full range of stand-off skills resumed when he created the next Wigan try with a glorious pass. He missed out Dunn to hit Stephenson precisely, and the centre then had the time and space to put Gill in the clear. The try still needed a good deal of scoring, and Gill completed the job with a marvellous sixty-yard straight-as-a-tram-track dash to the line; but there was no doubt that it had been made possible two passes earlier.

A 16–8 half-time lead is a good one in a Wembley final, and it looked even better three minutes after the break when Kenny struck again. Wigan won a scrum in midfield, and Ford passed immediately to Kenny; he hinted at a return pass, twisted out of Sterling's low tackle and raced at the Hull defence. Young Shaun Edwards, backing up alertly, was able to take the pass and score by the posts for Gill to convert.

Without Sterling to drive them on, Hull could have disappeared from the game at this point, leaving Wigan and Kenny to put on an exhibition. But Sterling had no intention of letting that happen. The same hunger which had driven him through the replay against Widnes and the two semi-finals against Castleford was driving him now, and Hull were carried along with it. Within a minute of Edwards's try, he was making for the corner on a diagonal run from thirty yards out, which made Kenny, for one, look as though he was standing still. Five yards from the line, he realised that he was not going to make it. He glanced up and back, assessed the situation and, as Edwards arrived to wrap him up with a tackle that would carry him into touch, he flicked the ball inside one-handed for Evans to drop over the line and score. Crooks missed the kick, but there was a feeling around the ground that, at 12–22, Hull might still do it.

It can only be guesswork but, if events in the fiftieth minute had worked out differently, perhaps Hull would have won. With both O'Hara and Muggleton wide on the left, Hull had a potential overlap; Sterling spotted the chance, but O'Hara, continuing his nightmarish afternoon, seemed to stumble as the pass arrived and could only paw at it ineffectually. Muggleton, hunting even wider than usual on the left touchline, could not gather the ball as it went to ground just behind him. But Ferguson, whom the BBC commentary team had, only moments before, written out of the script as he limped around, apparently waiting to be substituted, could. He was away on the forty-yard run to the line, and not even a hamstring pulled halfway there could stop him. With Gill's kick making it 28–12, that was surely the end of Hull. But nobody had told Sterling.

His determination undiluted by the hopeless position, he seemed even to increase his efforts. After sixty-four minutes, he drove to within a yard of the line, and good handling by Norton and Rose gave Leuluai the try. Then a short ball sent Muggleton to within six inches of the whitewash and, on the next attack, an exquisite pass sent substitute Divorty over. Crooks, in an unhappy kicking display, had failed to improve Leuluai's try, so another substitute, Schofield, took over – and missed as well. That left Hull still 8 points behind with five minutes to play, when Leuluai scored the one try of the afternoon that involved neither Sterling nor Kenny, taking Ah Kuoi's pass to sprint in for yet another spectacular score. But Hull had left themselves just too much to do, and were still 4 points in arrears when the hooter sounded.

Sterling, entitled to be exhausted if ever any footballer was, dropped to his knees; it was one of the most poignant moments in Rugby League when Kenny sought him out and consoled him. 'To win the Cup was something we both wanted,' Kenny said. 'I knew how he felt.' The moment when the two friends and rivals shook hands, Kenny stooping to meet the bowed and battered Sterling was, in its way, as moving as the embrace between Norm Provan and Arthur Summons after St George had beaten Western Suburbs in the 'mud-bath' Sydney Grand Final on 24 August 1963. That gesture has been immortalised in the design of the present-day Winfield Cup, which is presented to the winners. No one has yet made a statuette of the Kenny–Sterling reunion after those eighty dramatic minutes of striving to best each other at Wembley – but someone should.

To Kenny went the extra prize of the Lance Todd Trophy – the first Australian ever to win it. The voting in the press-box that day was decisive enough, but it took place before the Sterling-inspired resurgence of Hull. Many of us who voted for Kenny that day would, at full-time, have been at least as happy to give it to Sterling. The *Sunday Times*'s man at the game was the most outspoken in his preference: 'Kenny was voted man-of-the-match,' he wrote, 'but that was a travesty. Peter Sterling of Hull did enough prompting, enough creating and enough running to win four Cup finals.' In a less brilliant final, many of us reflected, the opportunism of Ferguson or the ball skills of the veteran Hull forward Norton would have been enough to take the trophy. The Kenny–Sterling argument simply came down to the old dichotomy between them; to whether you admire more the tireless ingenuity of one or the diffident genius of the other.

At any rate, Sterling had no complaints. Even five years later, he still regarded the final as one of his most treasured memories. Rugby League players generally retain little nostalgia for matches in which they have been beaten, but Sterling makes an exception for Wembley 1985. 'It's the only game in which I've been on the beaten side but still regarded myself as a winner just by being there,' he says. 'As a boy, I'd watched the final on TV in Wagga and thought, because of the transfer ban, that I would never get a chance to play in it. The blow of losing there was softened for me by the fact that the difference between the sides was Brett Kenny – one of the greatest players and one of the greatest mates I've had in the game. Being beaten by him was easier to bear.'

*

As Hull had already been beaten – by Wigan, in the week before the Cup final – in the end-of-season Premiership play-offs, Sterling was now free to return to Sydney. He did so, still enthusing about Hull and England, and predicting that he would play just two more seasons with Parramatta before emigrating to Britain to finish his career. That never happened; nor, in 1989, was Sterling able, because of injury, to take up a contract with Leeds. But nobody who saw his performances with Hull would ever forget Peter Sterling when they reflected on great half-backs.

For Brett Kenny, the aftermath of his Cup-final triumph was an unhappy one; one which soured, to some extent, all that he had achieved in Britain. Four days after Wembley, Wigan played St Helens in the semi-final of the Premiership trophy. Kenny did not want to play; after Wembley, he regarded his job as done and felt that any further games would be a pointless anti-climax. However, his contract with Wigan was to play until all the club's commitments for the season were over, and that included the Premiership semi-final and, if they won that one, the final. Wigan were beaten 14–37, although they trailed by only 3 points with fifteen minutes to go, and it was perhaps not surprising that the team as a whole should tire in the latter stages. But what did surprise people at that match was Kenny's role.

Ian Heads reported that Kenny 'was heckled by his own fans . . . when he turned in the lowest of low-key games . . . There were cries of "C'mon Kenny" and "Get into the game, Kenny" during his ultra-quiet performance . . . Kenny, booked to fly out to Australia, was sore and tired after Wembley. But I have never seen the Parramatta champion play a less effective game.' Alan Thomas, of the *Daily Express*, said that Kenny was 'almost anonymous' – and that was one of the more polite descriptions.

Brett and Julie Kenny caught their plane, but the player made matters much worse back in Sydney when he was quoted as saying that he had deliberately thrown a bad pass in order to ensure that Wigan did not score a try at a time when the match was finely balanced. Wigan were naturally disturbed by that statement, but joint-coach Colin Clarke confessed himself baffled by it. Kenny had played a poor match, he agreed, but he could recall no incident like the one the article described.

Kenny later took legal action over that article and accepted an out-of-court settlement. 'It created a lot of problems for me,' he recalls. 'I mentioned to a journalist that a few blokes had made jokes about me throwing the ball over someone's head, and it was written up as though that was what I had actually done.' He admits, however, that he was half-hearted about the match. 'I felt it was a bit hard to play in that game after the Challenge Cup final. It was hard to get into the swing of things. In a way, I wasn't too disappointed that we lost because, if we had won, I would have had to stay on.'

Julie Kenny, consistently unenthusiastic about Britain, has been firmly cast as the villainess of this episode, but the player himself says that he was equally anxious for a quick getaway. 'To be honest, I was never wrapped in the place either. We had a good time and people were good to us, but we were used to living in Sydney, and Wigan, well, it's just an old mining town.' He pleads guilty to homesickness and running out of enthusiasm – but not to throwing either the game or that famous rogue pass.

It was, nevertheless, a sorry end to a memorable season of football from Kenny. It was also always likely to be his only season in England. Wigan and several other clubs made repeated attempts to persuade him back, but none succeeded. Wakefield Trinity came closer than any in 1989, when Ray Price, his old Parramatta team-mate, approached him on their behalf. For a while, it looked as though they had got their man; but, in the end, Kenny stuck to what he had always said – that he would not be back.

*

The history of Australians at Wembley does not end with Kenny and Sterling; it continues unabated. In fact, a Cup final without an Aussie involved would now seem a little odd. In 1986, a diminutive aborigine from Redcliffe in Brisbane, Jamie Sandy, scored a try and had a fine game for Castleford, who also fielded loose forward Ian French. Losers, by a single point, Hull KR had John Dorahy, Peter Johnston and Gavin Miller who, unfortunately for him and his side, virtually played on one leg. In 1987, a Halifax side player-coached by Chris Anderson and also including fellow-Australians Grant Rix, Keith Neller and the illustrious veteran, Graham Eadie, at full-back, also won by a single point, against St Helens, who had former Brisbane Souths full-back Phil Veivers and St George stand-off Brett Clark in their line-up. The following year, Eadie and Neller, along with Martin Meredith, Tony Anderson and Robert Grogan, gave Halifax a new Wembley record of five Aussies in one side. But Wigan, with no Australians but a coach and four players from New Zealand, beat them 32–12. The same foursome helped to see off St Helens 27–0 in 1989, with Veivers returning to Wembley and Test players Michael O'Connor and Paul Vautin jetting in from Sydney to no avail. Then, for the next three years, Wigan coach John Monie stamped his authority over the old stadium, seeing off compatriots Bob Jackson, Phil Veivers (again), Graeme Bradley and Darryl Van de Velde, and including Gene Miles in his latest success in 1992.

But there has not yet been a Wembley which could challenge 1985 as the Aussie Wembley; and maybe there never will be one in which such outstanding players from Down Under play such memorable parts.

8
Too Much of a Good Thing?

When the Canberra Raiders came to Britain to play Widnes for the World Club Challenge in 1989, they went virtually straight from the airport to watch St Helens play New Zealand at Knowsley Road. It was a thrilling game, already well under way when they arrived but, for five minutes, there seemed to be nobody watching what was happening on the pitch. All eyes were on the stand, where Mal Meninga was eating a hamburger. That was the way, five years after he played for them, that the St Helens public felt about Meninga; the sight of him sitting on a tip-up seat was more compelling than the wholehearted efforts of the thirteen on the field.

If the 1984–85 season was notable for the Challenge Cup exploits of Brett Kenny, John Ferguson and Peter Sterling, it was also marked by Australian players elsewhere who captured the imagination to the same, devastating extent. Of all of them – and eighty-five Australians came to Britain that season – Meninga could be said to be the one who had the most dramatic effect. For Saints were in one of their aimless phases, showing no signs of recapturing their potency of the late 1960s and early 1970s and looking less and less likely to contest the major honours in the game. Yet the seeds of a startling change were sown on Great Britain's tour to Australia in 1984. Meninga, of course, had been one of the stars of the 1982 Kangaroos and, when it became clear that the ban was on its way out, he was always bound to be one of the prime targets for British clubs. You didn't need to know a great deal about the technicalities of the game to relish the sight of Mal Meninga in full flight. A huge, powerful man, he nevertheless moved with the smooth grace of a dancer; it was a combination designed to thrill crowds, especially in England, where his easy-going nature, his lack of obvious aggression or hunger, would not be counted against him in the way it could sometimes be in Australia.

Former St Helens player Ray French was in Australia to cover the Lions tour for the BBC, and he acted as the go-between for club and player. He watched Meninga play in a Brisbane club game for Souths and, afterwards, both Meninga and an impressive young team-mate, Phil Veivers, agreed to join Saints. Veivers was a member of a famous Australian Rugby League family but, at 20, he was largely unknown in his own right. He was to turn out to be one of the best value-for-money signings that any British club has made from Australia and become a long-term asset to the club. Meninga, however, was the big prize and, when Leeds started to make a move for him, French decided he had better get something on paper. He tells with gusto the story of how he dashed down to the Australian changing-rooms after the second Test in Brisbane and got Meninga's signature on a contract. It was, with all due respect to the commentator's own distinguished playing career, the most valuable run he ever made on behalf of St Helens.

More than most big-name Australian signings at this time, the capture of Meninga had a huge symbolic importance to the people of St Helens: it was proof that the club were prepared to go out and bring the best to Knowsley Road. The £30,000 that Meninga was said to be getting was the biggest figure to go into the bank balance of an Australian import, and the Saints fans were duly impressed; they had thought that the club's directors had lost that sort of flair and adventure. To say that his debut was keenly anticipated would be to understate the case dramatically.

That debut came against Castleford on 7 October, four days after Meninga and Veivers arrived at Heathrow. Steve Nicholson of the *St Helens Reporter* reflected the general sense of expectation in his column in the match programme: 'So the eagerly awaited day has arrived – the day Australian Test star Mal Meninga pulls on a red and white St Helens shirt. The signing of Meninga, one of the top centres in world Rugby League, has caused a great stir in the town, and the Knowsley Road board will be hoping this is reflected in this afternoon's gate. Meninga has been described by many as Saints' biggest personality signing since Tom Van Vollenhoven. And, as with all top sporting stars, the expectations of the public will be high . . . the question of public response is vitally important. The signing of the Australians, and Meninga in particular, has been a gamble. Saints fans have been demanding big signings over the last few seasons – and they don't come much bigger than Meninga. Now it is the turn of those fans and the stay-aways to repay the club by attending matches.'

As an expression of trepidation within the club over whether they were doing the right thing, that column was answered that very afternoon. The previous season, St Helens had averaged just 4656 at the turnstiles, well below the level of support at clubs like Leeds and, worst of all, historic rivals Wigan – and insufficient to run the club properly. The first two home games of the 1984–85 season attracted a total of just over 7000, and there were 7366 there to see Meninga make his first appearance as a Saint. That improvement was maintained throughout the season: Meninga, and the success he brought, were box-office magic.

On the field, his impact was immediate. He was only four minutes into his St Helens career when he used his phenomenal strength to stand up in Castleford's attempt at a tackle and lay on a try for winger Barry Ledger. That was his first touch of the ball; his second was a successful conversion. By half-time, he had set up another try and scored one himself, adding one more a minute from the end to seal a 30–16 win.

His previous season in Australia had not, overall, been the greatest of his career; he had taken some hurtful criticism – a recurring feature throughout his playing days – of his commitment and stomach for the fray. He was already appreciating the change in atmosphere at St Helens. 'I enjoyed it out there today,' he told me. 'They gave me a great welcome, and it's a pleasure playing in a team with such great ball skills. We just need to tighten up on our defence and we will be very tough to beat.'

His new coach, the former Great Britain international centre Billy Benyon, was jubilant – with just one reservation. 'He was magnificent out there today – the world-class player we knew he would be,' he enthused. 'There's just one thing that bothers me. People are going to expect this from him all the time. He's setting himself a standard he can't possibly keep up.' In truth, however, Mal Meninga was never designed to be an eighty-minute, thirty-five-games-a-season player. There were times during his season with St Helens when he looked diffident and slightly out of condition. When it really mattered, however, in the big matches, he was everything that Saints had hoped for, and more.

In the Lancashire Cup final and, most satisfyingly, against Wigan, Meninga produced a monster of a first half. I wrote in my match report: 'With a crowd of 26,000 at Central Park, Wigan, the air was heavy with a sense of occasion. And Meninga certainly made it something special for them. As early as the sixth minute, he sold a dummy near the Wigan try-line, did a quick spin and stretched out his big hand to score. Next, he had a hand in putting Roy Haggerty in for the second try, then put Sean Day away for the third with a gem of a pass. Just before half-time, he showed alarming acceleration to rip through for a fourth St Helens try in the corner. Wigan, although they fought back courageously after the break, were finished – wiped out by the irresistible force of mighty Mal.'

Saints won 26–18, and Meninga, inevitably, was man-of-the-match. It was part of a thirteen-match unbeaten run that started on the day Meninga and Veivers made their debut for the club, and Saints eventually finished second to Hull KR in the first division, their best campaign since they won the Championship a decade earlier. Meninga also managed to sign off in unforgettable fashion in the Premiership final. St Helens beat Hull KR 36–16, and the big man's deceptive pace was never better demonstrated. Twice he intercepted passes from Rovers loose forward David

Hall to score, the second time from a good eighty yards out. Phil Veivers also got on the scoresheet with a try and picked up his second winners' medal of what was to be a long St Helens career. Meninga's last act as a Saints player was a shoulder-charge which flattened Rovers substitute John Lydiat four minutes from time. It did Meninga little good either, and he watched the last rites from the St Helens bench, booed by the Humberside section of the 15,518 crowd.

St Helens supporters never gave up hope that Meninga would one day return to Knowsley Road. He did, but only as a member of two further Australian touring squads and as a spectator with Canberra. His name and face retained all their magical connotations, however. When a Lancashire publisher brought out a book six years later commemorating the long tradition of St Helens' derby games against Wigan, the Saints player featured on the cover was not Vollenhoven, or Alex Murphy, or any of the local heroes who had given long and distinguished service to the club; the only possible choice was a man from the other side of the world whose entire St Helens career amounted to a mere thirty-one matches. Such is the enduring status of Mal Meninga in St Helens that any other course of action would have rung false.

Something else that rang false thereafter was the attempt, as part of Fulham's transformation into London Crusaders in 1991, to bring Meninga to the capital. Their manager, Ross Strudwick, was of the opinion that his links with Meninga from years before in Brisbane would help him to swing the deal, and that he could find sponsorship to pay £1000 a match to a player of that stature for a short stay. Strudwick never received an answer.

*

By contrast with Meninga, Gavin Miller arrived in Britain that same season with little fanfare and as, at best, a fourth-choice import for his new club. Hull KR had wanted to bring back John Dorahy, but he was thwarted by his Australian commitments; the same applied to Noel Cleal, and then John Muggleton opted to join his brother-in-law, Peter Sterling, at Hull rather than play on the other side of the city. Rovers opted in the end for Miller, an unknown quantity and one of whom not everyone in Australia was inclined to speak well.

Miller had been through a turbulent time in Australia, to say the least. He had first emerged as a teenaged centre with Western Suburbs, later holding down the stand-off job at Easts and eventually being converted into a second-row forward at Cronulla. It was there that he became involved in events which forced him to the conclusion that his future lay outside Australia. In 1983, Cronulla were embroiled in a major financial crisis which meant that they were unable to pay their players. There was talk of a strike and Miller, as the players' spokesman, was widely regarded as a trouble-maker, a barrack-room lawyer, a view encouraged by his forthright manner and unwillingness to defer to people who thought that they knew what was best for him. Miller felt that, as the player who knew most about the administration of the club, he had no choice but to give a lead. 'But, looking back, it would have been better for me if I had not got involved,' he says. Clubs distrusted a player with such a pugnacious reputation off the field; Australian Rugby League was not ready for shop stewards. There was no future for him at Cronulla, and he spent an unhappy further season back with a badly floundering Easts before deciding that he would be better off on the other side of the world; he was to be proved wholly correct in that assessment. Apart from his 'rebel' image, the other criticism you would hear of Gavin Miller in Australia was that he was not as good a player as he thought he was. In Britain, he was to become the player on the field that he had always been in his own mind.

Miller started off in the 'A' team at Hull KR, and it was an injury to regular loose forward David Hall that gave him his chance in the top side. It was a position Miller had never played in Australia but, from first pulling on the No. 13 shirt against Oldham, he looked completely at home in the role. Miller had always been well respected for his defence, and his tackling stiffened Rovers considerably; but it was with the ball in his hands that he was a revelation. Never a ball-handling loose forward in the traditional British sense of standing wide of the rucks and directing operations, his style was to take on defences with his robust running and then put men through the gaps which he had created.

His first two seasons on Humberside saw him become one of the most influential players in the British game. He was a key figure, and a strong candidate for man-of-the-match, when Rovers beat Hull 12–0 to win the John Player Special Trophy in January 1985. He also played a prominent role in the club's Championship success that spring although, significantly, he was back in Australia by the time Rovers reached the Premiership final and folded to a Mal Meninga-inspired St Helens. The 1985–86 season was even more of a personal triumph, and Miller's grinning face, with the unmistakable nose going off in a direction of its own, became a fixture at virtually every award ceremony. He was man-of-the-match in the 22–18 Yorkshire Cup final win over Castleford, a game in which he scored two tries. In an unprecedented double, he was also the man-of-the-match in both Hull KR's drawn Challenge Cup semi-final against Leeds and in their victorious replay. Not surprisingly, he was also Rovers' player-of-the-year, and he became the first overseas player to be named Man of Steel as the outstanding figure of the season.

It was entirely logical that Miller should have been the lowest-priced favourite ever for the Lance Todd Trophy at Wembley, but that 1986 Challenge Cup final against Castleford turned out to be his one major disappointment of the season. What the book-makers did not know was that Miller had pulled a hamstring badly the day before the final. Rovers, understandably, tried to keep the injury quiet, but there was no way of disguising his pronounced limp when the team went to Wembley on the eve of the final for the traditional stroll around the pitch. A less important player would have been ruled out immediately, but coach Roger Millward, again quite understandably, gambled on Miller still being able to influence events. Miller did not play badly; he was able to tackle and he tried to get involved as a pivot, but he was simply incapable of running. All the same, Rovers would have won if John Dorahy had managed a dreadfully difficult last-minute conversion; instead, Castleford got home 15–14, with little Jamie Sandy the Australian hero of the day.

The main focus of Miller's career shifted back to Australia in succeeding years. His exploits in Britain had made him a desirable commodity again, and that limited his further involvement with Rovers. He played just fourteen games for them in 1986–87, stayed in Sydney the following year and ended his British career, rather unsatisfactorily, in 1988–89. That was the disaster season for what had so recently been such a powerful club: they were relegated to the second division and, although Miller's form and effort were beyond reproach, it all finished badly when he returned to Australia early to resume with Cronulla.

By this time, Miller's position in Australia was very different from what it had been when he first left for Britain. He had gone from being a Sydney reject, a perceived misfit, to playing for New South Wales and Australia. If ability and experience of playing in British conditions counted for anything, he would have been an automatic choice for the 1990 Kangaroos, but coach Bobby Fulton took the view that Miller could only be Miller if a pack of forwards was picked around him, specifically to fit in with his particular skills. Neither Fulton nor his selectors were prepared to do that, so Miller was denied a return to the scene of his rehabilitation. Despite that, he had every reason to be grateful to British Rugby League for the remarkable transformation it had wrought on his career. 'It was like being reborn,' he said once. Any number of Australians have given their careers a boost by taking some time out to play in completely different circumstances on the other side of the world; few have rescued themselves as dramatically as Gavin Miller.

*

A week before Miller had arrived on Humberside, Hull KR had announced the signing of another player who was to become massively influential in Britain – although not for them. Chris Anderson was an enormously experienced winger who had played for Canterbury in all their successes of the late 1970s and early 1980s. Although never a spectacular try-scorer, he had been highly enough regarded to tour with the Kangaroos in 1978 and 1982 and to win eight Test caps. He also knew all about League in Britain, having guested with Widnes in 1974–75 and played in the side that won the Challenge Cup that season.

Anderson had not come back to Britain to play on the wing, however. For one thing, such speed as he had possessed had gone, but he had always fancied himself a little closer to the action, at stand-off or centre. Hull KR could not see him in that role, and he played just two games for them before a phone call came from the man who was presently becoming the most enthusiastic collector of Australians, Halifax president David Brook.

Brook, through his company, Modern Maintenance Products, had sponsored Great Britain's tour to Australia in 1984. There he had watched a good deal of club football, and it had struck him that here might lie an answer to the problems that were lying in wait in the forthcoming British season for Halifax, the club to which he was lending his considerable financial clout. Halifax had been through some tempestuous times: in the mid-1970s, they had been the joke side of the second division, always hovering around the bottom of the table and actually beating the likes of Doncaster and Huyton for the wooden spoon on one occasion. In the early 1980s, they had twice been promoted and twice, with apparent inevitability, relegated the season after. In 1984, they had won promotion again, and therein lay Brook's problem. It was clear to him, and to everyone else connected with the club, that the team was no more capable of staying up than its predecessors had been. Nor was it possible for Halifax to buy their way out of the trap by investing heavily in the British transfer market; the players who could make sufficient difference were not available, and those who were would cost too much even for Brook's deep pockets.

In Australia, however, there was a depth of available talent to make the mouth water. Halifax were not equipped to bid for a Lewis or a Sterling, but what they could, and did, do was to bring over a large number of young, relatively cheap Australian players who were keen to come to Britain for the experience and the adventure. Brook struck up a rapport with Peter Moore, one of the leading administrators in Australian Rugby League and the driving force behind the Canterbury club. With some guidance from him, and from his own observations and a series of interviews in Sydney and Brisbane, Brook started to assemble a 'job lot' of Australians designed for the specific task of keeping Halifax in the first division in 1984–85.

It was significant that Brook's first Australian signing was Moore's son, Kevin. A broken leg limited his appearances to just four, but two other Canterbury players signed on the same day were to prove happier investments: Paul Langmack was already regarded as a fine loose forward, and Michael Hagan was seen as a potential successor to Steve Mortimer as Canterbury's scrum-half. By the end of August, six more Aussies had signed Halifax contracts: Ron Ryan from Balmain was to become Hagan's half-back partner, and the others were all from Brisbane clubs – forward Martin Bella and backs Bob Hudson and Tony Anderson from Eastern Suburbs, and two more forwards, Bob Arnold and Keith Neller from Valleys. Eventually, exactly a full team of Australian players, thirteen in all, joined Halifax that season. It was October before most of them arrived, and they did not bring instant success, although Halifax were, from the start of the season, picking up some useful points. Brook then decided to push his survival strategy to its logical conclusion; if he was to have a team largely composed of Australian players, the likeliest way to get the best out of them was by bringing in an Australian coach.

Chris Anderson came with the warmest recommendation from Peter Moore; to those who might surmise that this was primarily because Anderson was Moore's son-in-law and protégé, the only answer was his subsequent record. To bring him to Thrum Hall, however, involved kicking out the incumbent coach, Colin Dixon, who was popular with both players and supporters; he had, after all, just led them to promotion. Dixon, a real gentleman of the game, had the sympathy of many, which naturally made Anderson's early days at the club rather more fraught than they would otherwise have been. But the grand strategy of buying survival in that first season back in division one by bringing in Australian expertise was triumphantly vindicated. Fans who had been furious at the way Dixon had been treated were soon won over.

With Ryan and Hagan at half-back and the player-coach organising the threequarters from centre, especially in defence, Halifax gained ground steadily through the season. Two of Anderson's finest hours were in successive matches that his side drew: against Wigan and St Helens, with him marking Brett Kenny (moving to stand-off for that specific purpose) and Mal Meninga. Wins over Hull, Oldham and Castleford meant that, by early April, Halifax were safe from any threat of relegation: although the last three League games were lost – with most of the Australian contingent having returned home – Halifax finished tenth, 7 points above the best of the four relegated teams. The other three teams which had been promoted with them the previous year all went straight back down, along with Leigh. Brook and Halifax felt thoroughly justified.

It had not always been the smoothest of seasons, though. An important part of Anderson's philosophy could be summed up in the phrase: 'The team that plays together, stays together' – and the playing was not invariably confined to the field. The original Halifax Australians were great partiers, and Anderson believed that a few beers together – Poms *and* Aussies – could sometimes do more good than running through a move again on the training pitch. The difference was that most of the remaining British players were subject to the restraining influences of wives, girlfriends and having to get up the following morning to go to work; the Australians, in most cases, were not, and sometimes it showed.

The most celebrated, and potentially most tragic, escapade came when several members of the Australian contingent were returning from seeing off their team-mates Paul Langmack and Ron Ryan at Manchester Airport: there was a police chase, and Bob Arnold finished up in hospital after falling thirty feet from a bridge. His life was considered in danger at one stage, but he rallied to make a good recovery. The British papers the following week were full of statements from the club saying that the Australians had been warned about their future behaviour, although Brook, the man whose opinion mattered most, denied that the riot act had been read to them. 'I would never demean myself or them by treating them like little schoolboys,' he said. 'They have been the most committed and dedicated group of players you could wish to find – within the limitation that they are young men in a foreign country.'

Halifax were certainly not deterred from signing more

Australians, although circumstances determined that they would never again be able to sign them in the same quantities. A feeling gathered strength throughout the 1984–85 season that some clubs, notably Halifax and Leeds, were taking the whole thing too far. For evidence, the critics only had to point to the first-division match between the two clubs in January, in which no less than fifteen Australians took the field; Halifax had ten and Leeds five, with another, Ricky Lulham, on the substitutes' bench. It would have been more if Leeds's Queensland forwards Wally Fullerton-Smith and Gavin Jones had not been absent injured. The British players' association was thoroughly unhappy about the way that the lifting of the ban – which it had supported so strongly – was working out; a traffic which was largely one-way was doing its members no good at all. The Department of Employment was also making threatening noises, and the member clubs of the Rugby Football League decided that they would have to take action before the civil servants did. What they settled upon was a sliding quota of five overseas players per club the following season, going down to four and three in succeeding years. It was not to be quite as simple as that, because the situation would be complicated by several categories of exemptions; but the aim was clear – to reduce the invasion to manageable proportions. 'The clubs had no choice but to agree to a limit,' said the RFL's public relations officer, David Howes. 'It was either that or having masses of players turned back at the airports.'

Halifax were against the new limits, but they could hardly be said to have suffered as a result of them; they recruited so shrewdly for the following season that they prospered beyond their wildest dreams. The two Andersons, Tony and Chris, remained, and the other three vacancies were filled by Canterbury prop Geoff Robinson; forward Cavill Heugh, from their other favourite hunting ground, Brisbane Easts; and Queensland full-back Joe Kilroy. All three were huge successes. Robinson was a long-haired, bearded bear of a man – very much in the Hemsley and Hambly mode – who played the game with a complete disregard for his own well-being and was loved for it by the Halifax fans. Heugh was a more sophisticated type of forward who thrived on the opportunity to develop his ball skills in British conditions and who could kick goals as well, while Kilroy was one of the most charismatic and exciting players of his day. His dashing attacking play was one of the most spectacular features of the season. 'Smokin' Joe' – the nickname was later given a grim irony by a drugs conviction which virtually finished his career – was a hero.

Halifax had also made some astute signings in Britain: the Huddersfield back-rower, Paul Dixon, veteran scrum-half Gary Stephens from Leigh, and Castleford forward Neil James were three of the most important acquisitions. Especially after they had won just one of their first five League games, however, they hardly looked the stuff of champions. When they settled to the task, though, they became the hardest of sides to beat, going from September to late January without a League defeat. Much of that resilience could be traced directly to the part played by Chris Anderson; Tom Hopkins, in the short-lived Australian publication, *Inside League*, selected him as the most valuable of all Australian players in Britain. 'Australian fans who regard him as little more than a worn-out winger may be astonished to hear it,' he wrote, 'but Anderson at five-eighth [stand-off] has had a sensational effect on Halifax. From the pivot position he always fancied, Anderson calls the shots for the most suffocating defence in English football.'

Halifax, despite the built-in handicap of a ground high on the Pennines with even worse weather than the rest of the north of England, were determined to carry on playing whenever possible throughout a particularly cold February. Anderson's theory was that points in the bank would be worth a lot more than matches in hand come the end of the season, and he was proved absolutely right. It was little fun at the time, however, for players used to performing in much warmer conditions; Joe Kilroy came close to contracting hypothermia after one match against Hull KR and had to be carried into the hot bath. 'There was a layer of ice on top of the pitch,' he said when he stopped shivering, 'and water had somehow got underneath it. When the ice got broken, it all mulched up into a mixture of ice and mud and water. It was half an hour after the match before I could even move.'

That sort of suffering started to seem worthwhile in the spring when it became apparent just how strong Halifax's position had become. On 20 April, they went into the match against Featherstone Rovers needing just 1 point to ensure that they would be champions. Featherstone, the least enthusiastic of British clubs when it came to importing Australians – they had offloaded their Western Suburbs full-back, Rob Pethybridge, to York the previous November, saying that they preferred to manage with locals – needed a draw to guarantee that they would not be relegated. There were almost 7500 supporters at Thrum Hall, which had seen attendances down to the hundreds only a few years before. Joe Kilroy and Cavill Heugh had gone back to Australia to fulfil their club commitments there, but the tell-tale star that the Halifax programme had taken to placing alongside the names of Australian players was there by those of the two Andersons and Geoff Robinson. It was not Halifax's greatest display of the season; a 13–13 draw seemed almost too convenient for the two clubs and was made all the more unsatisfactory by the way that referee Paul Volante blew for time several minutes early. The town of Halifax was in no mood to quibble, however; they had done the unthinkable by winning the Championship – their first major trophy for twenty years – and it was abundantly clear that it was the policy of recruiting in Australia which had made it possible.

It was a case of 'follow that' for Halifax in 1986–87; astonishingly, they did. Limited this time to four Australians, Chris Anderson brought back Keith Neller after a year's absence and signed the versatile back, Grant Rix, from Valleys in Brisbane. His undoubted coup, however, was to persuade Graham Eadie to come out of retirement to take over from Kilroy at full-back. Eadie was a player whose standing in the game was secure. In many eyes, he had been Australia's best No. 1 since Clive Churchill and he had also achieved great success as an essential part of the fine Manly sides of the 1970s and early 1980s. But he had been in retirement for three years, having come to the conclusion that he could no longer be bothered with the daily grind of training; Anderson, his old Kangaroo tour colleague, was nonetheless able to convince him that he would be able to rediscover his appetite for the game in Britain.

It was a risky move for both parties. There are few sadder sights in sport – any sport – than that of a once-great player whose fine edge of skill, timing and athleticism has deserted him, going through the motions like a dismal parody of his old self. Few specialists would be more vulnerable to this sort of humiliation than a Rugby League full-back who had lost his pace. Eadie, to a great extent, had lost his. He could still work up a formidable head of steam if he was allowed to run from deep, and he could get across the field in cover defence well enough. When he was forced to turn, however, there was an ominous clanging of rusty gears and the sounds of straining metal. He looked certain to be caught out, but he very rarely was. One reason was that his reading of the game compensated to a large extent for any lack of mobility; I also had an inkling during his time in Britain that Eadie commanded so much respect that opponents were sometimes hesitant about exploiting a weakness. He always managed to give the impression that he was still capable of turning any such attempt into a damaging counter-attack.

With Eadie able to play the game largely on his own terms, it was again a very good Halifax side who finished a creditable fifth in the first division. But it was Wembley that made it unforgettable for Halifax fans who were, by this time, in a state of permanent euphoria, unable to quite believe the way in which the fortunes of their side had been turned on their head over the previous couple of years. Halifax beat Fulham, Hunslet and Hull KR on their way to a semi-final against Widnes, in which Grant Rix scored a brilliant solo try to give them a 12–8 victory. Their opponents in the 1987 final were St Helens, with Australians Phil Veivers and Brett Clark, the Western Suburbs stand-off, in their side. More dangerously for Halifax and Eadie, however, Saints had an abundance of pace with which to embarrass them in the wide open spaces of Wembley.

Halifax's great strength was the intensity of feeling for the occasion which took over the town during the run-up to the final. Both Eadie and Anderson had experienced the biggest occasions in their own country – Grand Finals and Test matches. Now, over a quiet beer in team-mate Mick Scott's pub on the edge of the moors, they both admitted that the build-up to the Challenge Cup final in Halifax made all those big days look comparatively low-key. As aforementioned, Anderson's view – a typical starting-point for Australian players and coaches – had been that the Championship, marking as it does nine months of continuous effort and achievement, was the big prize. 'I've changed my mind now I've seen how much the Cup means to this town,' he said. Eadie, as accustomed as any player can be to back-slappers and well-wishers, found that it went far beyond anything else in his long experience. He couldn't go anywhere in the town without being mobbed, he said, without complaint.

It could have all gone wrong on the day: Eadie had a hamstring injury – shades of Gavin Miller the year before – and Anderson was in trouble with damaged ribs. Anderson had a quiet game, having already decided to retire as a player at the end of the season, but Eadie turned a potential disaster into a triumph. There was only one moment which saw him exposed, when Mark Elia tore past him for a try immediately after half-time. But, to set against that, there was a series of try-saving tackles and a try of his own after fifty-one minutes. Still, some thought the choice of Eadie as man-of-the-match and winner of the Lance Todd Trophy a slightly sentimental one; an immensely well-liked player, he took the award at least partly as a gesture of relief from those of us who were delighted that he had come through with his reputation intact. Halifax won 19–18 in a thrilling finish, Saints twice going desperately close to grabbing a winning try in the dying minutes. The Halifax fairy-tale – for it surely owed little to logic and reality – was complete.

The rest, by comparison with that stirring storyline, is a footnote, and not always a very happy one. Halifax went back to Wembley in 1988, but they were already a team in decline and no match at all for a rampant Wigan. Tony Anderson, who had missed out on the final the year before when he was the odd man out on the quota, alone could draw satisfaction from playing and scoring a try in a 12–32 defeat. Keith Neller, Brisbane Brothers stand-off Robert Grogan and Martin Meredith, who had spent most of his career in Manly's reserve-grade side, were the other Australians in the Wembley side, along with Eadie, the captain. Halifax had found loopholes in the law that enabled them to exempt two of their Aussies from the quota, loopholes that were largely to be stitched up the following season. They finished eighth in the first division and were knocked out in the first round of the Premiership. Chris Anderson then resigned, going home to Australia and eventually taking over as coach of Canterbury, just as he had always seemed destined to do.

That allowed Halifax to make a blunder that was to undo much of the good work that had gone before. They wanted to keep Eadie at the club because he represented continuity and because he was hugely popular with the players and fans. At the same time, it was felt that some new ideas were needed. Because the Australian chemistry had worked so well in the past, the club became lured into the error of imagining that Australians would invariably fit neatly together, like Lego bricks. Yet the attempt to divide responsibility between Eadie, as coach, and Ross Strudwick, as manager, was doomed to failure; they were just too different, and anyone who had spoken to both of them should have known that. There are cases in sport of a creative tension between two men producing great results – the names of Clough and Taylor in soccer spring to mind – but there was just too much of a contrast between the temperament and approach of these two. Eadie was easy-going, laid-back, one of the lads; for all his time in Sydney, there remained a lot of the unhurried country bloke's attitude to life in his personality. Strudwick was more prickly, more intense, a believer in shaking people up and keeping them on their toes. He saw a team on its way down, and he blamed the deterioration on the Anderson–Eadie view of the club as a bunch of mates whose comradeship off the field was as important as their mutual commitment on it. 'The players here are more worried about whether they've got everything for their barbecue,' was the way Strudwick described the atmosphere he found at Thrum Hall.

Clashes between the two were inevitable. Before the season had got properly underway, Eadie resigned his position as coach; furthermore, when he had played only five games, he was crossed off the quota to make room for the play-maker Strudwick wanted in his side, Valleys stand-off Peter Coyne. Eadie was bitter, not least with the board of directors who he felt had colluded with

Strudwick's desire to be rid of him. It was a sorry end to a remarkable second career, but it was by no means the end of the drama at Halifax. The club was soon embroiled in what was to be an unsuccessful battle against relegation, and Strudwick's methods won little sympathy from the fans or, one often suspected, from the players. In February 1989, after just six months at Thrum Hall, he was sacked. It was not a simple case of his being a bad coach; his record in Australia – where he was, among other things, Wally Lewis's first real mentor – and the positive effect he had upon Fulham when he took over as the general manager of their struggling London operation show that he had something to offer. He was just the wrong man in the wrong place at the wrong time, and it is on his shoulders that many in Halifax laid the blame for the rude awakening from their dreamtime. The hate mail from the most disgruntled continued to arrive long after he had left Halifax.

*

Leeds, the other club involved in that famous – nay, infamous – day of Aussie overkill, did not rise and fall on the strength of their Australian connection to the same extent as Halifax. But a tremendous array of characters went in and out of the revolving doors at Headingley in the mid-1980s.

Ten were recruited, with varying degrees of success, for the 1984–85 season, and a real mixed bag they were: Terry Webb and Ricky Lulham were retained; Steve Bleakley, an unlikely-looking skeleton of a loose forward from Redcliffe who rejoiced in the nickname of 'Chicken Legs'; Tony Currie, a famous Yorkshire sporting name but, in this manifestation, a future Test threequarter; and Neil Hunt, a winger with a devil-may-care attitude and a huge side-step, came from Parramatta. The Queensland touring team yielded three more forwards, Wally Fullerton-Smith, Gavin Jones and Trevor Paterson. Fullerton-Smith was a good example of a player highly rated at home who found it hard to come to terms with the different demands of the British game. Defence was his strong suit, but he found that, in England, it wasn't always considered enough to tackle all afternoon and cart the ball up; British crowds and coaches, with their different criteria, looked for more evidence of ball-handling or break-making ability and, in Fullerton-Smith, they did not always find it. Jones was unlucky with injury, but Paterson was undoubtedly the pick of the imported forwards. Not particularly big, he made up for it with great strength and mobility, and a consistent enthusiasm that always saw him put in a wholehearted eighty minutes. He finished as Leeds's player-of-the-season, just edging out the exciting Currie – although that parochial honour might have gone to another if he had been at Headingley for the full campaign.

Eric Grothe was one of the 1982 Kangaroos who was a guaranteed crowd-pleaser in Britain. For a winger, he had an exceptionally strong physique; he had the power and size to have played anywhere in the pack. What made him extraordinary was the speed he combined with his physical presence, and Headingley had good reason to remember both. In the club match against Leeds on that unbeaten Australian tour, he had scored one of the more spectacular tries of a career studded with spectacular tries, taking a miscued kick on the full and sprinting fifty-five yards to score. When Leeds – always a club with a yearning for a great winger – started to bring over Australians, Grothe was just the sort of player they wanted.

He was the last of the Australians to arrive, various commitments keeping him in Australia until late December. When he did reach Britain, his arrival was notable in every sense. The Grothe family just happened to contain the six millionth passenger to fly into Manchester Airport and were welcomed in with champagne and, for some obscure reason, a Scottish pipe band. The welcome at Headingley on his debut against Leigh was just as noisy: an unforgettable roar that greeted him as he came out on to the pitch for the first time. 'The Guru' – so called for his use of meditation as an aid to pre-match relaxation – lived up to the reception by scoring a hat-trick of tries, one of them simple, the other two involving the flexing of those formidable muscles to shrug off tacklers along the touchline. Grothe's only problem was a sartorial one; the winger's shirt he had to squeeze into for that first match fitted him, he said, 'like a straitjacket'. Leeds had to adapt a prop forward's jersey for his next game, sparking off a vintage silly-season story on the sports pages about Leeds's monster winger. 'They really went to town over that, and how massive I must be,' he said. 'To tell the truth, I don't think I'm as big now as I was on the '82 tour.'

He was big enough, and fast enough, however, to break the strongest defence – provided he could get the ball. If there was a disappointment surrounding Grothe's spell with Leeds, it was that he did not get as many running opportunities as he should have, partly because opposing teams very sensibly concentrated on cutting off his source of supply, and partly because Leeds did not always move it very fluently through the backs. Grothe did not himself believe for a moment that anyone was trying to freeze him out, although there had again been reports in Australian newspapers before his arrival that suggested that all was not well in the relations between the British and Australian sections of the side. Grothe had read them and had been concerned, but found few difficulties when he got to Britain. In his short stay of sixteen games, he scored fourteen tries and looked, whenever he had a running chance, every bit as difficult to stop as he had in 1982.

Six weeks after Grothe arrived, what was intended to be the tenth and final piece in the Australian jigsaw was slotted into place. Like Halifax, Leeds saw the appointment of an Australian coach as the logical next step. Maurice Bamford was bowing out in order to concentrate on his job with Great Britain, and in his stead Leeds brought over Malcolm Clift, who had coached Canterbury with some success in the 1970s, but who had been out of the front line and serving as a committee-man with the club. The timing could hardly have been worse. Clift arrived and took control immediately before the Challenge Cup first-round tie with Widnes; Leeds lost 4–14 and, the following week, went down to Hull KR in the League. Rovers went on to win the Championship, but Leeds were no longer in the running for anything, although they did reach the semi-final of the Premiership Trophy, only to lose again to Hull KR, this time by a single point. By this stage, Clift and Leeds had decided that they would not stay together. 'It was wrong what they did with "Shifty" [Clift],' said Terry Webb, 'putting him in charge for that match when he's just got off the plane.' It was to be the end – for the time being – of thoughts of an Australian coach, but Australian players were still very much on Leeds's mind.

The following season, 1985–86, they, like Halifax, had to adapt to life under the new quota restrictions. They brought back Currie, a player of unquestionable class, and Webb, and they also added North Sydney stand-off Cliff Lyons. Lyons was another who adapted splendidly to British conditions and who was destined to return, both to Leeds and, briefly, to Sheffield Eagles; his experience was later put to effective use by the 1990 Kangaroos when they slotted him into the team for the second and third Tests of that Ashes series, wherein he helped turn potential defeat into a memorable triumph. It was not a consistent season for Leeds, however; two disastrous periods, each of nine games without a win, one early and one late in the campaign, saw to that. The club did reach the semi-finals of both the Challenge Cup and the Premiership, although they lost them both, the first to their nemesis, Hull KR, after a replay.

The 1986–87 season brought more new faces from Australia: the Cronulla centres Andrew Ettingshausen and Mark McGaw. 'ET', as he increasingly became known for convenience, was the more eye-catching of the two, blessed with film-star looks (he was to play a part in the filming of *The First Kangaroos*, the story of Rosenfeld and company on the inaugural Australian tour) and startling pace. McGaw was more of a solid citizen, very strong in the tackle and reliable and intelligent in all he did. Illawarra prop Peter Smith was the other Australian signed, but he was a major disappointment and did not last long. Major disappointment, in fact, just about sums up Leeds's season: they were humilated 0–40 by the touring Australians; their only cup run of any sort finished with defeat by Widnes in the third round of the Challenge Cup; and the catastrophe of relegation was only avoided by virtue of points difference.

A wholesale rearrangement of the furniture for 1987–88 produced better results. Leeds brought over an interesting cross-section of Australians: the young and highly promising Brisbane Souths centre, Peter Jackson; two very experienced backs from Sydney, Steve Morris (Eastern Suburbs) and Marty Gurr (Manly); and South Sydney forward Peter Tunks. Morris and

Gurr both gave highly effective service, and Jackson was to confirm his reputation not only as one of Australia's best young players but also as one who believed in enjoying life to the full. The Australian term 'larrikin' was coined for him, encompassing as it does the ideas of roguishness and lack of inhibitions. Tunks, night-club owner, restaurateur, bon viveur and Test prop, became an influential figure at Headingley, being appointed captain by Maurice Bamford – back at the helm by this time – and also having some input into the training. 'I only came for a holiday,' he said, ruefully. Leeds lost the John Player final by a single point to Wigan, with Jackson scoring a try, and finished fifth in the League.

Tunks's lifestyle at Headingley formed an illuminating contrast with that of one of the most respected forwards in the Sydney competition, David Gillespie, who was one of a number of Australians just across the city of Leeds who could not prevent Hunslet going straight back into the second division after finishing in last place in the first. It was something that Tunks rarely let Gillespie forget about. '[Hunslet] had promised him everything, the way some English clubs do,' he says. 'What they really meant was that it would take him forever to get it.' Tunks was unfailingly sympathetic: 'When they had copped a really good beating, I'd ring him up and "miaow" down the phone.' Calling a player a cat is the most common form of Australian Rugby League abuse, both serious and flippant.

'We used to get £250–300 a win, and there's David getting £20 a loss. I used to go round with a big wad of notes spilling out of my top pocket; I'd sit down in the easy chair and plaster a £10 note to my forehead. "I'm going to get you," he told me. "When we play you, I'm going to put you in hospital." He tried to, as well. I was doing everything – kicking on first tackle, throwing it back through my legs. Anyone watching must have thought it was two big kids playing a silly game, but he never caught me in possession, and we won anyway.'

Not content with tormenting his old mate Gillespie, Tunks turned his attention to the Hunslet coach, Peter Jarvis. He phoned him and pretended to be an official from the Australian High Commission. 'The fact that it was an Australian voice was enough to make him believe it. I told him that we had evidence that he had been bringing players into the country without work permits. "Not only is it an offence against the Rugby League by-laws," I told him, "it is also a criminal offence. You'll be very lucky not to do time over this or, at the very least, a big fine." All I could hear was him going "B-b-b-but". I let him stew for half an hour and called him back.'

Tunks was to have one of the most varied careers of all Australian imports. In 1990, he joined Salford but, after failing to establish any kind of rapport with coach Kevin Tamati, he only played eight matches for them before going to Sheffield Eagles in exchange for the New Zealander, Francis Leota, in November. He was again closely involved in coaching at Sheffield but, at the end of the season, with the Eagles relegated, he was on his travels again. At the other relegated club, Oldham, he was hired as non-playing coach, with a brief to reduce the club's crippling overheads. The way in which he did that during the 1991–92 season, largely by trading away players on lucrative contracts for younger, cheaper players of promise, earned him a reputation as something of a hatchet-man. Oldham were not promoted, but they did reach the divisional Premiership final, wherein they eventually went down 20–34 to Sheffield, having rallied from a 4–16 half-time deficit to tie the scores at 20–20 with fifteen minutes to go. The committee were well pleased with the job Tunks had done with limited resources – including one Australian, a little-known utility back who had been playing in France, Vince Nicklin – and rewarded him with a new, three-year contract. Three other clubs, all of whom would play in the first division the following season, also enquired about his availability – a sure sign of a growing reputation.

*

The one common feature of Leeds's cast of thousands in the mid-1980s is that none of them, after Webb and Mark Laurie in 1984, ever got their hands on a winners' medal. That has to go down as a poor rate of return for the club; other teams achieved far more despite having less to spend on overseas recruitment.

Castleford were a case in point. They brought over Ian French from Wynnum-Manly and Jamie Sandy from Easts, both in Brisbane, for the 1985–86 season and got excellent value from both of them. French was Brisbane's current player-of-the-year and was already being tipped for great things; Castleford coach Malcolm Reilly, himself one of the outstanding loose forwards of modern times, believed that French would go on to become one of the acknowledged masters of the position. In the event, however, due to injury and bad luck, that never happened; French's return to Britain was not as a Kangaroo, but to lowly Doncaster, to whom he gave similarly good service in 1990–91. Sandy was virtually unknown and the tiny Aborigine looked as though he might struggle, physically and climatically, in a British winter.

Castleford had reached the final of the Yorkshire Cup before the arrival of their Australians, only to lose 18–22 to Hull KR. But they were to reverse that result where it really mattered – at Wembley. French and Sandy – if that does not make them sound too much like a well-known comedy partnership – had played so well for Cas that there was little doubt that the club would go to the expense of flying them back for the final from Brisbane, where they had been obliged to return before the end of the British season. Sandy, always a nervous flier, was even less keen on boarding the plane at what was a time of heightened tension over international terrorism; he was not consoled by being assured that, at 5ft 4in, he presented a very small target.

French had an admirable game in Castleford's 15–14 victory, completely negating any hope that Rovers had of the injured Gavin Miller still being able to call the shots. But the individual moment of glory belonged to Sandy; his try, a little beauty on the hour, effectively clinched the game. Taking the ball from stand-off John Joyner, he beat three tackles on a forty-yard diagonal run for the line; it was an image that stuck in the mind of television viewers in Britain and Australia, as well as the 82,000 in the stadium. Bob Beardmore was chosen as the man-of-the-match and took the Lance Todd Trophy as a reward for a fine all-round performance; but the emotional choice would surely have been the little wingman.

Castleford, lacking the financial back-up of some of their competitors, often compensated in their overseas dealings by using their excellent contacts to seek out Australian players on the way up who would be able to add something to the side. The following season, they brought back Brett Atkins, this time from Canberra, but they also unearthed Chris Johns, the St George centre who was destined to become a Kangaroo tourist. Bob Lindner, already a Test player, came too, but only for a brief nine-match stay. Atkins and Johns both shared in the winning of the Yorkshire Cup, the second-row man scoring one of the tries that beat Hull 31–24 in the final at Headingley. Lindner was back again the year after but did not always live up to his obvious ability; Cas got better value from two players from St George, Michael Beattie, a very experienced and reliable centre, and John Fifita, a running forward who could be a most damaging attacer. Fifita, originally from Tonga, suffered more than most in the cold weather but had some cracking games, including one in which he put a hat-trick of tries past Hull. He and Beattie both played in the side that failed to retain the Yorkshire Cup, losing 2–11 to Bradford Northern in a replay.

Wigan, having failed to resign Brett Kenny or John Ferguson for the 1985–86 season, looked set for an almost inevitable letdown, at least as far as the impact from overseas players was concerned. It says a great deal for the new imports, Steve Ella and Greg Dowling, that they spent no time at all in the shadows of their predecessors. Ella had frequently played outside Kenny for Parramatta, but his opportunities to play in his favourite stand-off position had obviously been blocked by the other man's unbreakable grip on the No. 6 jersey. At Wigan, however, he dropped straight into the role, and the fans at Central Park had the privilege of making their own comparisons. As an architect of play for his threequarters, Ella probably fell slightly short of the exultant standards set by Kenny; as a support player and a sniffer-out of unconsidered half-chances, however, he was in a sublime class of his own. From the 34–8 Lancashire Cup final win over Warrington, in which he scored two tries and was voted man-of-the-match, to the John Player semi-final against Leigh two months later, Ella scored tries in eleven consecutive matches and was starting to put pressure on the record sequence established by a great Australian player of an earlier era, Eric

Harris. In all, he scored twenty-one tries in twenty-three games and fully lived up to his Sydney nickname of 'The Zip-Zip Man'.

Dowling, troubled by injury, was slower to make his mark; when he did, however, the Wynnum, Queensland and Australia prop made a deep impression. A twenty-five-match stint saw his know-how and mental toughness contribute immeasurably to the development of a number of Wigan's young British forwards, the highlight of which was a rare front-rower's hat-trick in the John Player Special semi. Even rarer was Dowling's drop-goal in the final of that trophy, in which Wigan beat Hull KR 11–8 to go with their Lancashire Cup win and their second place, to Halifax, in the first division.

The arrival of New Zealand coach Graham Lowe for 1986–87, the tightening of the quota and the presence that year of three South Africans – Ray Mordt, Rob Louw and Nick Du Toit – on the club's books meant that import spots for Australians were bound to be at a premium. Wigan did, however, import Ian Roberts, a South Sydney forward of great potential who had the extra advantage of having been born in London. His work-rate and sheer physical presence were extremely impressive, and the club hoped that he would see his future with Wigan and Great Britain, rather than with Souths and Australia. He was tempted, but nonetheless opted to resume his career in the country where he had grown up rather than the one in which he had been born. Although he had as bad a time with injury as any player of his generation, he did, after moving to a Manly club by then coached by Lowe, achieve in 1990 his ambition of playing for Australia. His twenty games with Wigan in 1986–87 saw him share in two of the major trophy wins of an unprecedentedly successful season: he played in the side that beat Oldham 27–6 to take the Lancashire Cup, and he soldiered on with the courage that made him so popular in England in the John Player Special victory over Warrington despite a spectacularly gory split lip that required ten stitches. After his return home, Roberts was also remembered when Wigan won the Championship by a massive 15 points and went on to add the Premiership trophy to their spoils; the only disappointment of a remarkable season was a defeat at Oldham in the first round of the Challenge Cup.

Warrington, already having secured from Fulham the unsung but immensely hardworking Bob Jackson, went in for ambitious moves in the Australian market in 1985: Phil Blake, a quick and dazzlingly talented back from Manly, was signed, as was Brian Johnson, an accomplished full-back from St George. The big capture, especially as far as the headlines were concerned, though, was Les Boyd. To say that Boyd was a controversial figure would be to understate the case considerably – there have been few players who could arouse such florid emotions. Although he was a Test second-rower of undoubted ability, his career in Australia had been more notable for scandal, misdemeanour and clashes with authority than it had for its playing achievements. 'The Baby-Faced Assassin' – as he was known in Sydney – was a name he hated (although I never discovered which half of it he objected to). But his career bore it out: it had always been punctuated, both at Wests and later when he moved to Manly, by suspensions. There were many who thought that Les Boyd was a persistently dirty and violent player who had often got off lightly.

Boyd's later troubles need to be set in their historical context. Rugby League in Australia in the early 1980s was haunted by a fear that it would lose its traditional grip on a captive audience by the shrinking of the identifiable working class. To maintain its position as the No. 1 sport on the eastern seaboard, the game decided that it needed to extend its appeal to a changing society – to families, to women, to people who did not consider themselves part of any class. Yet all the evidence was that this new constituency was repelled by what it saw as the brutal aspects of professional Rugby League; mothers, in particular, were reluctant to let their sons play a game which seemed to be inflicting so much damage on fully grown men. The disciplinary system was widely regarded as toothless, with notoriously dirty players getting away with nominal suspensions and returning to the field to transgress again. Enter Jim Comans, a tough-minded Sydney lawyer of unimpeachable integrity, to head a revamped judiciary and clean the game up. Boyd was not his first victim, but he was his most illustrious; the one who sent a shiver of apprehension through the queue of players who waited at the New South Wales

Rugby League headquarters on Phillip Street every Monday night to hear their fate.

On 17 June 1983, Boyd went into a tackle on Queensland second row Darryl Brohman during a State of Origin match in Brisbane, and his elbow left Brohman with a badly broken jaw. Boyd never denied the foul, but was shocked when the judiciary banned him for a year. The following year, just three matches into his comeback, Canterbury cited him again for gouging their hooker, Billy Johnstone, and Boyd was this time suspended for fifteen months. Although never one to claim to be an angel, Boyd felt, and continued to feel, that hypocrisy and double standards had been employed and that he had been punished so severely because of who he was, rather than what he had done. 'People do what I was accused of every week and get away with it,' he said.

Despite a reputation that was bad and getting worse, British clubs never lost interest in Les Boyd. Several, most notably Hull KR, tried to sign him during his first long suspension, before it was made clear to them that the ban applied anywhere in the world. During the currency of the second ban, Warrington decided that he was the man for them and put together a package to tempt him to Britain in June 1985. Within a couple of months, they had also signed another two forwards with notoriously uncompromising attitudes on the field: Alan Rathbone from Bradford Northern, and New Zealand Test prop Kevin Tamati, from Widnes. Asked whether that wasn't overdoing it just a little, Warrington chairman Peter Higham replied – half-seriously – that at least one of them would be suspended at any one time!

In fact, Les Boyd proved to be a pleasant surprise to those who feared that his short fuse and barely-controlled aggression would prove a liability in Britain. He was sent off once in his first season with Warrington, but found not guilty on video evidence; it was almost as if the other side of his personality had asserted itself as he crossed the world. Yet Boyd had never been the unmitigated thug of popular legend; he had done some dreadful things on the field, but he was one of the most thoughtful and considerate of players off it. A devoted and affectionate family man, he was also one of the most coherent thinkers about the game; away from Sydney, and a system which he felt had it in for him, he was able to rediscover his love for Rugby League. During the darkest days of his enforced absence from the field in Australia, he had made himself even more of a villain in the eyes of most of the public by openly condemning the game and comparing it unfavourably with Australian Rules. In Britain, however, he got back in tune with Rugby League to the extent that, even after he left Warrington, he was incapable of giving it up. He carried on playing, for virtually nothing, well into his 30s, for the country club, Cootamundra, and for the Northern Territory side under his old Kangaroo team-mate, Steve Rogers.

The Boyd of Warrington vintage was still a hard, aggressive player, but he also became a leader who could instil the value of discipline into the players around him, despite his own earlier failings in that department. A move to open-side prop helped, it seems, by keeping him physically occupied for the whole match. He had little time for any nonsense, and you could make out a case for saying that he had grown up as a footballer for the first time in his career.

Along with Jackson and Johnson – Blake had already gone back to Sydney after averaging better than a try a game during his stay – Boyd was in the side that beat Halifax 38–10 to win the Premiership at the end of his first season. Boyd was undoubtedly the dominant force in the match, running with obvious power and deceptive pace to score the first and last tries of that emphatic victory and claim the coveted Harry Sunderland Trophy as man-of-the-match – the second Australian after John Dorahy to do so. Johnson, coming on as a substitute, and Jackson were also among the try-scorers, and Warrington's controversial judgement in signing Boyd had been handsomely vindicated. Rathbone, who did not play, later claimed in a Sunday newspaper that the Warrington team had taken pills to enhance their performance at Elland Road that day, a claim strenuously denied by all involved.

Boyd, Jackson and Johnson were all back the following season, 1986–87, when Warrington surrendered the Premiership to Wigan at Old Trafford, and he was back again, for a shorter, injury-affected season in 1987–88. It was 1989 before he finally left for good, after four seasons which had proved to be far more than a footnote to his career. In many ways, Britain saw the very best of Les Boyd.

*

Boyd's successor in the Australian second row, Noel Cleal, was a very different style of player, but one whose footsteps also led him into British club football in 1985–86. Cleal, along with the ill-fated Steve Rogers, played for Widnes, while St Helens tried to perform the impossible task of replacing Mal Meninga by signing Ross Conlon from Balmain. Conlon had, in a moment of aberration by the Australian selectors, edged Meninga out of the national side for one of the Tests during Great Britain's tour in 1984. That was largely on the basis of his goal-kicking, which was undeniably excellent; but, in other respects, the comparisons were unflattering. One player, and a virtually unknown one at that, who did make a startling impression that year was Steve Halliwell, son of former Wigan centre Frank Halliwell, who had emigrated to Australia. Halliwell scored a club-record forty-nine tries for Leigh in the second division, largely as the result of his alert backing-up. Intoxicated by his own success, he moved on to St Helens and Wakefield the following season, but a combination of illness and the way first-division rugby exposed the rough edges in other aspects of his play meant that he never regained his effectiveness.

One of the best stories of the season revolved around the Liddiard brothers at Oldham. David Liddiard, a very fast full-back or winger from Parramatta, had been a good capture for the club, along with Mal Graham from Newcastle and Gary Warnecke from Easts in Sydney. But Liddiard also brought with him an unexpected bonus in the shape of his kid brother, Glen. He had come along purely for the trip but, after he had played with obvious flair for a local amateur side and for Oldham's 'A' team, he found himself in the first team, alongside his brother, just a few days after his 16th birthday. Both brothers played in the Challenge Cup semi-final in 1986 as Oldham strove to reach Wembley for the first time, and the game hinged upon their actions to a large extent. David's cross-kick created a try for Glen, but Glen subsequently had to leave the field with concussion and an uncharacteristic mistake under a high kick by David gifted Castleford a try that went a long way towards giving them victory.

Other notable Australians who caught the eye that season were South Sydney's Neil Baker, who played particularly well for Salford, and Test props Dave Brown (at Barrow) and Geoff Gerard (at Hull). Mike Marketo, a rugged reserve-grade prop from Balmain, had some outstanding matches for York, and two players who were to loom large over the next few seasons, Phil McKenzie and Greg Austin, made their bow with Rochdale Hornets. Brown moved to Hull the following season, 1986–87, and McKenzie began his long and mutually beneficial association with Widnes, while Austin went to Salford. St Helens had Pat Jarvis, a highly reliable Test prop whose dietary requirements outraged his landlady at the pub in which he was staying: Jarvis would eat little but boiled fish and mountains of vegetables, and had to drink the water they had been cooked in afterwards. Ian Schubert, the flowing-haired golden boy of the wing in the early 1970s but, by this time, a battle-hardened back-row forward, was a similarly charismatic guest with Leigh the same year.

The 1987–88 season brought a new cast of characters. Test full-back Garry Jack played for Salford and emerged with his massive reputation, the bush hat that he invariably wore off the field and his name for never buying a round all intact. When he had to leave in mid-season, Brisbane Souths player Steve Gibson made a seamless transition from wing to full-back to replace him. It was a huge compliment to Gibson – if perhaps a slight exaggeration – for coach Kevin Ashcroft to say that the club hardly noticed the difference. Former Test second row Rod 'Rocket' Reddy brought to Barrow his particular brand of mischief as the game's most notorious practical joker, and international utility back Dale Shearer played for Widnes. Two good forwards of contrasting temperament, the unflappable David Brooks and the fiery Terry Regan, did well at Hull, and Manly second row Glenn Ryan and Canterbury's poetry-writing centre, Peter Mortimer, were across the city at Hull KR.

Perhaps the most telling indication of the strength of the Australian migration at this time came in the form of the 'beach parties' instigated by Western Suburbs prop Bruce Clark and held, in the first instance, on the car park at Oldham, to whom he was attached in 1986–87. A couple of lorry-loads of sand would be ordered, and Australian players from right across the north of England would gather – regardless of the weather – to drink ice-cold beer in their beach shorts. As the idea spread, and man-made beaches appeared on Humberside and in the Pennines with increasing regularity, there was never any shortage of expatriate Aussie footballers to make up the numbers.

9
Flops, Crocks and Runaways

You can't win them all, and that applies just as much to the gamble of signing players as it does to the way a side performs on the field. Buried in among all the Australian players who have made a telling contribution in Britain are many others who, for one reason or another, left little behind but a feeling of disappointment.

British clubs have often been to blame themselves. A surprising number of imported players are bought 'blind' or, at best, with a few glimpses on video to go by. Sometimes a recommendation can come from somebody who owes somebody a favour; it does not always do the recipient club any favours in return. Some clubs do their homework meticulously, making sure that they have seen a player live and unedited and that they have spoken to him directly before they even think about making an offer. Those clubs, and Wigan in their Australian phase in the mid-1980s would be the classic example, rarely make mistakes.

Others persist in trying to force square pegs into round holes. They wait for what they think is going to be a strapping prop forward who turns out to be a 12½-stone back-rower, or the new scrum-half turns out to be a stand-off who has never fed a scrum in his life. Sometimes it can be a matter of different interpretations of the same role. A team that badly needs an incisive, try-scoring player in midfield might find that the fellow they have gone to the expense of bringing to Britain is an organiser – and they already have six organisers getting in each other's way. The strong-running, tackle-breaking second-rower who is so eagerly awaited transpires to be a workhorse whose only talent is for making forty tackles a match; nothing wrong with that, of course, but it might not be what his new employers wanted or needed.

An important skill, but one that not every club possesses, is the ability to spot the player who wants to come to Britain on holiday. Maurice Bamford, at his various clubs, had a rule of thumb that anyone who mentioned the dread word 'sightseeing' was suspect. Others make a systematic study of how many games a player has missed through injury during the previous season. But some boards of directors and coaches merely want an answer to the question: 'Is he a good lad?'

There is no accounting, however, for the intervention of two factors: sudden and serious injury, and the inexplicable failure of a player to produce the form of which he is known to be capable. When Warrington signed two Australian stars in 1931, it was Nelson Hardy, a centre or full-back who had played all three Tests against Great Britain in 1928, rather than Bill Shankland of whom most was expected. But it was Shankland who was the success in Britain, and the club's report on the season notes glumly that 'Nelson Hardy failed to produce anything like the football expected of him.' The same epitaph has marked the end of the British careers of many a player who arrived with a glowing reputation. Even Dave Brown, the most prolific point-scorer of his day, failed to adapt to British conditions as well as might have been anticipated. His dislike of the soft English grounds was a major factor in his decision to buy out the remaining season of a four-year contract with Warrington in 1939 and return to Australia.

Injury is no respecter of reputations, and there is, beyond the normal precautions of insurance in which Australians seem, historically, to have been ahead of their British counterparts, no legislating for it. Most notably, Arthur Beetson snapped his leg in Hull KR's Christmas Day derby against Hull in 1968, bringing his British club career to a premature halt; but at least he had got a few games under his mighty belt. For sheer brevity, he is beaten out of sight by Paul Taylor, the versatile Parramatta player who joined Wakefield Trinity in March 1990 after being released by his Australian club. Taylor lasted just a few minutes of his debut before being carried off with a wrecked knee – and him one of the most durable players in Sydney. He at least had the consolation of having played previously in Britain, with Oldham. Scott Gale, with Hull in 1987, was another who suffered serious injury in his first match in England. The gamble of bringing him back later that same season to play in the Challenge Cup semi-final was not a success, as Hull went down 3–4 to Halifax.

The saddest case of all, both for the player and for the British spectators deprived of the pleasure of seeing him play week after week, was that of Steve Rogers. He had been one of the thoroughbred players of the late 1970s and early 1980s and a fixture in the centres in the touring Australian teams of 1978 and 1982. Many British clubs had pursued him, but it was not until 1985 that Widnes succeeded in persuading him to come to England. It was to prove a dreadful year for Rogers. In the first game of the season in Australia, his jaw was badly broken in a late tackle, and he made just one more appearance, as a substitute, in Sydney. He arrived in England in September confident that the damage was repaired, and Widnes fans looked forward to seeing him and his Kangaroo colleague, Noel Cleal, at Naughton Park. But they never did see Rogers there; after just thirteen minutes of his debut match at Wigan, he went down in an innocuous tackle and lay there in agony, his right leg broken in two places. He never played again.

That same 1985–86 season saw Michael Pobjie claim the dubious distinction of becoming the first 'name' player from Australia since the lifting of the international transfer ban to be told to pack his bags and go home because he was not producing the goods. Pobjie, from South Sydney, had arrived at Salford with a reputation as a good young player with an excellent future in the game. After nine games, however, Salford coach Kevin

Ashcroft reluctantly told him that his form was unsatisfactory and that he had to go. Yet Pobjie resumed a perfectly decent career in Sydney, which included appearing for Balmain in their Grand Final defeat by Canberra in 1989. By coincidence, on the opposite side that day and responsible for the winning try of a dramatic match was Steve Jackson who, two years before, had gone to Warrington and failed even to get a chance in the first team. Complete failure in Britain has not always meant a loss of direction in Australia, any more than monumental success on one side of the world has been a watertight guarantee of it continuing on the other side.

Tony Rampling was another to depart the Willows ahead of schedule, in 1989–90, after allegations of unauthorised use of a phone in the press-box at the ground. Rampling, the former Souths, Easts and Gold Coast prop, had been hampered with injury during his only season at Salford, but his form when he was fit was good enough for them to plan to bring him back for another year. It was an expensive phone bill for both club and player; and telephones, as we shall see, do seem to be a recurring source of conflict, especially at Salford.

Brian Battese, another highly respected Sydney player, also had an unaccountably disappointing time with Salford in 1985–86, while St Helens's attempt to work the Brisbane Souths seam – source of Mal Meninga and Phil Veivers – fell flat the same year when prop forward Gary Greinke failed to impress. Featherstone released their Western Suburbs full-back, Rob Pethybridge, in mid-season – he was snapped up by York – and, especially after the appointment of Peter Fox as coach in 1987, the club rarely took any interest in Australians thereafter. Along with Doug Laughton, to name but one, Fox came to regard New Zealanders as better value for money although, in 1990, he would have made an exception for Wally Lewis.

*

Sometimes, it is players with proven track records who can be the biggest letdown. The 1988–89 season was a case in point, because there was then no more potent name among prop forwards than that of Sam Backo. A colourful character who had developed into a top-class front-rower after walking into the Canberra Raiders club and asking for a trial, he had tormented Great Britain during the 1988 Test series in Australia; a big man with explosive power and pace near the line, he scored a try in each of the three matches of the series. Backo was the one Australian forward that the tourists really could not handle, and he was a very hot property indeed; Wigan in particular showed a lively interest in his future plans. His capture by Leeds, therefore, looked a major coup; but his contribution was minimal. Backo started just eight matches, scoring a single try, albeit a valuable one to win the Yorkshire Cup semi-final against Hull, and spending most of his time on the substitutes' bench – 'getting splinters in my backside,' as he put it. When Leeds finally got some reward for their expenditure, both international and domestic, by winning the Yorkshire Cup, Backo was again on the periphery, coming on for just the last sixteen minutes of the 33–12 victory over Castleford. On the opposing side that day was Gary Belcher, full-back-in-waiting for the Australian Test side, and another major disappointment that season. Plagued by injury, he started only ten games for Castleford.

Backo's limited participation for Leeds, plus his extremely laid-back manner, inevitably led to mutterings that he was one Australian who had definitely come to Britain on his hols. In fact, circumstances were largely beyond his control. Leeds had spent heavily on their front row, buying two British Test props, Lee Crooks and Hugh Waddell; the then Leeds coach, Malcolm Reilly, who was doubling up as national coach at the time, saw the pair as important elements in his long-term strategy for both club and country. Backo, as a short-term visitor, came well behind them in the pecking order.

To a lesser degree, Halifax were unfortunate with Dan Stains, a very well-regarded forward with Cronulla. He arrived in 1989, at a time when the team was struggling, and he never lived up fully to his credentials. He went on to play State of Origin football for Queensland and to tour New Zealand with the Australian team in 1989; but there were few signs of that quality at Halifax, although at least he never took the abuse from the crowd that fell to Valleys stand-off Peter Coyne in 1988–89. Starting from the uncomfortable position of being the player who cost the idolised Graham Eadie his place at the club, Coyne's hesitant early form diminished his stock still further, and the Thrum Hall crowd rarely got off his back.

Rochdale Hornets had a similarly unhappy experience in 1990 with Western Suburbs forward David Gallagher. Coach Allan Agar had watched him on video and liked what he saw, especially his physical strength and high work-rate. Yet Gallagher was a shadow of the player Hornets thought they had signed during his time in England. After only five games, his contract was cancelled, amid some face-saving talk about a debilitating blood disorder, which may or may not have had substance.

The 1986–87 season in particular was a bad one for big forwards from Australia. Peter Smith came to Leeds as a prop with a wealth of Sydney experience behind him; he played only nine games, including being replaced in an embarrassingly lame effort against the Aussie tourists, before Leeds cancelled his contract in November. Noel Cleal had, for a player of his class, been a slightly fitful performer for Widnes the previous season, but they would have settled for the same from his brother, Les – they didn't get it. The Cleals had been a famed double act in Australian country football but, unlike Noel, Les had spent most of his career in the bush; he had achieved unprecedented success as a player-coach of country teams and was reckoned to be the one with the rugby brain. But Les, even bigger and more hirsute than 'Crusher', never adapted to British football and bowed out after eleven games, two of them as substitute.

Bruce Clark, of beach-party fame, did see out his full season at Oldham, but not to universal acclamation. After his departure, he became something of a *cause célèbre* at the club's annual meeting, where disgruntled supporters slammed the board for bringing over a player who looked so heavy and slow and more fitted to the local amateur leagues. In fact, 'Bruiser', as he was known, had some deceptive ball skills and would have looked better in a side that backed up his trundling runs.

The mystery of the year, however, was not a prop forward, but Kerry Boustead at Hull KR. There was no more established star in Australian Rugby League than Boustead, who had played twenty-five Tests on the wing and was rated by many as one of the best in his position that the country had produced. In 1986, Boustead, despite a broken leg the previous season, was still in his prime and rather fancied the idea of 'doing a Chris Anderson' in Britain: moving infield a place or two to use his great experience and his largely unimpaired pace a little closer to the centre of the action. He did get to play that sort of role – but mainly in the reserves. Boustead's form in the first team was so ordinary that he was dropped in mid-season and could not force his way back in; it was a humiliation for a player who had done so much in his career, but Boustead, to his credit, bore it cheerfully. He managed to retain his enthusiasm and he was an asset off the field and on the training pitch and no doubt helped the young players in the 'A' team a good deal. But, as he said himself, he had not come 12,000 miles to play reserve grade. How that indignity befell him remains one of the puzzling questions of Anglo-Australian Rugby League in the 1980s. It was not even a case of his career being in terminal decline, because he went back to Sydney and played on with some success for Norths.

Australian players in Britain have cut their own stays short for all manner of reasons, including the cold weather and the warm beer. In 1928, two South Sydney players, Albert Carr and Sid Harris, left Huddersfield in the lurch by doing a midnight flit to London and embarking on a ship for Australia. In 1953, Alan Walker, the Manly and Australian Rugby Union centre, joined Leigh, but he left after nine games to play county cricket for Nottinghamshire. Many other departures have been just as abrupt and a lot more acrimonious. Take the case of Steve Stacey, the Brisbane Easts and Queensland winger who joined Salford in 1984. Stacey was a success on the field, scoring six tries in seven appearances; but as soon as he was there he was gone, leaving a trail of claims and counter-claims that typify the way relations can sometimes break down between player and club.

Salford alleged that Stacey had walked out without giving any clue to his intentions, after being fined £100 for missing the team bus for his comeback match after a four-match ban for spitting at an opponent. It was further claimed that he had pocketed a £5000 signing-on fee, left unpaid phone bills totalling more than £500, and left the house with which the club had provided him in a deplorable state. 'To say that we are bitterly disillusioned would be putting it mildly,' said Salford chairman John Wilkinson. 'No player could have been better looked after. He had a good signing-on fee from us. We fixed him up with a brand new home, and one of our directors provided him with a car. He had a job at the club. We couldn't have done more for him.'

As might be expected, Stacey's version was somewhat different. 'I told the club I was coming home,' he insisted. 'Obviously, from their reaction, they didn't believe what I was saying. I'd had about enough of their broken promises. It was costing me money to be over there, and I just had to get home . . . They promised me accommodation. What I didn't expect was spending the first two weeks sleeping on the floor like a swaggy. After that, they moved me into a boarding house run by an elderly couple. It wasn't exactly ideal accommodation. The club also promised to fly my girlfriend over, which they didn't, and agreed to pay my telephone bills. From what I've heard, they now say I left owing people money for phone calls. It's them who owe the money, not me.'

The club had eventually found him a job, he admitted. 'It was working in the club's promotions department. But there was only one snag: there was no pay.' Needless to say, his car kept breaking down as well. Salford tried, without success, to retrieve part of Stacey's signing-on fee, or to prevent him from playing in Australia until he had made amends.

Mario Fenech was another Australian whose manner of departure left a sour taste with his British club. An involved set of circumstances took Fenech to Bradford Northern in 1986. He had been a strong candidate for a place on the Kangaroo tour that year, until he got himself sent off in South Sydney's last game of the season, against Balmain and his great rival Benny Elias. Fenech missed out on the tour and was also given a four-match ban, which would have ruled him out of the first month of the 1987 season in Sydney had it not been for a very inviting little loophole. It transpired that there was nothing in the laws of the game to stop a player banned in Australia serving out his ban with a club in Britain; thus, for the cost of a return air-fare, Souths could send Fenech to England to sit out four games, play a few and then fly home with his debt to society – or, at least, the New South Wales Rugby League judiciary – paid in full. Bradford knew that Fenech's stay would be a brief one; what they didn't expect was that he would take off like a scalded rabbit after just two games – one of them, ironically, against the Australian tourists, with Fenech at prop against a front row including his old sparring partner, Elias.

The newish Sheffield Eagles club had cottoned on to this same idea and brought Cliff Lyons to Britain to serve out a similar four-match ban that same 1986–87 season. Lyons fulfilled his part of the bargain by staying on for the agreed six games after his suspension was served, and he gave excellent value on the field. Two years later, Sheffield performed a similar service for Mark Geyer, the young Penrith second row who had also fallen foul of the disciplinary body. He, too, played half a dozen times and made a good impression that was confirmed by his selection for the Kangaroo tour in 1990. After that, the loophole was closed.

On occasion, the chemistry between player and coach has been so badly wrong that a swift parting has been inevitable. In the same season, 1986–87, that Les Cleal was attempting to follow in his brother's footsteps, Widnes also signed the South Sydney scrum-half, Craig Coleman. Coleman was a good player by any standards, but he and Doug Laughton, the then Widnes coach, failed from the start to hit it off. Coleman complained after he left that Laughton had ignored him and had made no effort to introduce him to his new team-mates. After just three first-team games, Laughton told him that he wanted him to play in the 'A' team; Coleman refused, packed his bags and left. He remained keen to make his mark in Britain, however, and succeeded in doing so in two rather longer – although not entirely controversy-free – stays with Hull and Leeds.

Neither Coleman nor Fenech set up any records for self-imposed brevity of sojourn in the United Kingdom. That distinction surely belongs, among players of any stature, at least, to Graeme Wynn. The long-serving St George and New South Wales forward came to England to play for little Chorley

Borough in 1988. He was both injured and under suspension at the time, which gave him time to look around and decide that it was not a very feasible proposition. He left without ever lacing a boot.

*

One theory about the likely trend of the traffic between Britain and Australia when the international ban was lifted was that many players with their best years behind them, and even some out-and-out has-beens, would head for England to garner some easy pickings in their declining years. Some players undoubtedly extended their careers considerably; but it was rare for players who were regarded as completely finished to take the British ticket. Graham Eadie and Ray Price both made comebacks in Britain three years after their Australian retirements, but they got away with the gamble rather handsomely and thus have no place in this chapter. John Donnelly, however, had an altogether stranger swansong in Britain.

'Dallas' Donnelly was a larger-than-life figure, a prop forward of the old school who was as famous for his unbridled exploits off the pitch as he was for the impression he made as a player. On tour with Australia in New Zealand in 1975, he was reputed to have eaten the goldfish from a display tank in a hotel foyer and, for a period, his presence was not welcomed at his own Sydney outfit, Western Suburbs' leagues club. If he was still around, he could not sue you for saying that he was partial to a beer or two.

His 30th birthday past and Wests in the throes of being relocated to Campbelltown, Dallas decided that he wanted to see Britain. He touted himself around a number of clubs but, looking even more battered and lived in than he was, only Southend Invicta showed much enthusiasm. In any case, Dallas liked the idea of living in London which, as far as a man from Gunnedah, deep in rural New South Wales, was concerned, was right next door. He cut an outlandish figure, training along the promenade of a seaside town which scarcely knew that its Rugby League team existed. It was a depressing season, in which Southend won only four matches before accepting the inevitable and folding; but Donnelly soldiered on loyally, playing seventeen games and scoring one of the rare tries of his career in a heavy defeat by Bradford Northern in the first round of the Challenge Cup. Dallas had achieved his ambition; he had lived in London. Three years later, he was dead after collapsing on the beach near his home; he was mourned by all who had met him, in Sydney or in Southend.

That same Invicta side featured a player of an even earlier vintage than Donnelly: Chris Wellman, who had played in the 1973 Grand Final for a Cronulla side that also included Englishmen Tommy Bishop and Cliff Watson, and was well into his fourth decade. He was another cornerstone of the blighted Southend team, playing fifteen games in that grim season.

The start of the 1990s saw the birth of a significant trend in relations between British clubs and Australian players: the mid-season switch. First to perform this tricky manoeuvre was Jeff Hardy, a versatile and highly effective player from Illawarra, who started the 1989–90 season with Sheffield Eagles, playing mainly at centre and stand-off. Sheffield wanted to keep him for the whole season, but Hardy could not be certain of his plans. In the event, Illawarra released him, and no other Sydney club came in to snap him up – a good example of form in Britain cutting little ice back home in the southern hemisphere. By that time, however, Sheffield had gone elsewhere, signing up Kiwi Tawera Nikau to fill what they thought was going to be a vacant import spot, so Hardy went to Castleford to replace the departing Ron Gibbs. It was an ideal move for Hardy; like a lot of Sheffield players, he was living in the Castleford area – right next door, in fact, to his former Illawarra team-mate, Steve Larder, who was already with Cas. Hardy was again a great success, playing this time in the second row, and there was no particular bitterness over his swap – just a feeling on Sheffield's part that it could have worked out better from their point of view.

The same could not be said about Greg Mackey's move from Warrington to Hull. Mackey, an aggressive but shrewd half-back who had played for South Sydney, Illawarra and Canterbury, was an immediate hit with Warrington when he joined them at the start of the 1989–90 season on a short-term contract. His ability to pull the strings in midfield and his educated kicking game had a lot to do with Warrington's excellent start to the season: of his nine games for the club, eight were won and one drawn, with one of the wins coming against Oldham in the Lancashire Cup final, when Mackey created two tries in the first ten minutes to put the Wire on the way to a 24–16 victory. At the same time, however, Mackey's situation in Australia was changing. Canterbury, struggling to make ends meet and anxious to prune their playing staff, paid off his contract, so opening the prospect for Warrington of keeping him on a long-term basis. According to Mackey, they failed to make him a realistic offer; according to Warrington, he prevaricated while he waited for a better offer from elsewhere.

Whatever the niceties of interpretation involved, Hull saw their chance. Coach Brian Smith, himself a former Souths and Illawarra man, knew Mackey of old and regarded him as the organising half-back that he was lacking. Insisting that he was doing nothing unethical in offering a player a contract when his existing club had failed to do so, Smith signed him for Hull. Warrington lost their next five matches – although not even a cocky little half-back like Mackey would claim that his absence was the only reason for that – and Hull, once the New Year came, improved steadily. That improvement carried on the following season, when their outstanding form – with Mackey captaining the side from stand-off – put them on top of the first division for a while in mid-season. Unlike the Hardy transfer, Mackey's move caused considerable acrimony between the two clubs. 'I'll never be able to play at Warrington without being booed,' he predicted accurately. 'But they don't know the full story.'

The acquisition of Mackey led to a change of a different sort at Hull. David Liddiard, who had played so elegantly at Oldham four years earlier, had been brought to Hull in 1989 to address another of the perceived weaknesses of Smith's team – a lack of real pace out wide. He had showed every sign of being at least a partial solution to the problem, scoring four tries in his first seven games and rapidly becoming a favourite with the Boulevard crowd. Yet the need for a player to call the shots was an even more urgent one; Smith knew that Mackey would fit the bill, even though it meant that an overseas player had to be sacrificed. Hull's two Australian Test forwards, Steve Folkes and Noel

Cleal, were retained; Liddiard was told, painfully, that he was out. A niggling neck injury was a factor in the decision, but not a crucial one. 'It wasn't a pleasant thing to have to do, because David had been playing well and was very popular; he was a real crowd-pleaser. But it wasn't a difficult decision, either, because I knew what needed to be done,' said Smith. Replacing a popular player can be a bad way to start off at a new club, but it says a lot for Mackey that he was accepted almost immediately.

Mackey's influence continued under Smith's successor, Noel Cleal. Although Hull slipped down the first division after Smith's departure in January 1991 and eventually finished third, the half-back led a magnificent late surge to carry off the Premiership trophy. After beating St Helens and Leeds impressively in their first two matches, Hull faced Premiership specialists Widnes at Old Trafford. It was not the worst time to be playing Widnes, with Martin Offiah having announced his intention to leave and coach Doug Laughton rumoured, correctly, to be packing his bags himself. In their uncertain mood, Widnes were no match for Mackey, who controlled the game for Hull from first to last; he created the first try of a 14–4 victory when he dummied to kick and passed instead to Richard Gay, and also the decisive third when his pass sent in substitute Gary Nolan. Mackey joined John Dorahy and Les Boyd as Aussies who have won the man-of-the-match award named after their fellow-countryman, Harry Sunderland.

Two unlikely Australians also took their share of the glory: Damien McGarry, discarded by Balmain, and Brad Webb, a South Sydney junior who had dropped out of the game altogether, occupied the centre positions at Old Trafford. The following season, they were gone, along with Great Britain prop Karl Harrison – sold to Halifax – and the French scrum-half, Patrick Entat, whose financial expectations were too high for a club constantly on the verge of fiscal panic. Mackey moved to scrum-half for 1991–92 and missed Entat badly, with the inevitable result that neither he nor the team were as effective. It could never be said, however, that the decision to grab Mackey had proved to be anything other than one of Hull's wiser moves.

*

Hull's neighbours, Hull KR, made an even more difficult, controversial and unpopular decision at the start of the 1990–91 season. Of all the Australian imports in the 1980s, none had scored tries with the regularity of Greg Austin. He had scored tries for Rochdale Hornets, he had scored tries for Salford and, in their promotion campaign the previous season, he had scored thirty-eight of them for Rovers – a return second only in the country to Martin Offiah. Astonishingly, however, they chose to release him after just four games of the new season, in one of which he had scored six tries! There was a rationale behind this apparently bizarre move: Rovers felt that their great need was for forwards, and that the only way to give themselves a chance of surviving in the first division was to greatly strengthen their pack.

With the financial pressures that were to cause them further grief later in the season already gathering, Rovers could not compete for the signatures of British players who could make a difference – forwards like Kevin Ward, for instance – so they looked abroad. The man they got was James Goulding, a New Zealand Test prop who had been in particularly bullish form during the Kiwi tour the previous season. His signing meant that someone had to go: either Austin, who had tried and failed to get himself reclassified as a British-based player for quota purposes, Australian Test prop Bryan Niebling, or the newly-arrived Kiwi back, David Watson. Watson had just signed a five-year contract, while Niebling was the side's key forward; Austin was the odd man out, his tries regarded as a luxury that could, at a pinch, be dispensed with. Bitterly disappointed by his treatment and touched by the Rovers fans' continuing attachment to him – they chanted his name incessantly during matches he played for them after the news of his likely demise had leaked out – he packed his bags. Yet he did not have as far to hump them as Liddiard, who had gone back to Australia to resume his successful career with Parramatta; Halifax grabbed him and, predictably, he was a regular try-scorer for them as they won promotion from the second division. Ironically, at the season's end, Austin was followed to Thrum Hall by none other than David Watson after Rovers discovered, after just one year, that there was no way that they could afford to honour the rest of his contract.

Austin finished that season with forty-seven tries – second, for the second year running, only to Martin Offiah. For the second year running, too, he was on the losing side and failed to score in the second-division Premiership final, Halifax going down 20–27 to a Salford side that included another long-serving Australian, Steve Gibson, at full-back. In 1991–92, with Offiah sitting out the first half of the season while Wigan and Widnes haggled over his eventual £440,000 transfer, it seemed that this might finally be Austin's year to top the try-scoring lists. He shared the lead as late as the end of March, but his total of thirty-three was overhauled by Shaun Edwards, whose total was swollen, it must be said, by his team-mates in a rampant Wigan side presenting him with a number of gift tries to ensure that he stayed ahead of the field. Performances like his five tries against his old club, Hull KR, still reinforced Austin's standing as the most prolific try-scorer borrowed from Australia since the lifting of the ban.

One of the most remarkable changes of horses in mid-season – voluntary in this case – was performed in 1988 by John Cogger, a player who gave tremendous value on the field in Britain but managed to fall out with two clubs in rather spectacular style. Cogger had always been an unusual character; as a young player with Western Suburbs in Sydney he had been notable for a number of things – his long blond hair (which, even by that time, and even in Australia, was out of fashion with everyone but him), his diminutive stature for a forward, and his ferocious aggression. Cogger, influenced by the success his elder brother, Trevor, had enjoyed at Leigh the previous year, had first come to Runcorn in 1986. Trevor cannot have marked his card all that thoroughly, because John was somewhat taken aback to find his first game watched by the proverbial two men and a dog. 'And that's a good gate,' someone told him. 'The dog doesn't always come.'

Nevertheless, he returned for two more seasons and invariably looked a cut above the rest of his perennially struggling team-mates. Plenty of bigger clubs would have been glad to have him because, apart from his high work-rate and fiercely committed tackling, he also had the happy knack of sniffing out tries. For the 1988–89 season, Runcorn, rather than lose him, put him on quite a handsome contract – and this at a club where few players knew with any certainty what a contract was. Yet it was that contract, and the accident of a draw against Wigan in the first round of the John Player Special Trophy in November, that forced him into a most uncomfortable corner.

Runcorn were drawn at home but agreed, for sound financial reasons, to forego that advantage and play the match at Central Park. The Runcorn players spotted a rare chance to make some money out of losing matches, and argued for a sizeable bonus, win or lose; the board of directors offered them a better winning bonus, but far less in the event of their inevitable defeat. It was not handled very well on either side, and the upshot was that the entire first-team squad went on strike. Cogger's instinct was to do the same: he felt that the players were in the right. But a phone call from a director warned him that he, unlike them, was a contracted player; refusal to play would put him in breach of that contract and would allow the club to reclaim his house, car and return air-ticket and withhold his cash. 'I would have been broke and homeless in a foreign country. I was left with no choice but to play.'

He did, along with a rag-bag outfit of local amateurs, gnarled veterans and coach Bill Ashurst, who came out of retirement at nearly 40 and was sent off twelve minutes after coming on as substitute. Runcorn were beaten by a competition record 2–92, but it was not the torment of continually lining up behind the posts for yet another conversion attempt that distressed Cogger: it was what he heard when he was there. In the crowd were most of his striking team-mates, and it was not a pleasant experience to be jeered at and called a blackleg or worse by men he had played alongside.

It was inevitable thereafter that he would leave, but he did stay at Canal Street until February 1989, and even served for a month as player-coach, before he was rescued by Oldham. His impact there was immediate, with three tries in a win over Featherstone and two in the defeat of Castleford. His contribution came too late to save Oldham from relegation, but he had proved his worth. He did so again the following season as Oldham won promotion straight back to the first division and reached the semi-final of the Challenge Cup, but it ended in some confusion and recrimination when Cogger went back to Sydney with several games still remaining to visit his sick father. Mr Cogger Snr recovered, but John did not return; at one stage, his baggage was lost and he became stranded in Hong Kong. Soon, however, the whole thing degenerated into an argument about money. He was on the transfer list and then off it, and did not regain his role as club captain. Somehow, his considerable heart did not seem to be in it any more: his suitcases seemed not to be the only thing he had left behind.

Cogger was involved in one more unusual incident. In a Cup tie at Batley, he was attacked by a woman in the crowd who grabbed him by the hair as he celebrated an Oldham try. He was promptly sent off for 'inciting the crowd' with a gesture after he had freed himself from the woman's clutches. Life was rarely dull with Cogger around.

*

Runcorn, whose two years and more without a win made them the most unsuccessful team in the history of British Rugby League, also figure in the most bizarre little cameo appearance by any Australian player since Alby Rosenfeld met his wife-to-be. Kerry Gibson was that most unlikely proposition – a one-armed Rugby League player. He had been born in the Sydney suburb of Burwood with a normal right arm and a left one that was stunted and withered and close to useless. Incredibly, however, he still managed to be an outstanding sportsman at school; his rugby was good, his cricket was better, and his one real frustration was that his favourite sport, boxing, was one that was utterly barred to him. 'If I'd had two good arms, I'd have been a fighter,' he said; he certainly lacked nothing in aggression and determination. Gibson also used to joke that he was a pretty useful swimmer – 'Although I tend to go round in circles,' he said.

That was typical of the way he set out to make light of his handicap and, to a large extent, he succeeded. As a back-row forward, he played in one of Western Suburbs' junior teams for a season and then had a profitable year with a country club at Lower Clarence. Even more surprisingly, he then went back to Sydney and played in reserve grade for Wests in 1983 and 1984.

He also had a short period playing for Wynnum-Manly in Brisbane before Tas Baitieri, the catalyst for an influx of Australian players into France in the 1980s which was smaller than its English equivalent but still significant, fixed him up with a club on the outskirts of Paris. From there, he decided to chance his arm – as he himself would phrase it – in Britain.

Springfield Borough were also hosts briefly in that 1987–88 season to Castleford-bound Gary French, before he suffered a back injury that threatened to end his career; but it was not a difficult club at which to get a chance. Making up the numbers to field an 'A' team was never easy, and they were not inclined to inquire too deeply into the antecedents of newcomers who seemed like they might know how to play the game – or even count their limbs too carefully. Gibson played, and there was talk – mainly from him – about the club offering him a contract. When they failed to do so, he went instead to Runcorn, another club where a bloke with a pair of boots under his arm always had a chance of getting a game.

Kerry Gibson did play twice for Runcorn's first team. The second, and last, time just happened to be against Springfield. Gibson, never short of aggression, was still furious with Borough coach Stan Gittins, who he believed had blocked his bid for a contract there; but nobody knew just how furious he was. As the teams walked down the tunnel at Springfield Park at full-time, he found Gittins and caught him with a beauty of a punch. 'I might have only one arm,' he said afterwards, 'but I can punch all right with that.' Runcorn kicked him out with little ceremony; the last thing they needed was a player who swung punches at opposing coaches.

Gibson had a couple of plans in mind. There was a remake of *Bridge on the River Kwai* being filmed in the Philippines, he said, and he had been offered a role as one of the prisoners-of-war. It must have been, at least since *The Fugitive* disappeared from our television screens, one of the few opportunities for a one-armed actor. He was also keen to get into coaching. 'I could have gone all the way as a player with two arms,' he said, and perhaps he could; he was convinced, at any rate, that he could certainly do so as a coach. 'I know people. I understand their psychology and I know Rugby League like the back of my hand.' He paused for a moment. 'Like the back of my right hand, of course.'

And with that, Kerry Gibson, surely one of the strangest cases among all the Australian players who did not quite make it in Britain, or made it and lost it, moved on to pastures new.

10
The Clipboard Jungle

Towards the end of the 1980s, the nature of the Australian influence on British Rugby League changed markedly. It was Arthur Beetson, in Britain coaching the touring Queensland side in 1983, who first articulated what was to become the conventional wisdom: 'What you need out here,' he said, 'is not so much Australian players as Australian coaches.' His belief was that it was not the intrinsic superiority of its players that had put Australia so far ahead of Great Britain at the time; it was the way that it organised and prepared its players, which it did both differently and better.

Beetson was not angling for a job himself. Although his friendly ties with Hull KR made his the first name to leap to mind when they were looking for a coach several years later, Artie never had any great desire to uproot himself from Australia. Others were to put his theory into practice.

In a sense, Graham Lowe's period at Wigan was something of a trial run for Australian coaches in Britain. Although one must not forget for a moment that he was a New Zealander, his approach to the role owed more to his time as a coach in Brisbane than it did to his home country. Lowe's triumphs at Central Park – and his record shows him to be one of the most successful coaches there has ever been – encouraged other clubs to look further afield than the domestic merry-go-round. The equally startling success of Chris Anderson, first as player-coach and again after he hung up his boots, had the same effect and, if Leeds and Malcolm Clift failed to make a go of it, that hiccup failed to discredit the idea.

Rod Reddy was the next, taking over as player-coach at Barrow midway through the 1987–88 season. At the start of the following season, he was joined by three others: Ross Strudwick began his ill-fated spell at Halifax; Darryl Van de Velde arrived at Castleford; and Brian Smith took command at Hull.

Van de Velde, like Strudwick, had emerged from the Brisbane competition which, until the advent of the Brisbane Broncos in 1988, had been a powerful entity in its own right. He had coached Redcliffe with a fair degree of success and had earned a reputation as an innovator: he was, for instance, the first coach in Brisbane to leave the touchline and watch the game from an elevated position, keeping in touch with the dug-out by walkie-talkie, and the first to apply techniques of self-analysis and self-criticism to the running of a rugby team. In West Yorkshire, however, his name conjured up little other than images of a Dutch detective. A close-knit club and community like Castleford, traditionally coached by one of their own – Malcolm Reilly had been there for thirteen years before a brief interregnum under Dave Sampson – seemed an unlikely destination.

Not surprisingly, Van de Velde – known variously in Castleford as Truck Van Rental and DV^2 – looked to Australia for some playing reinforcements and came up with Gary Belcher, the future Australian full-back, well enough known to him from Brisbane, and Manly forward Ron Gibbs. Injury reduced Belcher's value to the club, but Gibbs, despite, or perhaps because of, his reputation as a firebrand, was a great hit.

In the early days of Van de Velde's reign, it seemed he could do no wrong. The only game lost in the first fifteen of that 1988–89 season was the Yorkshire Cup final, in which a Leeds side featuring Andrew Ettingshausen and Cliff Lyons finished 21–12 ahead. It was January before Castleford lost in the League, by which time they were out on their own at the top of the first division. Unfortunately, the defeats started to come with increasing regularity after that: there was a run of nine matches without a win and Cas, it turned out, were just being Cas – playing brilliantly for half a season and then hibernating for the rest, in their time-honoured style.

The following year, Steve Larder replaced Belcher at Wheldon Road, and Van de Velde also brought Gary French to join the returning Gibbs on the overseas roster. Larder, a full-back from Illawarra who had learnt his football in the Northern Territory, and French, understudy to Wally Lewis and Allan Langer at Brisbane Broncos and once with the late, lamented Springfield Borough, both gave the coach a good season, while first Gibbs, and then his replacement, Jeff Hardy, pepped up the pack. Gibbs, however, cemented his fearsome reputation in a controversial incident, one which chilled the relationship between Van de Velde and Hull coach Brian Smith – never a very warm one – to freezing-point. Smith reported Gibbs to the Rugby Football League for what he claimed was a calculatedly dangerous tackle on his stand-off, Welshman Gary Pearce. Smith's allegation was that the forward had perfected a tackle aimed at the knee of the non-kicking leg just as it was supporting the entire weight of Pearce's body. Rubbish, said Van de Velde; Gibbs had merely been diving to try to block the kick and had not even been looking at Pearce, let alone aiming deliberately at his knee, at the time of the impact. The RFL's disciplinary committee studied the video of the incident and suspended Gibbs for four games, later reduced to two on appeal – a result that struck both sides as an unsatisfactory compromise. On a less serious level, Gibbs was also banned from wearing gloves after allegations over their involvement in injuries during a nine-a-side tournament.

It was ironic that Van de Velde, a coach who confessed his astonishment at the prominence given to knock-out competitions at the expense of the Championship, should unwittingly turn Castleford in 1990–91 into Yorkshire Cup specialists. Two years after the defeat by Leeds, Cas, who had resigned the three Australians with whom they finished the previous season, Larder, Hardy and French, won a trophy Van de Velde firmly believed should be abolished by beating Wakefield Trinity 11–8. French missed the final, and both he and Larder came under increasing pressure for their places as Castleford, aided by what was for them an unprecedented spending spree, built up their playing staff.

A year later, they did it again, beating Bradford Northern 28–6, with Graeme Bradley, newly signed from the Penrith Panthers during their trip to play Wigan in the World Club Challenge, at centre. Thereafter, for a time, it looked as though Castleford might mount a challenge for the prize that Van de Velde would value more – the first-division Championship; but, like everyone else, they were eventually left trailing by Wigan. Not even reaching the Challenge Cup final fully compensated Van de Velde for that falling away, but everyone else in the town seemed excited enough about it. By that stage, Bradley, a failure in the centres who was clearly on his way to being shown the door, had made a highly successful switch into the second row and was man-of-the-match for his strong running and cover-tackling in a hard-fought semi-final victory over Hull.

Van de Velde was a study in cultural bafflement during the run-up to the final. Although the preparation was meticulous, with training twice a day, special diets and the players swearing off beer, he remained detached from all the excitement. 'I'll be glad when all the hype is over,' he opined. 'I've said all along that there's too much emphasis on knock-out competitions and I'm not going to change my mind now.'

Victory against Wigan might have converted Van de Velde to the Wembley-enthusiast wing of the movement, but that was never much of a possibility from the moment that Wigan capitalised on early mistakes to grab the first try through Martin Offiah. Bradley, who ran strongly enough in a much perkier second-half performance by Castleford, was equally dismissive: 'Just another match to me,' he said. His coach remained sanguine about the 12–28 defeat, and it was no doubt the overall inconsistency of his team in the League, rather than their failure to land the Challenge Cup, that made him think long and hard about his future in West Yorkshire. In the end, the challenge at hand proved too attractive, and Van de Velde signed a one-year extension to his contract in late May.

*

Hull had been in a dreadful state when Brian Smith landed, and it showed: the first six Championship matches of the 1988–89 season were all lost. Doing it tough was nothing new for Smith; after making his name as a successful lower-grade coach with South Sydney, he had taken on the difficult job of trying, against the odds, to establish an Illawarra club without stars, money or traditions as a force in the Sydney Premiership. Hull had plenty of tradition, but no money and few stars. Smith went back home, to players he knew, to try to put that right, and the three players he brought in all played major roles in a season which improved the longer it went on. David Moon, with a background at Souths and Illawarra, was the least known of the three but proved to be a sharp and effective threequarter. David Boyle was one of the honest workmen of Sydney football, an unflashy but hard-working and dedicated forward; he had a galvanising effect on the young Hull pack, with his attitude to training and match preparation rubbing off on them to very good effect. Although he hobbled through the latter stages of his stay with a stubborn injury, Boyle, in his own quiet way, was an inspiring influence at the Boulevard.

Craig Coleman was something different again. He had already played for, and then deserted, one British club, Widnes, and he had a reputation in Sydney as a rogue and a rascal, as well as a very good player. At Hull, he filled the need for a play-making scrum-half to perfection. If there was one criticism of him, it was that he could have run with the ball himself more often; but his passing of the ball – particularly his ability to pick out a wide runner with a visionary long ball – more often made you think that he was doing it exactly right. His short-kicking game was another string to his bow, and he formed an effective partnership with stand-off Gary Pearce, who took care of the long-range kicking.

The impact that these Australians had on the Airlie Birds was best seen on one memorable evening when Hull went to Wigan and, with Coleman leading the way, won magnificently. Smith's barren first few weeks seemed a long time ago. Hull eventually finished fourth in the League, one place ahead of Castleford, and reached the final of the Premiership trophy. They were beaten there 10–18 by Widnes and were not helped by the fact that all three of their Australians had returned home – Coleman after a particularly messy tug-of-war with Souths – but it was still an impressive first season for Smith.

His second season saw the improvement continue, particularly when Greg Mackey arrived from Warrington in place of David Liddiard, to join forces with Australian Test forwards Steve Folkes and the legendary pig-wrestler, Noel Cleal. Hull started the following season, 1990–91, like the proverbial house on fire, with Mackey, Cleal and a little-known former South Sydney junior, Brad Webb, as their three imports. Cleal played the unusual role of specialist substitute to good effect, turning several matches by coming on and running at defences already showing the strain of tackling what was a very big pack assembled by Brian Smith. Cleal was also becoming increasingly involved in the coaching side of affairs at the Boulevard and, when Smith announced that he was leaving in January to take up an appointment with St George in Sydney, 'Crusher' was the logical replacement. He was forced to abandon plans to be a player-coach, however, by a knee injury that forced him to retire, and Damien McGarry, a young centre from Balmain who was one of a number of Australian players made jobless at home by the introduction of the salary cap and the draft system, came in as his replacement on the import quota. McGarry made a try-scoring debut in Smith's farewell match, an emotional evening which saw Hull run riot against Leeds as a vivid testimony to the revivalist role played by the young coach during his three years on Humberside.

Noel Cleal had a difficult act to follow: there was only one way to go from the position he inherited, he observed, and that was down. Under Cleal, Hull lost more Championship matches than they won over the remainder of the season and finished third, 8 points behind the champions, Wigan. But Hull then proceeded to do what they had been unable to achieve under Smith by going on to win a major trophy – the 1991 Premiership.

Cleal felt let down during the close-season that much of the basis of the Premiership-winning side was undermined without anything being put in its place. McGarry and Webb returned to Australia after their brief taste of glory in Britain, and Karl Harrison and Patrick Entat departed for financial reasons. Wayne Portlock, an experienced Sydney first-grader with Easts and Norths who had been player-coaching at Young in New South Wales, was added to the squad for 1991–92, along with David Ronson, a back from Manly who had played in the first World Club Challenge against Wigan in 1987; but the club was still crucially weakened. The St George prop, Peter Spring, replaced the disappointing Portlock in mid-season when it became clear that extra forward power was the priority, and Hull reached the semi-final of the Challenge Cup before losing to Castleford. In the League, however, it was a thoroughly difficult season. With two matches to go, Hull were in danger of being relegated, and the board reacted by sacking Cleal.

The dismissed coach was so angered by the decision and its timing that he took the peculiar step of calling his own press conference to tell his side of the story. Hull had verbally offered him a new two-year contract only days before the sacking, he said, and he also accused the club's directors of cynicism in their choice of moment: 'If we go down, they're geniuses. If we stay up, they're geniuses. It's all about justifying their own position.' In the end, Hull stayed up on points difference. Having had his say, Cleal returned to Warialda in northern New South Wales to relax, hunt a few wild boar and consider his future.

*

Rod Reddy, in his first full term in charge of Barrow in 1988–89, did extremely well to guide what was largely a young and inexperienced side to promotion. He, too, brought in some carefully chosen helpers: Tim Dwyer, a centre or full-back from Manly, could contribute little because of injury, but Cavill Heugh, now an Illawarra player, was every bit as good as he had been for Halifax three years earlier, and Jeff Burns, from Brothers in Brisbane, was a regular scorer in the centres. Barrow finished second in the division; it would have been better for them if it had been fourth. 'I was promised money for the new players we knew we needed in the first division,' said Reddy. 'My mistake was believing it.' Without that investment, the hopelessness of Barrow's position in division one quickly became apparent. Reddy was outspoken in his criticism of a board of directors which he accused of letting down both him and the Barrow public, and was duly sacked. Barrow were relegated with the worst record ever by a first-division side, but Reddy, one of the most ebullient characters in Rugby League, did not disappear quietly from the scene. He subsequently became heavily involved in the formative stages of the Soviet Rugby League, and eventually returned to Australia, as Brian Smith's assistant at St George.

In 1988–89, there was a further impressive contingent of Australian players who came to Britain to ply their trade, although their varied fortunes began to raise doubts about the wisdom of investing good money in a short-term, hit-or-miss import. The two high-calibre Test players who joined St Helens had a predictably fluctuating relationship with their coach, Alex Murphy, although Paul Vautin was a more obviously valuable addition than Michael O'Connor who, for all his undoubted class as threequarter and goal-kicker, found few opportunities to show what all the fuss was about. Vautin, too, came in for some flak early in his stay, although Murphy later became sufficiently taken with him to make him club captain. There was no doubt that Vautin enjoyed his rugby in Britain, and he was talking eagerly about staying in the northern hemisphere to finish his career. Primarily regarded as a defensive workhorse in Sydney, he found that the looser British style of play allowed him to expand his repertoire: 'He's made more breaks over here than he had in his whole career in Australia,' joked O'Connor, and it wasn't far from the truth.

Not for the first time, everything turned sour around the time of Wembley. Saints, as unfathomably inconsistent in the League as ever, had qualified for the Challenge Cup final by beating Widnes 16–14 in the semi, and Murphy had already announced his intention of bringing Vautin and O'Connor back from Australia for the big occasion. Manly, by this time heartily sick of sharing their players with British clubs, proved less than cooperative, demanding a compensation payment which Murphy described variously as blackmail and extortion. It all seemed a pointless exercise, however, when Saints were overwhelmed 0–27 by Wigan in an embarrassingly one-sided final, with neither Australian making any kind of impact; it was not surprising that Murphy's reaction later was to say that he would never again fly in overseas players for a final. Vautin still insisted that he was keen to move permanently to Britain, but he eventually chose to wind down his career in Sydney, with Eastern Suburbs, instead.

The victors at Wembley, Wigan, dominated the honours that season without an Australian in their side, although the other teams who left some sort of mark on the campaign owed at least something to men from Down Under. Leeds's 33–12 Yorkshire Cup win over Castleford and third place in the first division made it a successful trip for Ettingshausen and Lyons, while Salford could feel well pleased at not only avoiding relegation, but also reaching the final of the Lancashire Cup. Their tiny aboriginal half-back from Manly, Paul Shaw, was a case of Jamie Sandy revisited and, if anything, he was an even greater crowd-pleaser. Shaw's form in the early part of the season was outstanding and, even though his club lost the Lancashire Cup final 17–22 to Wigan, he was the man-of-the-match. Unfortunately, Shaw's size and elusiveness made him the target for some shameful tackling. At times, it seemed like open season for tacklers going high on the little man, and concussion became a constant companion. Not surprisingly, his form and confidence were eventually affected, and his impact trailed off.

Steve Ella returned to Britain and was a major success for Wakefield Trinity – another club whose main ambition was to stay up – until a shoulder injury ended his career, but Warrington were never as consistently fearsome in the forwards as they should have been with Steve Roach and Les Davidson alongside Les Boyd. Even with Phil Blake also at Wilderspool, scoring tries from all over the field, the Wire still finished only one place clear of relegation.

The three clubs that did go down all spent a good deal on importing Australian players, without it having the desired effect on their results. Halifax, with former Great Britain international

Alan Hardisty taking over in February from Strudwick, were one; Oldham, with Paul Taylor, the Canberra pair of Chris O'Sullivan and Ashley Gilbert and, at the end, John Cogger, were another. Gilbert never made much of an impact and actually spent part of his stay in the 'A' team, while Taylor – never the luckiest of players with injury in Britain – played only nine games. Rock bottom, however, were Hull KR – such a force not long before – despite the presence of Gavin Miller and two other Australians, former international centre Chris Close and Cronulla front-rower Michael Porter.

Moving in the opposite direction, along with Rod Reddy's Barrow, came Leigh and Sheffield Eagles, the latter bolstered by Mark Geyer's flying visit and by the acquisition, via Bramley, of Warren Smiles. Smiles, originally from New South Wales, had come to Britain by way of player-coaching in Perth and, after Bramley showed little interest in him, he turned out to be a handy utility forward for the Eagles, both in their promotion campaign and in their first season in division one.

*

The 1989–90 season saw further additions to the Australian coaching colony in British Rugby League. Brian Johnson, their former full-back, had taken on the job at Warrington midway through the previous season, after Les Boyd had turned it down. John Monie, the Parramatta coach, took over from Graham Lowe at Wigan; he was, as he pointed out, accustomed to the idea of following a tough act, as he had been Jack Gibson's successor at the Eels. More surprisingly, the veteran Sydney coach, Ron Willey, came out to take charge of one of the most insular of British clubs, Bradford Northern, while Halifax turned to John Dorahy, with his proven record in Britain, to try to take them back into the first division at the first attempt.

Two of those new appointments failed disastrously. Willey, a staunch Anglophile, seemed to relate more easily to the country he had seen as a Kangaroo tourist in the 1950s than to the place as it was in 1989. The players, in turn, seemed to resent an outsider; Willey's record as one of the most durable coaches in Australia meant little to them, and he was treated with little respect. Behind his back, they referred to him as 'Ron the Relic' and 'The Fossil'. There was some initial encouragement when the side that had won through to the Yorkshire Cup final before his arrival took the trophy by beating Featherstone by 20–14 – Canberra half-back Ivan Henjak was in the thirteen that day, although Western Suburbs winger Graham Mackay missed out – but the relationship never worked. In March, Willey left for home, amid a confusing cross-fire of variations on the themes of sacking and resignation. Thereafter, under player-coach David Hobbs, Bradford suddenly looked as though they wanted to play and they eventually reached the final of the Premiership trophy, where they lost 6–28 to Widnes after the departure of both Henjak and Mackay.

Dorahy's tenure at Halifax also produced some early results, not least when the club reached the final of the Regal Trophy, beating three first-division sides – Salford, Featherstone and St Helens – on the way. Dorahy was playing himself and was still capable on occasion of looking the high-class footballer that he had always been, although he was dissatisfied with his own form overall. Alongside the long-serving Tony Anderson, he brought in Brian Hetherington, a most experienced centre, and Lindsay Johnston, a prop from South Sydney who had previously played for Hull KR. The full Australian contingent played in a particularly spiteful final against Wigan at Headingley, and Dorahy rediscovered all his old big-match magic in a first half in which his side more than held its own. The turning point came when Johnston, who had also been playing particularly well, was sent to the sin-bin for punching; Wigan scored two tries during his absence and were eventual 24–12 winners.

That, for Halifax fans, was a brief taste of the good old days, but the real priority for Dorahy was to get them back into the first division. Their inconsistent form against mediocre opposition destroyed that hope and, at the same time, the club's financial predicament – the result of such ambitious spending in the recent past – was worsening. Anderson was sold to Oldham to help keep the wolf from the door, and there were increasing mutterings about the amount that Dorahy, with his young family and old-style Halifax contract, was costing the club; he, in turn, was less than enamoured with having his better players, like Anderson and Les Holliday, sold from underneath him. Although he was under contract for a second season at Thrum Hall, it was no shock when it was announced that he would not be coming back for more. Future Australian signings, said chairman David Brook shortly before he gave up control of the club, would only be players who were considerably younger and considerably cheaper.

Monie's first season was altogether more propitious. The new man at Wigan was an unqualified success; his debut treble of Championship, Regal Trophy and Challenge Cup was a haul that had eluded even Graham Lowe. Quiet and determinedly low-key by comparison with his immediate predecessor, Monie's reputation increased steadily as the season went on. One doubt that had been expressed about him was whether he would have the force of personality to keep the lid on the simmering mix of temperament and talent that was the Wigan first-team squad. Lowe had needed to take a hard line on occasion with his 'big three' of Ellery Hanley, Shaun Edwards and Andy Gregory, and keeping them all at the club and – a few brief altercations aside – on the field was considered to be one of his major achievements. It said a lot for Monie and his calm, methodical ways that 1989–90 was the quietest season on the Central Park tom-toms for some time; there were no fall-outs and no drama, just a rugby team that won matches.

One piece of traditional Wigan enterprise made a telling contribution to the season's success. The down-side of signing high-grade footballers from overseas is that their country is liable to want them back from time to time, and such was the case for the New Zealand tour of 1989: after a protracted argument, Wigan had to release Kevin Iro and Adrian Shelford for the duration of the trip. That left an undeniable hole in Monie's team, but Wigan discovered that there was nothing to stop them filling it by temporarily deregistering the two New Zealanders and bringing in a couple of other players to fill their places on the overseas quota – indeed, a club with an insatiable appetite for paperwork could, in theory, register a different set of overseas players every week, although nobody has quite gone to that extreme yet. Wigan were interested in a number of Australians for the short-term contracts at Central Park: previous favourites John Ferguson and Ian Roberts were possibilities, and so was long-time target Gene Miles. The two signed, however, were Phil Blake, already with two seasons at Warrington behind him; and South Sydney prop and 1986 Kangaroo tourist Les Davidson, who had been at Wilderspool with Blake the year before. They did the job admirably. Davidson took on the role vacated by Shelford with great enthusiasm and looked thoroughly at home in the British game. Blake impressed Monie enormously; he knew him well enough as an opponent in Sydney, of course, but even so admitted to being pleasantly surprised by the seriousness underlying his obvious flair and panache. He made his mind up quite early that he would like to bring Blake back for a longer stay the following season.

Of the eleven games the two Souths men played for Wigan, only two were lost: one, surprisingly to say the least, by a single point at Oldham in the semi-final of the Lancashire Cup, the other at home to Castleford in the first division. No ground had been lost, however, and Wigan's Championship win by 4 points over second-placed Leeds owed no little something to Blake and Davidson's high-class papering over the cracks.

Wigan had an uncharacteristically poor start to the 1990–91 season, and it seemed that perhaps Monie had been right to want Phil Blake for his last import spot rather than the All Black Frano Botica, the player his directors signed instead. Wigan went far deeper into the season without winning a trophy than had been their wont but, the further they went, the more likely they looked to put that matter right. In the end, the side were revealed as an oddity in modern British Rugby League, in that they won the double of Championship and Challenge Cup without an Australian player on their books. The influence and reputation of John Monie, however, continued to grow.

It was a popular fallacy that anyone could have coached Wigan to a high level of success that season, so well-endowed were they with players of outstanding ability, but a programme of eight League games in seventeen days at the end of the first-division season would have stretched any but the best-run operation to breaking-point. The way Monie marshalled his increasingly threadbare resources through that gruelling period was exemplary, although he himself said that 'No club should ever have to go through what we have gone through.' For the second year running, Monie was named coach-of-the-year. He also agreed to stay for another season at Central Park, adamant that it would be his last before returning to relaunch his interrupted coaching career in Australia.

For all his previous success at Wigan, Monie had problems at the start of the 1991–92 season. After prolonged and convoluted negotiations, Ellery Hanley was sold to Leeds for £250,000 and, as had always seemed likely, another regular match-winner, Kevin Iro, joined his former Wigan coach, Graham Lowe, at Manly. It needed something special to compensate for the loss of players of that calibre, and chairman Maurice Lindsay went to Australia in search of that something.

The bush telegraph worked overtime as all manner of names were bandied about. Wigan even joined St Helens and London in vain pursuit of Mal Meninga but, in the end, Lindsay's efforts were concentrated on two players: Terry Hill, an exciting young centre whose turbulent early career was in the process of taking him around the points of the compass in Sydney, from Souths, to Easts, to Wests; and Gene Miles. If there was one player who had been chased more persistently by British clubs than Wally Lewis since 1983, Miles was the man, and it had usually been Wigan doing the chasing. Lindsay had liked the idea of him in a cherry and white jersey from the very first and, had it not been for the formation of the Brisbane Broncos in 1988, he could well have been enticed to England earlier. By 1991, however, it was clear that Miles's usefulness to the Broncos was, at least in their view, coming to an end. A lucrative season in Britain made perfect sense.

Although the latter years of Miles's Australian career had been spent in the pack, Monie made it clear from the start that he saw him as a replacement for Iro in the centres, rather than for Hanley at loose forward. The question was whether he could move successfully back to his original position at the age of 31, and the initial signs were not too good. After a smooth enough debut against Featherstone Rovers which was marked with a try and a hand in three others, Miles damaged a thigh muscle in training and struggled through the Lancashire Cup semi-final defeat by St Helens. 'I probably shouldn't have played,' he said. 'But you don't like to cry off when you've just arrived in town.' Miles's over-anxiety to get on to the pitch brought a couple more setbacks, and it was December before Wigan's increasingly impatient supporters saw him fully fit and firing on all cylinders.

Wigan never lost again all season – a stunning sequence of victories that brought them an unprecedented hat-trick of Championship, Challenge Cup and Premiership. There were many contributory factors towards that flawless record, but the commanding form of Miles was one of the main ones. Anyone expecting barnstorming runs to score frequent tries on his own account might have been mildly disappointed but, as a provider of chances for others, Miles was without peer during the second half of the season. In January, Wigan drove a corporation dustcart through the world transfer record established by the sale of Hanley by paying Widnes £440,000 for Martin Offiah. With the fastest player in the world directly outside him, Miles's value to Wigan was hugely increased. The presence of Offiah gave him *carte blanche* to stretch his unorthodox passing ability – one-handed scoops and basketball-style overhead dunks included – to its limit. 'Most of my passes are a long way from the coaching manuals, but he's got great hands,' said Miles of his new partner. Not surprisingly, he was very much involved in helping Offiah to a record-breaking ten tries in the 74–6 Premiership semi-final victory against Leeds.

If there was one factor which had drawn Miles to Britain, however, it was the prospect of playing at Wembley. His partner in the centres for Australia, Brett Kenny, had told him all about the experience of playing there for Wigan and, as Miles put it: 'Brett isn't the most excitable of blokes, so anything that has that effect on him must be pretty special.' Wigan's record of reaching the Challenge Cup final in the four previous seasons was a theme upon which Lindsay played heavily during his talks with Miles in Brisbane. Miles was persuaded that he would be very unlucky indeed not to reach the twin towers in a season with Wigan.

The side were as good as their chairman's word. Despite a tough draw that gave them ties against Salford, Warrington and St Helens, they won through to the semi-finals, where Miles played outstandingly and scored two tries in a record-breaking 71–10 win over Bradford Northern at Bolton. Then, briefly, it seemed that Miles's injury problems had returned: he missed the last Championship game of the season, against Warrington, with a calf injury, and Monie wanted him to sit out the Premiership first-round tie against Widnes six days before the final. 'I always try to leave it up to the player, but I thought Gene should give it a miss. I even sent Andy Gregory round to persuade him, and he can usually wear anyone down.' Gregory, preparing for his eighth Wembley final, seemed the ideal man to convince Miles that a visit there was not something to be put in jeopardy. Miles, however, felt that he needed the run-out, played the full eighty minutes against Widnes and came through safely.

Miles was one of the pre-match favourites for the Lance Todd Trophy but, in truth, he did not have one of his most eye-catching games of the season. He relished the occasion, though, and reflected afterwards that 'that's what I came for.' The question of whether he would be coming back for more was left open. Miles himself had enjoyed every minute of the British experience, once he had shaken off his early injury problems; but his family responsibilities increased with the birth in England of his second child – part, perhaps, of a future team of British-born offspring of visiting Australian players – and his wife, Debbie, was not as enthusiastic about Wigan as he was. When he announced his intention to delay a decision on a second season with Wigan until he got back to Brisbane, the club feared the worst, but his much-delayed and relatively brief time with Wigan had been worth the wait for both parties.

The possible blow of losing Miles was softened, in any event, by Monie's decision to have one more season in Britain. The new heights touched by Wigan during the 1991–92 season – the Premiership having previously eluded both him and his predecessor, but now being claimed with a stunning 48–16 victory over St Helens – emphasised his value to the club still further, and the task of replacing him was one that Wigan were anxious to put off for as long as possible. There was a very short list of possible candidates, beginning with Tim Sheens at Canberra and probably ending with Miles's old Broncos boss, Wayne Bennett. Nor was Monie likely to be short of options in Australia: apart from the continuous reports of his achievements in British domestic competitions which had filtered back, the World Club Challenge victory over Penrith and Wigan's spectacular success in the Nissan World Sevens in Sydney kept his stock rising in his home country. As the end of his Wigan contract loomed, four Sydney clubs, plus consortia hoping to establish Winfield Cup clubs in Auckland and Perth, approached him about his future plans. But so did Lindsay and, not for the first time in his dealings with Australians, he got his way: Monie agreed to one more year, and this one definitely the last.

*

Brian Johnson had put Warrington through some intensive pre-season preparation prior to the start of the 1989–90 campaign, and it showed – no side looked as full of running in the early weeks of the season. They opened with a convincing win over Wigan, who were still waiting for Monie to finish his commitments at Parramatta and were slower into their stride; in fact, it was the end of October before Warrington lost a game, by which time they had won the Lancashire Cup, beating Oldham 24–16 at St Helens. Greg Mackey, soon to decamp to Hull, was a major influence at scrum-half, but the star turn was Bob Jackson, coaxed out of semi-retirement and the odd social game in Sydney to make a comeback with the Wire. He scored two tries against an Oldham team destined for promotion, captained by John Cogger – who played with typically fierce commitment – and also featuring Brett Clark. Warrington met Oldham again in the semi-final of the Challenge Cup, beating them this time by 10–6 and setting up a final against Wigan. However, that proved an altogether less satisfactory day out for them and for Jackson; he lasted just thirty-five minutes of the overwhelming 14–36 defeat before going off injured.

In 1990–91, Warrington continued to show themselves capable of winning honours, at least in the knock-out competitions. Johnson brought Chris O'Sullivan – formerly with Oldham – from Canberra and also revived the British career of Don Duffy, a second-rower once hailed as a future international at Parramatta but who had played his overseas rugby in the relative obscurity of Fulham and Carlisle. O'Sullivan played, and set up the only try, in a dour 12–2 win over Bradford Northern in the Regal Trophy final; Duffy and Bob Jackson were both injured. However, Warrington still could make no impression on the first division. 'We can beat anyone in a one-off game,' Johnson said. 'But it takes so much out of us that we could never sustain it for a whole season.'

That continued to be the story at Warrington, although O'Sullivan's chequered career in Britain had another twist left in it. In the summer of 1991, he took on what many people already regarded as the impossible task of coaching Swinton to safety in their first season back in the first division. It was soon clear that Swinton were not up to it but, with O'Sullivan calling the shots on the field and with the help of two of his former Canberra Raiders team-mates, Craig Bellamy and Mark Lowry, they at least attained some measure of respectability.

Towards the end of the year, however, Swinton announced that there was simply no money left to pay the three Australians. There was no criticism of them, on or off the field but, if Swinton were going down, they might as well try to go down within their means. O'Sullivan, Bellamy and Lowry accepted the situation with dignity, helped Swinton to one of their better results of the season when they lost 10–18 at home to Leeds, and signed off in the Boxing Day derby against Salford. O'Sullivan, one of the most resilient of characters, was still not finished. Despite a long-running dispute with Canberra over money, he returned for a last fling with the Raiders and even found himself back in first grade when Ricky Stuart was injured. He was philosophical about his Swinton experience: 'They could have done their sums better,' was his understated view of the episode.

*

Oldham ended their 1989–90 promotion season on a high note with a thrilling 30–29 victory over Hull KR in the second-division Premiership final at Old Trafford. Brett Clark was there for the big occasion again, but Tony Anderson had succumbed to serious injury almost as soon as he arrived from Halifax, and John Cogger was absent in Sydney. In the opposition line-up were Greg Austin and former Test prop Bryan Niebling, who collected second-division runners-up medals to go alongside the Championship of the division which they had helped Rovers to win.

Other notable Australian contributions that season came at Leeds, who shuffled their overseas allocation restlessly throughout the year. They brought over Craig Coleman, and he again showed what a good scrum-half he was, although not, perhaps, a full replacement for the player they had expected to have in their No. 7 shirt, Peter Sterling. Injury, several changes of plan and a good deal of fobbing-off stopped Leeds ever getting their hands on the man they still regarded as the best in the world in his position. When Coleman went home, another South Sydney player – although a far less well-known one – was given a chance in his place, and David Cruickshank was making a spirited bid for a long-term future at Headingley until he was suspended and lost his opportunity. Two Parramatta forwards, the returning Mark Laurie and Craig Izzard, both appeared for Leeds, with Izzard looking particularly impressive.

Others worthy of mention in 1989–90 were Bruce McGuire, the Balmain and Australia forward who joined Sheffield Eagles, and Chris Johns, the Brisbane centre who joined Rod Reddy's doomed ship at Barrow. They, like the Leeds, Castleford and Hull contingents of Australians, had no medals by which to remember their campaigns. Nor did Wakefield Trinity's main signing, although he was arguably the most memorable figure of the season.

There was a definite sense of foreboding when Ray Price, one of the greatest Australian players of his day, announced that, at 36 and after three seasons out of the game, he was making a comeback with Trinity. His contemporary, Graham Eadie, had got away with it at Halifax; but a forward – and one whose whole style had been built around fitness and continuous involvement? Surely not. There were times, to be sure, when Price himself must have thought that he had made a mistake. Although he had kept himself formidably fit and had never actually stopped training with his old club, Parramatta, the wear and tear of match-play is something different again. Price was rarely free of back pain during his season in Britain and was plagued, much to his own disgust, by a series of other, lesser injuries. He proved, however, that his mental toughness was unimpaired. Playing largely on his resources of will-power, he still managed to be an inspiring presence for Wakefield, exerting a particularly strong influence on the young forwards around him.

Ultimately, Trinity, despite the addition of two other Australians who did well in their first season in Britain – Parramatta centre Brian Jackson and a young Queenslander spotted in an amateur game in Yorkshire, Chris Perry – were not good enough to upset the big guns. But the Price influence could make them awfully difficult to beat. They might not live alongside his memories of Grand Finals, State of Origin matches and Ashes Tests, but a couple of his own performances in games that Trinity lost – both against Wigan, in Challenge Cup and League – were vintage Ray Price: all passion and determination. 'I don't have anything to prove to anybody, except myself,' he had said when he arrived; although Wakefield would have loved to have him back for at least one more season, he considered by spring 1990 that he had confirmed to himself that he could still be recognisably Ray Price on the rugby field, and that there was no real need to go through it all again. It is doubtful whether the impression he made upon the club could have been any deeper if he had played on into his 40s. His only regret was that he had not been able to help Wakefield to get to Wembley and to experience the atmosphere that Parramatta team-mates like Brett Kenny and Peter Sterling had told him so much about.

Wakefield came up with a new idea for the 1990–91 season – or at least one which had been in abeyance since Harry Sunderland's days as secretary-manager at Wigan – by importing an Australian administrator. Journalist Neil Cadigan had been involved in the deal which had brought Price to Belle Vue and he was hired as general manager, with a particular brief to raise the profile of the club. As Price's playing successor, he brought in the almost equally experienced Chris Mortimer, who had spent a decade in the Canterbury side before having a final season – and playing in the Grand Final – with Penrith. Mortimer showed glimpses of what a positive influence he could be during an encouraging first half of the season, although he had still to arrive when Trinity reached the final of the Yorkshire Cup. As the team's overall form went into decline, however, he also struggled, and the Belle Vue fans, brought up on a recent diet of Ella and Price, showed their disappointment with him by subjecting him to more than his share of barracking. Things went from bad to worse for Mortimer when a serious knee injury in March threatened to end his career. The season was an anti-climax as well for Chris Perry; never at his best on muddy grounds, he found it hard to hold his first-team place during the winter and was a substitute in the Yorkshire Cup final. Nevertheless, he re-emerged more strongly in spring to help Wakefield's battle against relegation in the centres.

By the end of 1991, Cadigan, worn down by the apparently open-ended nature of his responsibilities at Wakefield, had resigned to return to Australia. One of his last contributions was to set up the signing of Geoff Bagnall, the experienced Gold Coast scrum-half, who was an immediate success at Belle Vue. Within a few weeks, Bagnall's obvious leadership qualities saw him join the small group of Australians to be appointed captain of their British clubs and, in the face of increasing interest from other clubs, Wakefield tied him up on an extended contract after he had helped them into the Premiership competition for the first time in over a decade.

Besides Price, the 1990–91 season saw another old warhorse, Bryan Niebling, give Hull KR the forward leadership they needed in their first season back in division one, although his effectiveness was similarly reduced by a recurring series of injuries. Rovers also came very close to agreeing terms with the one Australian coach whose influence, via the success of his Australian touring teams, had been instrumental in re-opening Rugby League's international trade routes: Frank Stanton. The club's parlous financial state led to that plan being aborted, which led, as surely as night follows day, to his name being linked with Leeds. Yorkshire's premier club endured a most disappointing season, despite continuing to invest heavily in the hope of real success. Cavill Heugh, whose contract at Barrow Leeds had bought out the previous season, was one of a number of players who seemed unsure of their role, and neither Heugh nor Doug Laughton, the coach who eventually occupied the seat temporarily filled by Stanton's wraith, could help rectify that in 1991–92.

Meanwhile, back in 1990–91, several Australian players got a long, hard look at the wrong end of the first-division table. Robert Grogan, once with Halifax, and – briefly – Dave Gallagher shared in Rochdale Hornets' doomed campaign. Brett Clark, always good value in British conditions, was the pick of Oldham's trio; Tony Anderson had too many injury problems to be seen at his best, and John Cogger never quite recaptured his central position in the scheme of things at the Watersheddings after his confrontation with the club during the close-season. Sheffield Eagles seemed to have come up with an outstanding signing in Ian Russell, the Illawarra loose forward who had not been far away from a Kangaroo tour place after an excellent season in Australia. He had his moments, but never made quite the impact that was expected of him and at one stage was dropped to the 'A' team. All three clubs were relegated.

In the second division, Steve Gibson had little trouble shining in a Salford team that ran away with the title. His rangy running and spectacular tackling continued to make him a particular favourite at the Willows, as Salford won the battle to stay up the following season. Gibson then signed on for a sixth season with the club and announced his intention of becoming the first Australian to earn a ten-year testimonial with them. At St Helens, Phil Veivers was considerably closer to that landmark as he ended his eighth campaign with a losers' medal in the 1992 Premiership final.

Others to catch the eye over the past couple of years have been Wally Gibson, an enterprising full-back with Huddersfield, hopeful of returning home to make his mark in Sydney, who won the third division's inaugural player-of-the-year award for 1991–92; and Ken Kerr, an unknown centre who proved a revelation with the improving Workington until a broken leg curtailed his activities for 1991–92. By this stage, an interesting development in the history of the importation tradition had been the grant of an extended quota to Fulham in deference to their distance from the Rugby League heartlands; in 1990–91, their most notable guests were Brisbane half-back Craig Grauf and big Cronulla forward Mark Lee. Ross Strudwick, in his second year as coach, now took on the extra duties of secretary and general manager. Performances were often heartening; crowds, even with a change of grounds to Crystal Palace, much less so, although Fulham received rewards for their continued survival in the shape of promotion to the new second division for 1991–92, and selection as one of the first two sides to visit the Soviet Union. In 1990, Trafford Borough brought in three good players from South Sydney – Darren Brown, Darren McCarthy and Steve Mavin – to fill in until a trio of New Zealanders arrived. They then argued that they, like Fulham, should be allowed extra overseas players, since their needs were similarly dire – but to no avail.

Fulham's trip to Russia in the summer of 1991 produced one of the more tortuous examples of self-advancement among the expatriate Australian football community. Greg Pearce, who had come to Fulham from New South Wales country football via Hemel Hempstead, had already decided that, after three seasons, it was time to move on. He played so well on the tour that he became a marketable commodity – a rare case of a player going to a most unlikely spot in order to be 'discovered'. Gary Stephens, who had coached Ryedale-York on the Soviet trip, took him to Leeds when he went there as assistant coach. When Pearce could not break into the first team at Headingley, he moved to Halifax for 1991–92, where he thrived as loose forward and goal-kicker.

Strudwick's third season with what was now London Crusaders brought the usual revolving cast of Australian players: notable among them were the prolific try-scoring centre from Valleys, Shane Buckley; Ipswich scrum-half Ray Ovens, subsequently to retire after two brain operations; and a Rugby Union player from Brisbane, Ben Olsen. Strudwick, with typical ingenuity, argued that Olsen should not count as an overseas import because he had a passport from an EEC country, Denmark. Yet the difficulty that the Crusaders had in fielding a credible side without sailing close to the wind on their import quota brought them into conflict with Huddersfield after their match in the first round of the new divisional Premiership. The Rugby Football League's concession to London was that they could have eight overseas players on their books, but could only use four in any one match: Huddersfield claimed that, on the evidence of their ears alone, there were far more than that speaking broad 'Strine' in their match. An inquiry into the complaint by the RFL's board of directors ruled that the case was not proven, but a second inquiry into London's registration of overseas players was ordered. Meanwhile, Oldham also complained that the import rules were being broken in their play-off semi-final against London.

*

An argument of a different sort centred on a player whose career in England makes him one of the most remarkable imports from Australia ever to immerse himself in the British game. Phil McKenzie was a nobody when he arrived, along with Greg Austin and his brother, Tony, to play for Rochdale Hornets in 1986. His Australian career had certainly been nothing special: he had joined the Illawarra Steelers, but had played mainly in the lower grades with just a handful of games in the top side. Despairing of ever making it, he had drifted away and into country football with Picton in the Group 6 competition not far from Sydney. It was not much of a pedigree for a young hooker trying his luck in Britain, but Rochdale soon found that they had stumbled on something a bit special.

McKenzie's pace and eye for a gap brought him nineteen tries in thirty-two appearances in that first season in Britain – a freakish rate of scoring for a hooker. More important for his long-term prospects, he made a favourable impression on Widnes coach Doug Laughton when the two sides met in a Challenge Cup tie; Widnes won, but McKenzie's sparkling running from dummy-half caused them all manner of problems. Laughton knew that he would need a replacement for veteran hooker Keith Elwell in the near future, and the name of Phil McKenzie was filed away for reference. The following year, he duly became a Widnes player, and a vital component in the exciting and effective side that the club was assembling. Pace was the key word as far as Laughton was concerned, and his side had it in abundance, in virtually all positions. If a hooker was to gel effectively with the rest of the side, it followed that he needed to be outstandingly quick as well. McKenzie was – not just in the sense of being able to accelerate through a chink in a defence, but also in having the capacity to make tactical decisions at speed. With his passing ability, his kicking game and the pace to go on his own, McKenzie was a unique hooker. He had so much rugby about him that Widnes were able to use him at half-back and loose forward on occasion without him looking remotely out of place.

McKenzie was an important element in all the triumphs of the new Widnes side: two Championships, three Premierships and a memorable victory over Canberra in the 1989 World Club Challenge, to name just the major events. It was clear to him that his future lay in Britain; surprisingly enough, his declaration that he would like to spend a close-season playing in Sydney had elicited little response. He also made the decision that he wanted to become a British player in the fullest sense, by qualifying and playing for the Great Britain team. McKenzie had the Scottish antecedents that he sounded as though he should have, carried a British passport – always a useful document for Australian players to have up their sleeve – and had married a Rochdale girl. 'My future is here, my children were born here, and I feel more British than Australian,' he said.

The meeting of the game's International Board in New Zealand in 1990 considered the case of players like McKenzie and decided in favour of a residential qualification that would allow them to play for their adopted country after living there for five years. For McKenzie, the magic date was September 1990 – just in time to make him available for the Test series against Australia. It should have been one of the most significant dates in the whole, complex history of cross-pollination between the world's two main Rugby League-playing nations.

McKenzie lost few opportunities to reiterate just how pleased and proud he would be to play for Great Britain, and there was no shortage of voices raised in his support. The plain fact of the matter was that he was the best hooker in Britain; with all due respect to some fine British-born players like Lee Jackson and Martin Dermott, he had extra dimensions to his play to which they could not aspire. Opposing players and coaches consistently picked McKenzie as the hooker who presented the greatest threat; if ability had been the sole criterion, he could not have been left out.

Unfortunately for McKenzie and his ambitions, it was not as simple as that. Although it was never said officially that he would not be considered for the series, there was a strong feeling among some of the most important people in the British game that his Australian upbringing ruled him out of contention. Appealing strongly and directly to their players' nationalist emotions had been part of the Great Britain Rugby League side's strategy of regeneration since coach Maurice Bamford had had them clustering around the Union Jack before the New Zealand Test matches of 1985. Bringing an Australian into this atmosphere – for it still played a part under Malcolm Reilly five years later – was not thought desirable.

It seemed a misguided view. Much improved as British Rugby League was by this stage, it could still ill afford the luxury of leaving out the best available player in a specialist position. The most wrong-headed of all the arguments advanced against McKenzie's inclusion, and one that was often heard, was that 'the Aussies wouldn't do it' if the positions were reversed. That really was the most extraordinary thing to say at a time when the country was being entertained by an Australian touring party managed by a Welshman (Keith Barnes), coached by a Warringtonian (Bobby Fulton – like Barnes, a much-capped Australian Test player), and with a vice-captain (Ben Elias) born in Beirut. Anyone who knows the highly pragmatic Australian attitude to the business of putting winning sports teams on to the paddock also knows that they would cheerfully have selected Saddam Hussein, if he qualified according to the rules of the day and if he was the best man in his position. British Rugby League was not quite ready to take that leap forward in the story of Australian involvement in its domestic affairs, and so McKenzie missed out.

Ironically, when his chance did come the following season, McKenzie was not able to take it. The Great Britain management decided that the man from Wollongong could be an asset after all and announced their intention to play him in one of the Tests against France in early 1992, with a view to assessing his suitability for the Lions tour that same year. Unfortunately, the twin considerations of form and fitness conspired against McKenzie. He was left out of the Widnes team that beat Leeds in the final of the Regal Trophy and struggled through large sections of the season with various injuries. The chance to stake a claim to a little piece of Anglo-Australian Rugby League history had gone.

Index